Online Teaching and Learning

New Roles for Participants

Online Teaching and Learning

New Roles for Participants

Rajiv Ranjan

CENTRUM PRESS
NEW DELHI-110002 (INDIA)

CENTRUM PRESS
H.O.: 4360/4, Ansari Road, Daryaganj,
New Delhi-110002 (India)
Tel: 23278000, 23261597, 23255577, 23286875
B.O.: No. 1015, Ist Main Road, BSK IIIrd Stage,
IIIrd Phase, IIIrd Block, Bangalore-560085 (INDIA)
Tel: 080-41723429
Email: centrumpress@gmail.com
Visit us at: www.centrumpress.com

Online Teaching and Learning: New Roles for Participants

First Edition, 2011

ISBN 978-93-80921-67-9

PRINTED IN INDIA

Printed at Tarun Offset Printers, Delhi-110053

Contents

Preface

E-learning comprises all forms of electronically supported learning and teaching. The information and communication systems, whether networked or not, dish up as exact media to apply the learning procedure. The idiom will immobile the majority likely be utilized to reference out-of-classroom and in-classroom educational understandings via technology, even as move forwards keep on in look upon to devices and curriculum.

E-learning is fundamentally the computer and network-enabled move of abilities and knowledge. E-learning submissions and procedures include Web-based learning, computer-based learning, fundamental classroom opportunities and digital collaboration. Content is delivered via the Internet, intranet/extranet, audio or video tape, satellite TV, and CD-ROM. It can be self-paced or instructor-led and comprises media in the form of text, image, animation, streaming video and audio.

Abbreviations like Computer-Based Training, Internet-Based Training or Web-Based Training have been used as synonyms to e-learning. Today one can still find these terms being used, along with differences of e-learning such as e-learning, E-learning, and e-Learning. The conditions will be utilized throughout this article to point to their authority under the broader vocabulary of E-learning.

Author

1

Introduction

TEACHING IN ONLINE LEARNING ENVIRONMENTS: OVERVIEW

WHAT IS ONLINE LEARNING

The term online learning includes a number of computer-assisted instruction methods.

Two parallel processes take place in an online environment:

- Students become more active, reflective learners.
- Students and teachers engage in learning through the use of technology and become more familiar with technology by using it.

Online learning is most effective when delivered by teachers experienced in their subject matter. The best way to maintain the connection between online education and the values of traditional education is through ensuring that online learning is "delivered" by teachers, fully qualified and interested in teaching online in a web-based environment.

Approaches to Online Learning

Two approaches to online learning have emerged: synchronous and asynchronous learning. Synchronous learning is instruction and collaboration in "real time" via the Internet.

It typically involves tools, such as:

- Live chat
- Audio and video conferencing
- Data and application sharing
- Shared whiteboard

- Virtual "hand raising"
- Joint viewing of multimedia presentations and online slide shows

Asynchronous learning methods use the time-delayed capabilities of the Internet.

It typically involves tools, such as:

- E-mail
- Threaded discussion
- Newsgroups and bulletin boards
- File attachments

Asynchronous courses are still instructor-facilitated but are not conducted in real time, which means that students and teacher can engage in course-related activities at their convenience rather than during specifically coordinated class sessions.

In asynchronous courses, learning does not need to be scheduled in the same way as synchronous learning, allowing students and instructors the benefits of anytime, anywhere learning.

Course Software

Rather than creating your online course from scratch, a number of software programmes are now available that make it easy to develop an online course. These programmes include features such as threaded discussions and document sharing and pre-designed design layouts to make the course design process easier. Check with the campus technology specialists to learn more about the preferred software for online learning in your department.

ADVANTAGES OF LEARNING ONLINE

Online learning offers a variety of educational opportunities:

- *Student-centred learning*: The variety of online tools draw on individual learning styles and help students become more versatile learners.
- *Collaborative learning*: Online group work allows students to become more active participants in the learning process. Contributing input requires that

students comprehend what is being discussed, organize their thinking coherently, and express that thinking with carefully

- *Easy access to global resources*: Students can easily access online databases and subject experts in the online classroom.
- *Experiential learning through multimedia presentations*: New technologies can be used to engage and motivate students. Technology can also be used to support students in their learning activities.
- *Accessible for non-traditional students*: Online delivery of programmes and courses makes participation possible for students who experience geographic and time barriers in gaining access to higher education.
- *Draws on student interest in online learning*: Many students are interested in online learning. In a recent survey conducted by the Office of Academic Planning and Assessment at UMass Amherst, more than 50% of students surveyed said that they were "very interested" or "somewhat interested" in taking an online course.

ADVANTAGES OF TEACHING ONLINE

Teaching online courses can:

- *Offer the opportunity to think about teaching in new ways*: Online teaching can allow you to experiment with techniques only available in online environments, such as threaded discussions and webliographies.
- *Provide ideas and techniques to implement in traditional courses*: Online e-mail discussions, a frequently-used practice in online learning, can be incorporated into traditional courses to facilitate group work. Other techniques, such as web-based course calendars and sample papers posted on the Internet can easily be incorporated into a traditional course.
- *Expand the reach of the curriculum*: Online teaching can expand existing curriculum to students on a regional, national, and international level.

- *Professional satisfaction*: Teaching online can be an enormously rewarding experience for teachers. Teachers often cite the diversity of students in online courses as one of the most rewarding aspects of teaching online.
- *Instructor convenience*: Teaching online can offer teachers conveniences not available in traditional classroom settings; for example, at-home office hours and flexible work schedules.

CHALLENGES OF TEACHING ONLINE

A recent American Federation of Teachers report on distance learning, faculty must be prepared to meet the special requirements of teaching at a distance.

Some of the challenges for instructors of teaching online include:

- Familiarity with the online environment
- Capacity to use the medium to its advantage
- Being available to students on an extended basis electronically
- Providing quick responses and feedback to students

Yet, the proponents of online learning argue that these obstacles can be overcome by employing such techniques as the following:

- *Become familiar with the technology used in your online course*: Long before your course starts, become familiar with the technology used in your online course, including hardware and software, and spend some time exploring their options. An online course requires a high level of computing power and reliable telecommunications infrastructure. Make sure you have access to both.
- *Use the online medium to your advantage*: The online environment is essentially a space for written communication. This is both a limitation and a potential of online learning. Written communication can be more time consuming, but "the ability to sit and think as one composes a question or comment also can raise the quality of discussion." Additionally,

shy students who have trouble participating in a classroom discussion often feel more comfortable in an online classroom. Online classrooms can be developed with this fact in mind to take advantage of these considerations.

- *Keep connected with students*: Use the technology of the online environment to help you keep in touch with students. Communicate frequently with students, both individually and as a group. A main part of this focuses on how to connect with students. While keeping connected with students can be a challenge, the online environment offers a number of interesting pedagogical opportunities.

COMMON QUESTIONS

Q.1 What is an online course?

Ans. An online course is offered in part or wholly via the Internet.

Q.2 Who can teach an online course?

Ans. Faculty members as well as graduate students may teach online courses at UMass.

Q.3 Will an online course echo a course I have already prepared?

Ans. It can, but be aware that many changes will be necessary for the course to "work" online. You may find it professionally stimulating to create an entire course anew.

Q.4 Why would I want to teach an online course?

Ans. Do you want to experiment? Do you want to travel during the semester, have other scheduling complications, or want the convenience of working from home? Are you interested in reaching students whom you might not otherwise have a chance to teach? These are some of the reasons why instructors choose to teach online.

Q.5 Where are online courses taught?

Ans. Anywhere. Most courses are taught entirely online and students and professors never or only rarely meet face-to-face. Other courses are taught with a strong on-campus component.

Q.6 When are online courses taught?

Ans. Mass has many options for teaching online. Interested teachers can contact their own departments or the Division of Continuing Education.

Q.7 How do I learn to teach an online course?

Ans. The places to look for information include your department, online teaching tools such as e-College or Blackboard, the consultants at Continuing Education, or the instructional technologist at your campus. Also, colleagues who have taught online courses can be an invaluable resource. You can also gain experience with the online learning environment by developing a course homepage for your own classroom-based course.

COMMON TERMS

Following are some common terms used in online courses:

- *Lurking*: Reading threaded discussion responses without posting a response. Students who lurk in online courses are like silent students in traditional courses; they listen but do not speak. In online situations where you do not know how many people are "listening," lurking can be problematic if others do not know you are present.
- *Threaded discussion*: An asynchronous discussion. In threaded discussions students may post responses to a prompt at any time. Threaded discussions allow students to work at their own pace, allow the teacher to respond more thoughtfully since all the responses are not posted simultaneously, and are easier to coordinate than expecting all students to be online at the same time.
- *Webliography*: An online bibliography of web-related resources. Often online teachers will use a web-based bibliography to help students identity appropriate Internet resources.

TEACHING AN ONLINE COURSE

PREPARING TO TEACH ONLINE

As you plan your online course, it is helpful to remember that in any environment "good teaching is good teaching". Experienced online instructors stress that teaching online is less about the mechanics of distance education and "more about what makes for an effective educational experience, regardless of where or when it is delivered".

Many teachers have found the Principles of Good Practice in Undergraduate Education to be a useful framework for thinking about how to enhance student learning in their classes.

Principles of Good Practice in Undergraduate Education:

- Encourages contact between students and faculty, especially contact focused on the academic agenda.
- Develops reciprocity and cooperation among students, *i.e.*, teaching students to work productively with others.
- Encourages active learning, *i.e.*, doing and thinking about the learning process.
- Gives prompt feedback and helps students understand how to respond.
- Emphasizes time on task by providing repeated useful, productive, guided practice.
- Communicates high expectations and encourages students to have high self-expectations.
- Respects diverse talents and ways of learning and engenders respect of intellectual diversity.

An additional good practice that does not appear on this list, but that many experienced online instructors mention as being essential to successful teaching, is:

- Includes a well-organized course, the structure of which is clearly communicated to students.

Use these eight best practices as a framework for thinking about your online course. Of course, it is also important to acknowledge that some aspects of good teaching, such as faculty-student contact and cooperation among students, are particularly challenging to accomplish in an online environment. This recommendations on how to accomplish these goals, despite the complications that may exist.

PREPARING STUDENTS TO LEARN ONLINE

Students new to online learning may initially find this kind of learning disorienting without the physical classroom space and guidance from the physical presence of a teacher. Other students may initially misperceive learning online as "easier" than learning in a physical classroom space. In reality, students often find the workload in an online course heavier because they must cover course material on their own and type their discussion comments.

There are a number of suggestions for how to help prepare students for online learning:

Clarify computer skills/terminology:

- Provide guidelines that the minimum technological requirements needed for the course.
- At the beginning of the semester, provide a detailed worksheet with instructions on how to complete the technical tasks required for completing course work. For example, while it may be clear to you how to post a message for many students, such tasks are new. Also, while some students may be familiar with one online environment, do not assume that they are familiar with all online environments.

  Some examples of information to provide include:
  - Where to find information online
  - How to post a message and homework assignments
  - How to access course readings and take online exams
- Describe how to seek help immediately when having trouble
- Explain online conventions for tone, such as using ALL CAPS for emphasis. Set rules for using abbreviations and emoticons.
- Provide a tutorial on computer basics.
  - *Tip*: If you cannot provide a tutorial on computer

basics, try working with a local community college to schedule a series of computer orientations. One Online Fellow scheduled five 2-hour computer orientations at a local community college to help her students learn computer basics. The college's IT staff setup 15 computers with updated browsers and word processing. Students learned basic computer operation as well as word processing skills. The final tutorial was dedicated to navigating library databases and the World Wide Web. The collaborative effort helped ensure student success for those students unfamiliar with online learning.

Explain the differences in learning online versus learning in a traditional classroom:

- Emphasize the amount of time needed for taking an online class and the importance of working independently. Because all class discussions are written, students must be prepared for the amount of time needed to type their comments. A 3-credit online course can easily require more than six hours of time, especially for students who type slowly.
- Emphasize the extensiveness of reading and writing in an online course. Because all class assignments are provided in written format with no opportunity for class questions, teachers detail class assignments thoroughly in online courses. Consequently, students must become careful readers in order to ensure that they understand the assignment.
- To help students understand the communication differences of learning online, provide a detailed worksheet with instructions on communication guidelines.
  - *Tip*: Conventions for Communicating Online to this stage for an example.
  - *Tip*: One instructor uses the following explanation to clarify to her students the definition of a threaded discussion post:

(i) How much to post, and what makes a "good" post?: These are hard questions to answer because discussions are organic, developing and evolving depending upon what is said by whom... In general, posting only once is not enough to really engage in a discussion. I am expecting probably 3-6 posts depending upon the amount of time I've allotted for the discussion and how in-depth your posts are... What I expect and hope to see is a dialogue evolving, with give and take, back and forth, questions asked and ideas explored like in a face-to-face class discussion... So as you post be cognizant that you are engaging in a discussion. Do not post long pages of responses—probably a couple of paragraphs at most, sometimes a sentence or two can be effective, especially if you're asking a question.

Address students' concerns on cyber-culture anxiety:

- Encourage questions and comments about technology.
- Use a survey to assess student technical knowledge at the beginning of the semester.
  - *Tip*: The Pre/Post Survey example in this stage for ways to assess student technical knowledge.

Clarify expectations:

- Post guidelines for participation on the class homepage. For example, explain to students how many days each week they should login to the course website. In online courses, it is not uncommon to expect students to login every week day.
- Give a detailed, conspicuous course outline. Because you must clarify course expectations only in writing, make sure that you give students enough detail to complete class assignments. Even simple assignments like a journal need detailed explanations.
  - *Tip*: One instructor uses the following explanation

for the weekly journal exercise. She posts this explanation in every unit to remind students weekly of the assignment:

(i) Your journal is the place for you to keep thinking about, wrestling with, exploring the issues we've discussed online. Feel free to add your own day-to-day observations about issues related to our course. Your journal is only read by me. I will never comment on your observations; I only check to see if you've completed the assignment. Length: 1-2 paragraphs Due: Every Friday by midnight EST

- Set clear expectations with regard to student performance/activity. Help students understand expectations for the course and encourage them to ask questions. One way to help students understand course expectations is to post examples of model assignments. You can post examples of model assignments from other webpages or upload sample papers. Most online course software programmes allow you to easily upload files, such as MS Word and Excel documents.
- Remind students frequently of course expectations.
  - *Tip*: During the semester, one instructor posted reminders to keep students up-to-date with the course material. Following is an example of one such reminder:

    (i) Have you read your James McBride?: If you haven't started reading The Colour of Water, you better get reading! It's almost Monday and the weekly exercise is due Wednesday. Look for the threaded discussion posting on Monday morning. Hope you had a great weekend! I look forward to getting your response papers on Monday night!

Explain the time-frame in which e-mails will be answered. For example, on Monday, Wednesday, and

Friday only, or within 2 business days of receipt.

- Emphasize courtesy to fellow students. Because students can not see verbal or visual clues from other speakers, encourage them to be tactful in their responses or include parenthetical clues for humour or emotion.
  - *Tip*: One instructor describes courtesy to her students with the following explanation:
    (i) Our online discussions will be class discussions, meaning the same respect we would show each other in an actual classroom, as suggested also show in a virtual classroom. In fact, because the online environment is primarily a verbal environment where we communicate through writing, it lacks the physical and auditory clues that accompany face-to-face discussion, which may lead to more misunderstandings, particularly when a person is using humour. But being polite and respectful does not mean that you can't disagree or question each other's interpretations of our texts. But be sure to do so in a polite way, rather than "I think you're wrong and here's why" write instead, "Sally, I think you are saying Y [paraphrase what person wrote], but I wonder if there isn't another way to look at that same incident. The way I see it, X really happened..." etc.

TEACHING AND LEARNING CHALLENGES

STRUCTURING AN ONLINE COURSE

- Course Planning
- Course Organization
- Communication

Experienced online instructors and students alike emphasize the need to have a clearly structured and well-planned course when teaching and learning online. Structuring the course effectively means planning the course well in advance of when it is being taught, thinking through the organizational structures and qualities that will help students learn, and understanding that the online environment presents a number of communication challenges.

Course Planning

Designing a course always takes a great deal of time and thought. That is no different with online courses. At the same time, the online environment offers particular obstacles and opportunities for both instructors and students. As you think through the course elements, pay particular attention to the course components that may serve as stumbling blocks to student learning online. One particular tension that emerges is the need to have a clear and organized structure, while allowing flexibility for making adaptations mid-stream.

- Develop your course before the semester begins: Often new faculty discover that developing online courses is time-consuming and that transitioning a successful traditional course to an online setting can be difficult. Experienced online instructors suggest developing your course well in advance and with a clear, concise objectives statement. The better prepared you are, the better your online teaching experience will be.
- Allow flexibility in your course design: Although it is important to make course expectations and due dates clear, it is also important to build in flexibility to your schedule. Building flexibility into your course structure will allow you to compensate for unexpected technological problems as well as give you opportunities to respond to student feedback.

Course Organization

Students in online courses are in particular need of a clear organizational structure. Keep in mind that each student is experiencing the course on his or her own–without the opportunity to turn immediately to a neighbour if confused or unclear about something in the course. In addition, students in online courses do not have the imposed structure of attending class at a consistent time and place each week they do not have the traditional "markers" of handing in papers in class or coming to the classroom to take a test. For all these reasons, it's important to think carefully about how to appropriately organize your course to encourage student participation and facilitate student learning.

- *Chunk the syllabus into parts*: Divide the course syllabus into discrete segments, organized by topic. Self-contained segments can be used to assess student mastery of that unit before moving forward in the course.
  - *Tip*: Use an "Assignments" page for course assignments. On that page, outline each assignment in a paragraph, explaining its purpose in helping students, and provide explanations and guidelines for evaluation.
  - *Tip*: Another way to divide the course is by time. One instructor uses the following organization, in which each unit is labeled by week and author, for her literature course.

    The first two weeks of her course:

    (i) Course Home
      - a. Syllabus
      - b. Calendar
      - c. Lounge
      - d. Questions

    (i) *Week* 1: Kyoko Mori
      - a. Who is Kyoko Mori?
      - b. Reading Notes
      - c. Weekly Exercise
      - d. Journal
      - e. Threaded Discussion

    (i) *Week* 2: Esmeralda Santiago
      - a. Who is Esmeralda Santiago?
      - b. Reading Notes

c. Weekly Exercise
d. Journal
e. Threaded Discussion

- Break assignments into chunks with "touch points": Because students work at their own pace in an online course, it works best to develop guidelines that require students to come back to the course website often. Chunking assignments helps students keep up with the work. In addition, use "touch points" at which point students do something–write in a journal, send an e-mail, enter into a discussion–to help chunk course content and give the course more structure.
  - *Tip*: A literature instructor chunked one unit as follows:
    (i) *Assignments for their eyes were watching god*:
      a. *Background information*: Before you begin to read Their Eyes Were Watching God, please read the background information that I have provided.
      b. Read stages 1-10 and write a two-page, single-spaced reading response that you will put in your Journal on the course homepage journal link. This response will be more informal than an essay, and is due by MIDNIGHT, JULY 23.
      c. Finish reading the book and POST at least twice to your group discussion board 8 p.m. July 25.
      d. Respond to your group discussion board several times by noon, July 26.
- *Provide due dates for assignments*: Each assignment should have a clear due date and time. In addition, multiple due dates every week keep students on track with course requirements.
- *Provide multiple opportunities for graded activities*: Assess students on writing assignments, standard test formats, and class participation. The online course

format offers a number of opportunities for graded written assignments, including threaded discussions, papers, web research, and online exercises. Multiple measurement points will stimulate students to become involved in multiple activities and keep them participating in class.

- *Give credit for participating in online discussions*: Give students credit for the substantive learning that students provide for each other through online discussions. In many online courses, these discussions are essential for advancing the course goals. By assigning credit for participation in online discussions, instructors can deter "lurking," where students listen to the conversation but do not participate.

Communication

In considering how you communicate with students about course goals and your expectations, it is again important to remember that students experience your course on their own and will come to the course with varying levels of technical expertise. Place important information in a variety of places, and repeat it often, in order to enhance the chances that students will pay attention to it.

- *Give students a clear overall understanding of the course structure*: Students need a clear message of the "vision" of the course so provide them a sense of the overall landscape of the course.
  - *Tip*: Use a Table of Contents layout design to help first time online students understand the structure of the course. The Table of Contents style is similar to printed material.
- *Post course syllabus, policies, expectations, and objectives on the course website*: You will most likely not be available to respond immediately when students e-mail questions regarding assignments or due dates, so posting your syllabus on thc course homepage will eliminate confusion.

- *Tip*: Students will access the course homepage at any time of the day or night. You can't always be online to answer questions, so make the assignments easy to find and easy to understand.

- *Setup a housekeeping clearinghouse part on your webpage*: To cut down on the number of individual questions, set-up a housekeeping clearinghouse part on your webpage where students can post a question and get answers about general course information. Encourage students to go to this part of the course before asking the instructor.
- Use printed materials if a student requests: Have a printed workbook of course syllabus and other critical course information available for students who request printed copies.
  - *Tip*: For engineering courses with heavy math content, provide detailed lecture notes, solutions, and other course materials in PDF format before the lecture date or online access date. This will allow students to download and print course material in advance.
- Structure online discussions: Structure the course to capitalize on the threaded discussion format. Use existing textbook material or website readings for "lecture" and guide students through activities and threaded postings for active learning.
- Remind students frequently of due dates: Use a technique like "Nag Notes" to remind students of due dates and other requirements.
  - *Tip*: One Communication professor uses "nag notes" to remind his students of due dates.

    For example:

    a. I've posted the topics proposed thus far. Browse to PROJECTS/PAPER No. 1. Reminders:
    b. For Wednesday, Read the Birkerts piece, "Into the Electronic Millennium."
    c. For Monday, Read Postman's and do the

IT/HC in the News Discussion Forum assignment.

CREATING COMMUNITY

- Student-to-Student Interaction
- Faculty-to-Student Interaction
- Tone

In an environment where instructors do not necessarily meet students face-to-face and where students may never have an opportunity to meet their peers in a physical classroom, developing a sense of community can be particularly challenging. At the same time, a sense of a community–where students are able to work cooperatively with peers on course material, have the opportunity for positive interaction with the instructor, and where the learning environment is respectful and motivates students to do their best–is key to a positive and successful learning experience. This part provides a number of solutions for creating community in the online classroom. The Online Fellows are quick to point out, however, that creating community is a challenge, and classroom dynamics must be monitored throughout the semester to ensure that students continue to engage thoughtfully in course content and continue to work together productively.

Student-to-Student Interaction

As the Principles of Good Practice in Undergraduate Education make clear, student learning in any classroom is enhanced when students have the opportunity to connect with each other about their academic work. For the online instructor, facilitating student-to-student interaction is made particularly challenging because students do not naturally have a chance to get to know each other before class or in face-to-face conversations. Therefore, it is important to structure opportunities where students "have" to interact with each other. It is also important, however, that the instructor develop methods for monitoring the success of these interactions.

The Online Fellows offer the following recommendations:

- *Limit the size of discussion groups*: Rather than having

an entire class talk in one large group, break the class into smaller discussion groups of four or five students. That way, students can get to know each other in a more intimate way.

- *Allow students to post student-to-student communication to get answers to questions*: Encourage students to discuss among themselves. Do not respond to every comment—interject and guide the discussion. Encourage students to introduce themselves to the group at the beginning of the semester.
- *Pair each student with a "buddy" in the course*: The buddy system gives students a source of support in the online classroom. Some instructors match students with varying technological experience. Other instructors prefer to match students who possess similar technological skills. Pair students just as to the goals of your course or the assignment.
- *Encourage peer response*: Post student papers online and ask each student to select a partner to critique each other's work. Be sure that students know their paper will be posted.
- *Structure opportunities for personal interaction*: Incorporate opportunities for students to tell you something about themselves in a "student lounge" or meeting place. A "student lounge" can also be a place where students can share with each other, meet each other virtually, and learn more about each other without your presence.

Faculty-to-Student Interaction

The Principles of Good Practice highlight the importance of faculty-student interaction in promoting learning. The online environment is not necessarily conducive to this goal, because neither the instructor nor the student can rely on regular face-to-face interactions to reinforce one's willingness to be helpful and approachable. Experienced online instructors, however, have identified the following ways to help enhance faculty-student interactions:

- *In your written communication, present yourself as accessible to students*: Students in an online course must feel that you are approachable. Often the demands on teachers are greater in online courses, so it is important to explore the variety of ways you can send a message of availability. One way to bridge the distance between faculty and student is to address students by name. Praise student-initiated contact.
  - *Tip*: To make yourself seem approachable to students, try using a more informal tone. For example, "Today, as you all are well aware, our class officially begins. Please begin working on the assignments for July 15-21. You have a couple of assignments due tonight"
- *Schedule an in-person meeting of the entire class*: If possible, meet with students in person for one session at the beginning of the semester. Meeting in person helps students associate names with faces and can be an effective, timely way to accomplish many of the administrative tasks central to your course.
- *Generate frequent communication*: Students need to have a sense the instructor is really "there," not "missing in action." This means responding in a timely manner to individual questions or issues that are raised in discussion groups. It also means making your presence known by participating in online discussions, giving students regular feedback on their work and their comments, and being flexible enough to make changes to the course mid-stream based on student feedback.
- *Assign discussion group leaders or project team leaders to facilitate group work*: Assigning team leaders is one way to ensure that students receive ample feedback. Make sure that the team leader disseminates information to every member of the team. Part of the responsibility of the team leader should be to report to you frequently on the progress of the team.

Tone

Remember that in the virtual classroom, neither the instructor nor the student has the visual cues of face-to-face communication. This also means students have fewer methods for determining whether their efforts are comparable to those of their peers and for assessing how they are doing in the class. Students will use the cues that are available to help them understand the classroom climate. Therefore, how the instructor shapes the course climate through written comments and the tone of communications to students is particularly important.

- "Humanize" the course: Remember that although you are teaching online, you are still teaching real people, so it helps if you and students can put names with faces. Develop a portion of the course website to post pictures and brief bios of students.
- Avoid general broadcast questions: An online course is not a collective but many individuals all reading messages separately. So, a broadcast message like "Are you doing the reading?" is hard for a student sitting at his/her own computer to interpret.
- Consider the tone of your own responses to students: Attitude comes through in writing. Are you sounding impatient? Supportive? Praise and model appropriate tone.
- Use private e-mail for sensitive communications: Use threaded discussions for group conversations. Use private e-mails to comment on individual student contributions and criticism.

ASSESSING STUDENT LEARNING

WHAT IS ASSESSMENT

The word "assessment" has taken on a variety of meanings within higher education.

The term can refer to:

- Standardized measures imposed on institutions as part of increased pressure for external accountability,

- The process faculty use to grade students' course assignments, or
- Activities designed to collect information on the success of a course, a programme, or a university curriculum.

The suggestions in this stage focus on the latter two components of assessment:

- Testing/evaluating student performance and providing feedback to students for grading purposes
- Assessing whether the course itself is "working" for student learning: what is going well, what isn't, and how do you know?

This second definition of assessment–determining what's "working" in the classroom– is particularly important in the early stages of innovative course design because assessment makes it possible to:

- Make informed improvements to current practices
- Document success to share with funding agencies, department chairs, etc.

At its best, assessment should be valuable to the teaching/learning process and not another add-on or "make work" of little use to instructors. In fact, assessment activities can be helpful in promoting all of the Principles of Good Practice.

EVALUATING STUDENT PERFORMANCE FOR GRADING PURPOSES

In assessing online learning, it is important to create a "mix" of assignments that cover the multiple dimensions of learning that online courses can employ. Traditional tests become a smaller part of the grade as you move towards encouraging student interaction on group projects and other activities.

Different forms of assessment include:

- End of semester paper
- Weekly tests
- Group projects
- Case study analysis
- Journals

- Reading responses
- Chatroom responses
- Threaded discussions participation

Communicate Expectations

Students in online courses are in particular need of clear information about course requirements and instructor expectations. Therefore, develop specific grading guidelines for course assignments and activities ahead of time so students know in advance what is expected of them.

For example, articulate what are appropriate responses to questions in online discussions, what is a substantive answer versus a superficial response, etc. Providing students with specific examples of the kinds of work you are looking for is also helpful.

Keep Track of Student Performance

The gradebook option in online software packages makes it possible to store all information about students' performance in one place. Many also make it possible for students to look up their own progress on assignments.

Give prompt feedback:

- At the start of the semester, clarify the type of feedback you will be giving so students have a clearer sense of what to expect from you.
- Students want feedback on assignments, but it is often difficult to provide much feedback when you use a number of varied assignments throughout the semester. One instructor uses system to provide a quick response to students.
- A number of grade book features have a comment part where the instructor can give specific feedback to a student on an assignment that can only be seen by the instructor and that student.

Design effective tests:

- Be clear from the start about what is allowed and what is not permitted when students take a test online.

- Because it is difficult to ensure that students taking an online exam are not using their books, some faculty encourage open book exams but place a time limit on how long students have to complete the test. These instructors believe that if a student knows where to go in the text book to get the information they need in a timely fashion then that student has clearly done the reading, and the issue of memorizing the information is less important. Some online course software allows you to limit the time that students may view test questions and post test answers.
- Unlike many traditional classes where students never see their completed exams after they hand them in, students in online courses can usually go back and look at the exam questions at a later date. While this can be a useful learning tool for students, it can lead to additional questions from students about exam content or the wording of a question.

Encourage active learning:

- Help students become more reflective learners by asking them to set their goals for the course at the beginning of the semester. At the end of the course, ask them to return to their goals to reflect upon what they've accomplished.
- The majority of students focus their academic effort on those elements of the course that will affect their grade in the course. Be sure that your grading policies reinforce the activities and assignments you value and that you take advantage of learning activities that are particularly suited for an online course. For example, if you want students to meaningfully participate in online discussions, be sure to include participation as part of the grading scheme.

Evaluate participation in threaded discussions:

- Require students to participate in specific numbers of threaded discussions.

- Have interactive learning activities account for a high percentage of the course grade.
- Identify the qualities you look for in discussions and grade students just as to those criteria.

ASSESSING WHETHER THE COURSE IS "WORKING"

Assessing whether your course is "working" provides feedback to understand what is useful to students. Josh Bersin in "Measuring E-Learning Effectiveness: A Five-Step Programme for Success" offers a helpful framework for thinking about the kinds of information you can use to determine your course's success. We also provide some specific assessment techniques.

Five Steps to Measure Effectiveness

- *Enrollment*: Is the audience showing up? If students are not enrolling in your course, then they might not know about the course or do not know how to enroll in the course. If the course is an elective course, the course may be named poorly or not located correctly in the catalog.
- *Activity*: Are they making progress? Typically, if the content is appropriate for the audience, students will progress at a reasonable rate. You may find that students move quickly and then stop at a particular point. Such information is valuable to help you assess the usability, relevance and performance of the course content.
  - *Tip*: Use minute papers or muddiest point exercises to provide feedback. Minute papers and muddiest point exercises work even better in an online environment because students can share them with each other, so students see what other students are thinking about.
- *Completion*: Did they finish? Students who truly complete the course can provide valuable feedback. However, many course software will "flag" a student "complete" even if that student has not completed

all the course assignments. Make sure that you can accurately track which students have completed all the course work.

- *Scores*: How well did a student score? In online learning environments, you often can not gauge why a student has scored highly on a quiz or assignment. Did they really learn the material or copy from someone else? Multiple assessments will allow you measure incremental progress towards the final learning goal, so you can measure what exactly a student scored well on and where they have fallen short.
- *Feedback/Surveys*: Did they like it? Feedback is a vital part of online learning. Regular feedback will provide you important details about the course content, assessments, and technology.
  - *Tip*: Collect mid-semester feedback and alter the course just as to student suggestions.
  - *Tip*: Survey students at the end of class about their progress. What worked in the course and what didn't?

ACADEMIC LIBRARIES IN E-TEACHING AND E-LEARNING

The noted psychologist B.F. Skinner, referring to the first days of his 'teaching machines' in the late 1950s and early 1960s, wrote, "I was soon saying that, with the help of teaching machines and programmed instruction, students could learn twice as much in the same time and with the same effort as in a standard classroom."

Academic libraries are the forefront of knowledge when it comes to systems and services that suit the needs of the information seekers. It remains for them to act at the institutional, national and international level to ensure that this knowledge is brought to bear in e-learning to the benefit of teachers and learners directly. With the advent of computers, the nature of libraries has changed dramatically. Computers are being used in libraries to process, store, retrieve and disseminate information. As a result, the traditional concept of library is being redefined from a place to access books to one which houses the most advanced media including CD-ROM, Internet, and remote access to a wide range of resources. Libraries have now metamorphosed into digital institutions. Gone are the days when a library was judged by its quantitative resources. Today, libraries are surrounded by networked data that is connected to the vast ocean of Internet-based services.

Moreover, electronic resources relevant to the professions are developing at an unprecedented pace. Academic libraries are considered to be the nerve centres of academic institutions which support teaching, research, and other academic programmes in various ways. Demographic changes, technological advances and globalization have totally changes the concept of education. The teaching-learning is a delicate process which needs to be standardized throughout the world. The important question today is no longer whether to implement e-teaching and e-learning in academics but how to run it well and how to get the best out of it.

E-TEACHING AND E-LEARNING

The prefix "e" has become increasingly evident on the lives of people in ways many could not have imagined less than ten years ago. With relative ease, the "e" is used with activities like real estate, retailing, banking, entertainment and now education. The "e" stands for electronic and it relates to the use of the Internet to undertake the wide range of activities. As we become more familiar with the language of the Internet we find just how much it pervades our daily lives in the dot.com age.

We readily recognize as an Internet web site and see it plastered on vehicles, billboards, hot air balloons, merchandise and in the electronic and print media. Educators are now beginning to hear terms like e-teaching, e-learning and e-education as these subtly become part of our regular vocabulary. Academic libraries serve the educators, including the new generation of teachers who will work in an Internet environment in both regular and virtual classroom situations. They will come to terms with new concepts of working in temporal and spatial settings.. E-teachers collaborate, build and discover new learning communities and explore newer resources in their interaction with information, materials and ideas with their students and colleagues. The e-education involves e-teaching and e-learning along with the various other administrative and strategic measures needed to support teaching and learning in an online environment. It will incorporate a local, regional, national and international vision of education. An Academic Library must have an effective e-learning strategy must be a good combination of the technology and the content it carries.

It must also focus on critical success factors that include building a learning culture, marshalling true leadership support, deploying a nurturing business model, and sustaining the change throughout the organization. Again, e-learning encompasses both the acquisition as well as use of knowledge distributed and facilitated by electronic means. "E-Learning is Internet-enabled learning. E-Learning provides faster learning at reduced costs, increased access to learning, and clear accountability for all participants in the learning process. In today's fast paced culture, organizations that implement e-Learning provide their work force with the ability to turn change into an advantage.

ACADEMIC LIBRARIES AND E-LEARNING

Academic librarians generally serve the subject academicians to provide information regarding teaching, learning and research. Though not everywhere, yet e-learning has been integrated in the curriculum of most of the university by different faculties. From the library side it has been a great opportunity to integrate the library resources and services in support of learning, research and outreach. In recent years several bold steps have been taken to integrate e-learning with the academic work. Most of the modern academic libraries are digital and e-learning can effectively take place in a digital environment. Academic libraries apply appropriate communication technologies in support of e-learning and e-research by providing seamless access to electronic resources and services. Electronic resources include online catalogues, databases, multimedia, online journals, digital repositories, electronic books, electronic archives and online/electronic services. The utilization of cutting edge technologies by academic libraries to provide access to resources and services in support of learning, teaching and research has benefited both on-campus, part time as well as distance learners. Both students and lecturers can undertake learning and research without being in the library.

An academic library, faculty and academic development department managing e-learning may use appropriate technologies to facilitate learning and access to resources and services. It is quite understandable that an e-learning environment can provide both students and faculty with a sustainable infrastructure and seamless access to knowledge, course content, information resources and services, all from integrated service point.

The initiative which should be taken by The academic libraries should take an initiative towards establishment of an e-learning support centre which would undertake training of the academic staff in integrating the educational technology into the curriculum to provide access to the content. As a part of this initiatives an Educational Technology unit will develop e-learning smart classrooms, along with video conferencing and assignment tools enabling flexible learning and teaching with the students studying at their own place. The academic library must have a holistic approach in e-learning whereby different traditional and digital methods and media are integrated in learning and teaching.

As faculty and instructors have began to adopt e-learning strategies as a part of their teaching repertoire, libraries played a key role, helping to find and organize resources to complement programmes and courses making use of e-learning in order to provide support to students working through their assignments. OCLC have suggested that resources must be integrated for academic libraries at the point of need to make these more effective. The role of the academic library for e-teaching and e-learning process can be carried out if the library has two types of requirements filled up:

- Technical and Functional requirements
- Technical and Cultural requirements

Technical and Functional Requirements

- Display and integrate a variety of information windows as part of a learning activity
- Aggregate access to content in any given learning context
- Provide bibliographical tools that permits easy searching and reference completions
- Provide access to tools that render and present content in user customised formats
- Integrate plagiarism software into course management systems to encourage good practice and to assess reliability of content.

Technical and Cultural Requirements

- Embed library resources in course management systems
- Integrate third party commercial information services
- Customise portal facilities for storing personal preferences
- Provide easy access to virtual reference services at the point of need.
- Embed training modules to assist in information seeking.

As a part of e-learning an academic library must provide the services to its students and staff from remote access which include:

- New acquisitions to indicate newly acquired materials for each department.
- View your patron record to see materials borrowed by an individual customer with an option to renew the borrowed materials without visiting the library.
- Request for materials that are borrowed by another

user. Upon return of the material, communication is sent to the user who made the request to come and borrow the material.

- Users can suggest additional items that the library should acquire based on their need. The request can be made online.
- Materials placed on reserve by lecturers for specific courses.
- E-mail communication is provided through the system to enable a two way communication between the user and the library.
- Online charges and fines are made available to users.
- Searching for past examination papers by faculty, department and course numbers providing access to full text.

ROLE OF ACADEMIC LIBRARIANS IN E-TEACHING AND LEARNING

Nowadays academic librarians are a part of e-learning process and are actively participating by providing online and in person modules, guides, subject and class based lists, as well as reference. The librarians offer classes and courses on research strategies, help students in determining useful scholarly resources, work with the faculty in planning and developing distance education courses to integrate concepts of information literacy throughout the curriculum. Faculty need support in these activities because the ability to articulate information needs, find appropriate information resources and critically assess the results of an online search are key to success in e-learning and this leaves the faculty to focus on course content.

In the case of libraries what is good for the online student is also useful for the campus based student. By a study it was seen that the librarian facilitating the e-learning are establishing a positive relationship between the academic achievement and use of open shelf library books. The librarians should play a dedicated role in supporting instructors and administrators to realise the potential of e-learning through the provision of service models unique to libraries. Librarians somewhere have found to develop web based modules to support course integrated instruction session, encourage students to actively follow the librarians' presentation using their own topics for selected searches. Students receive immediate feedbacks on search strategies during the session and can return at any time to refresh their skills for subsequent assignments.

Reference staff use the material to guide students in using information resources specific to their assignments at the reference desk. This blended approach to information literacy offers students and instructors with an ability to address diverse learning styles and encourage active participation along the presentation to a 24/7 access that may foster increased student contact with the librarians. Many librarians specially university librarians are working with online course developers as well as instructors in traditional courses to provide online guides and help for library research, these include modules that introduce students not only to specific resources but to critical evaluation of resources, specific about thesis preparation and the like.

As with face to face library connection, these modules are very effective when integrated into course and research material provided by the instructor.

The requirements on the part of the Librarian to be a part of e-learning are:

- Must be proactive in questioning the selection of learning management systems and complementary e-learning tools by faculty and departments.
- Actively seek representation through appointments to committees that deal with selection, management and governance of online instructions systems on their campus.

COMPETENCIES FOR ONLINE TEACHING

Information technology is changing the way people live and learn. Not surprisingly information technology is also transformation the nature of teaching. These remarks provide a framework for thinking about such changes and exploring work in progress that is relevant to the development of competencies specific to teaching online.

COMPETENCE, COMPETENCIES AND CERTIFICATION

Competence refers to a state of being well qualified to perform an activity, task or job function. When a person is competent to do something, he or she has achieved a state of competence that is recognizable and verifiable to a particular community of practitioners. A competency, then, refers to the way that a state of competence can be demonstrated to the relevant community. The International Board of Standards for Training, Performance and Instruction, a competency involves a related set of knowledge, skills and attitudes that enable a person to effectively perform the activities of a given occupation or function in such a way that meets or exceeds the standards expected in a particular profession or work setting. The structure and assessment of competencies may differ from one community of practice to another and even within a community. To facilitate a common understanding of competencies in the context of online and distributed learning some specifications have been elaborated. Typically, a competency is divided into specific indicators describing the requisite knowledge, skills, attitudes and context of performance. There are different ways to validate that a person has demonstrated the relevant competencies. One of them is through a certification process.

Teacher certification is a common practice, and the notion of teacher competencies is fairly well established. However, competencies are generally associated with highly formalized professional activities and not applied to ill-defined tasks. Ill-defined tasks certainly include many forms of teaching. This narrow view of competence runs counter to common sense and professional practice, but brings into attention the mainstream approach to elaboration of teacher competencies where it is essential to clearly identify the conditions of teaching. The delivery environment is a particularly relevant condition to identify competencies for online teaching.

ONLINE AND CLASSROOM TEACHING

Information technology can be integrated into both online and classroom settings, but the interaction between these technologies and new approaches to learning and instruction may vary. The range of activities available in online settings and the multiple conditions of time in which they take place are evidence that the technology demands placed on online teachers are somewhat more significant than those associated with classroom teachers.

Much of what has already been published with regard to online teaching has focused on technical skills and requirements of successfully moderating and facilitating online discussions and chat sessions. This body of literature suggests that becoming an effective online moderator requires training and that there are competencies unique to online environments. In online asynchronous discussions, the moderator's competencies involve allowing learners time for reflection, keeping discussions alive and on a productive path, and archiving and organizing discussions to be used in subsequent sessions.

In online synchronous discussions, the moderator must establish ground rules for discussion, animate interactions with minimal instructor intervention, sense how online text messages may appear to distant learners, and be aware of cultural differences. How are these competencies unique to online teaching?

At the applied level, animating discussions, displaying cultural sensitivity and so on, apply to all teachers. At the environment level, however, the ways in which a teacher demonstrates such competence is quite different, which suggests that there are competencies unique to online settings. Belisle and Linard the use of IT in teaching calls for additional competencies adapted to new roles and circumstances. Teaching competencies and online teaching competencies have generally been considered separately. However, efforts to interrelate the two are being undertaken by IBSTPI in association with the research centre for Télé-université, Université de Québec.

IMPLICATIONS OF COMPETENCIES FOR ONLINE TEACHING

The current interest in competencies for online teaching is coming from business and industry, primarily with regard to technical training and professional development courses offered in online settings. It is quite likely that some of the interest in competencies for online teaching is a result of hastily-crafted online courses and inadequate preparation of online facilitators.

Clearly technology offers the potential to create and implement highly engaging and effective online environments to support a wide variety of learning goals. It is also quite clear that our capacity to make effective use of information technology in educational settings is impaired by inadequate preparation of teachers and by a shortage of properly trained instructional designers and educational support personnel. The development of competencies for online teaching should lead to the associated development of training for online teachers and to the certification of online teachers.

To develop competencies for online teachers is not without challenge. Competencies are dynamic in nature, and they largely depend on the relevant social context. The constant transformation of IT makes the development of competencies for online teachers a continuous process and demands continuing professional preparation and training for online teachers. Such endeavors will improve our ability to make effective use of technology in learning and instruction.

QUALITY STANDARDS IN ONLINE TEACHING AND LEARNING

The challenges associated with online teaching and learning demand new approaches to quality assurance beyond the framework within which higher education institutions currently operate. As Taylor and Richardson assert, there is a need for quality assurance systems which consider "the standard of online information", and at the same time, support academics in the development of high quality online resources. This document presents an approach developed by the

University of South Australia, which addresses both these aspects of quality - providing the standards by which online courses are judged, and supporting academics as they develop their own scholarship of teaching in the area of online learning. The Boyer notion of scholarship is a framework for considering academic work that can be applied to online teaching and learning within universities.

Boyer identified four scholarships - discovery, teaching and learning, integration and application. His approach is predicated on an understanding of the communal basis of all scholarly activity: that scholarship by its very nature is a public rather than private activity; that it is open to critique and evaluation by others; and that a field of study is progressed through the scholarly activity of building new ideas which are then open to the same processes of public scrutiny. All of the scholarships are exposed to the same rigorous approaches of peer review as a way of gaining quality, transparency and accountability. Within this framework the scholarship of teaching and learning has emerged as a major theme in the higher education sector. Central to this notion of the scholarship of teaching and learning is that of the 'learning community' - the recognition of the value of relationships and practices that occur in and through the work practices of staff. One way to support and stimulate this kind of collegial activity is to provide structured opportunities for discussion and reflection through a checklist of agreed good practice.

Taylor and Richardson advocate the application of this approach to the design and construction of information and communication technology based teaching resources, arguing that independent peer review requires "...the development of an explicit and shared understanding of the scholarship underlying the design and development of these resources". Such shared understanding, just as to Taylor and Richardson can also form the basis for validating the quality of the resources. This document describes the development of a checklist and supporting website, in which shared understanding about the scholarship of teaching and learning in resources developed for online delivery is made explicit.

The principles underlying the development of this approach are as follows:

- The criteria for the standards of development have been gathered from the full range of relevant academic literature surrounding online teaching and learning. This affirms the work of academics in the area and provides it in a highly practical form which is accessible to a broadly-based audience.
- The approach locates responsibility for the quality of teaching and learning with the academic staff responsible. Staff can use the items to guide the development or redevelopment of their own courses through reflective processes.
- The instrument and its associated website provide an opportunity for just-in-time academic staff development by providing the accepted standards, information about how to meet these and examples of how others have done this.
- The instrument provides a framework to involve other academics in the process of peer review.
- The website is designed to provide a model of best practice, and has been validated using the W3C Mark-up Validation Service, and the W3C CSS Validation service, and complies with W3C Web Content Accessibility Guidelines 1.0.

REVIEW OF OTHER INSTRUMENTS

In order to pursue this approach, the authors reviewed a range of instruments available through the Internet. Several generic descriptors for online course development and evaluation were identified. Since online teaching and learning is still a developing area of academic activity within universities, and many staff engaged in online approaches have limited expertise, the authors were interested in identifying instruments that provided an educative and explanatory dimension which supported the evaluative function. In effect, this required the instrument to be both comprehensive in scope and specific in detail. A review of the instruments available identified several problematic issues. First, several had been developed to address particular aspects of course development and were partial in their scope rather than comprehensive.

Second, many of them were very general, open-ended instruments. Although there may be some justification for this in terms of providing a generic framework, these instruments make considerable assumptions about the level of expertise of those involved in the processes of online teaching and learning.

Third, some instruments were found to be comprehensive in their scope, but unnecessarily complex because the instrument and supporting online materials were not integrated. Finally, most of the online instruments were found to be inaccessible for users with disabilities. The authors noted features in some approaches that were consistent with the objectives of the proposed checklist of agreed good practice. Of particular note is the Michigan Virtual University's Standards for Quality Online Courses and the accompanying Excel-based Course Evaluator tool.

The standards addressed in the MVU instrument include several criteria proposed for a checklist of agreed good practice including; instructional design, accessibility, usability and technology. However, the authors were concerned about the complexity of this instrument, and in particular, the lack of a seamless integration between the Excel tool and the supporting online material. Furthermore, the authors contend that aspects relating to accessibility and usability need to be embedded within criteria relating to instructional design, interface design, use of media and technological issues, rather than treated as separate considerations.

DESIGN AND DEVELOPMENT

Since the instruments reviewed failed to adequately address all of the needs that the authors had identified as important characteristics of a checklist of agreed good practice, it was necessary to develop a new review tool designed to meet those needs. In doing so, the authors recognized the need to build on the experience gained from the review process which had indicated some consistency in the priority placed on certain criteria. For example, Michigan Virtual University's standards for quality online courses, the peer review proforma developed by the Griffith Institute for Higher Education, the Electronic Learning Institute's criteria and standards used in evaluating Web-based instruction and delivery guidelines, and Lyn Knowitall's expert review checklist all consider instructional design issues, interface design and/or appropriate use of media and technological issues.

The proactive evaluation model proposed by Sims also places importance on criteria relating to instructional design, interface design and elements of content utility, including the accessibility of the content. Similarly, the MVU standards consider accessibility issues, using the W3C Web Content Accessibility Guidelines 1.0 Priority 1 criteria as its benchmark. This review of the literature and available evaluation approaches informed the authors' decision to structure the review tool and associated website around the following areas of consideration:

- Instructional design
- Interface design
- The use of multimedia to engage learners
- The technical aspects of interactive educational multimedia.

The authors opted to embed criteria relating to inclusivity in items associated with all four areas of consideration, since issues such as accessibility impact on the instructional design, usabilitity, use of media and technical functionality of online course materials.

The review of instruments also identified a range of different approaches employed to measure the extent to which the various items listed under these major areas of consideration meet the stated criteria.

These approaches include the complex quantitative rating system delivered via an Excel spreadsheet in the MVU's evaluator, simple yes/no checklist formats utilised in Electronic Learning Institute's criteria and standards used in evaluating

Web-based instruction and delivery guidelines, open-ended qualitative questionnaire formats employed in the Southern Regional Education Board's criteria for evaluating Web sites, and the CIDOC Multimedia Working Group's multimedia evaluation criteria, and quantitave measures using a rating scale approach with provision for qualitiative responses to open-ended questions, as exemplified in the Griffith Institute for Higher Education's peer review proforma. Based on this analysis, the authors decided to adopt a combined approach, employing a 5-point Likert scale to and a free form text area for comments.

This approach was considered to be appropriate for the design and development of a checklist of agreed good practice, since a combination of quantitative and qualitative measures will most likely yield comprehensive results. In developing this tool, the authors acknowledge that such instruments have inherent limitations, since as Owston observed "....no single model or framework is likely going to satisfactorily capture the complexity of pedagogical, technical, organizational, and institutional issues inherent with Web-based learning".

However, the tool is not intended to be used in isolation from other academic practices. It will be most valuable when it is part of a wider framework of course and programme development and evaluation or established peer review processes. To a very significant extent the intention of the review tool is to generate scholarly discourse around online teaching and learning within the rich environment of an academic community.

Summative and formative evaluation has been an integral aspect of the development of the review tool from the point where the authors identified the need to develop an instrument within their own institution. This involved reviewing a range of instruments which were deemed inadequate for the purpose and audience.

After much research, a paper version was developed and circulated to a reference group of online enthusiasts and other interested staff. Feedback was incorporated into a revised version. Using this version, the course materials of a volunteer academic were reviewed and the results were presented to a seminar of staff involved in online teaching and learning. Further revisions were made and a beta version developed. In the next stage of the evaluation, academic staff, professional development staff and students at the University of South Australia will be invited to take part in a trial using the beta version and their feedback incorporated in the final version of the review tool and the online website.

DESCRIPTION OF THE REVIEW TOOL

The preceding part describes the design and development of a review tool comprising a paper-based checklist of agreed good practice and supporting website which provides an educative function, addresses issues relating to inclusivity, and is constructed around four main areas of focus - instructional design, interface design, use of media and technical aspects.

Educative Function

The educative dimension is central to both the just-in-time approach to professional development and approaches which involve more formal educational development. The associated website supports this educative function through the inclusion of features such as hyperlinks to explanations and the relevant literature that are accessed by selecting a "more" link alongside each checklist item, an exemplars part, and additional resources.

There is often confusion among reviewers about the difference between general statements about the overall goals and clearly specified objectives. By selecting the "more" link the reviewer can check their understanding of these terms and also learn more about effective techniques for specifying objectives or learning outcomes from the hyperlink references included in the related explanatory screen.

Inclusivity

Items relating to inclusivity such as gender, culture and accessibility have been embedded across the four parts of the instrument. The decision to embed these items rather than to extract them into separate categories was based on the view that essentially the items reflect good teaching and ought to be seen in a more integrated way. Since the supporting website was designed to provide a model of good practice, it has been necessary to ensure that that it too meets W3C Web Content Accessibility Guidelines 1.0.

The accessibility design features incorporated into the design of the site are as follows:

- All pages validate at HTML 4.01 transitional using the W3C MarkUp Validation Service.
- Cascading style sheets are applied for layout and style, and have been validated using the W3C CSS Validation Service.
- Alt text attributes and captions have been applied to all visuals and image maps.
- Redundant text links are provided as footers on each page.
- Care has been taken to ensure that sufficient contrast is provided between foreground and background images, and that content does not rely on colour alone.
- The primary natural language of all Web pages has been specified.
- All tables linearise appropriately.
- Use of scripting languages and reliance on non-html languages has been avoided
- Links open as new pages rather than as new windows.
- All links can be accessed via keyboard control as well as mouse control.
- Menus are grouped logically and skip links are provided.

Areas of Focus

The review tool is constructed around four sets of considerations: instructional design, interface design, the use of multimedia to engage learners, and the technical aspects of interactive educational multimedia.

Instructional Design

Instructional design criteria consider how the strategies and techniques derived from learning theories are applied to the solution of instructional problems in interactive multimedia applications.

The importance of pedagogically driven instructional design in the creation of educational multimedia is well documented.

The features considered in instructional design criteria include:

- Whether the learning objectives are clearly stated;
- The appropriateness and accuracy of the content;
- The sequencing of instruction;
- Whether the topics are applied in "real" contexts;
- Assessment strategies and
- The appropriate use of feedback.

Interface Design

Interface design critieria address the quality of the end-user interface and how it affects "... users' perception of the product, what they can do with it and how completely it engages them". Reushle and Sonwalker contend that interface design and related usability factors will have a significant influence on the success of instructional interactive multimedia.

As Sonwalker explains, "Users interact with online Web courses through a graphical user interface, so the design of graphic elements, the colour scheme, the type fonts, and navigational elements can all affect how a course is organized and perceived by students". Interface design criteria address all of these usability factors as well as accessibility criteria since as Dey advises "the interface needs to be accessible to as wide an audience as possible".

Use of Media

Effective use of media is a key aspect of educational design. This area of concern considers issues relating to the effective use of interactive multimedia, writing style and accuracy of text and copyright. The term interactive multimedia is used to identify the capacity of digital media to facilitate a range of interactive experiences; the aim being to promote active learner engagement. Evaluation of the appropriate use of of interactive multimedia considers the ways in which multimedia technologies are integrated into the teaching and learning process to support the learning objectives, promote learner control and "...actively engage learners in creation of knowledge that reflects their comprehension and conception of the information...".

Multimedia components such as animations, video and audio also present challenges for users who have disabilities, and those living in locations with restricted bandwidths. The criteria must therefore also consider accessibility features, such as the provision of synchronised captions to avoid precluding certain groups of students from engaging in the learning experience.

Technical Aspects

The technical aspects of interactive multimedia are considered in reviewing educational applications because software and hardware problems can undermine learners' confidence and their ability to form good models of how computers work. Accroding to Sonwalker, the issues influencing the technological success of online courses include available bandwidth, target system configuration, server capacity, browser software, and database connectivity. In addition to these factors, evaluation of the effectiveness of interactive multimedia applications in online education needs to consider the extent to which the course materials are accessible to all users across different platforms and browsers, if plug-ins are required whether the user is informed and links are provided, whether all hyperlinks are active and the overall robustness of the application.

STANDARDS FOR QUALITY ONLINE TEACHING

The most important factor affecting student learning is the teacher. Everyone understands, on a personal level, the importance of teachers to their educational success. Teachers who know their subject, understand how to teach and can adjust their teaching to student needs will be successful in raising student achievement, research shows. Teacher expectations also are a significant factor in how much and how well students learn. Online learning provides the opportunity for every middle grades and high school student, regardless of where he or she lives or attends school, to have access to a quality teacher. Many of these students benefit by being challenged academically by an online teacher who, in some cases, possesses stronger academic credentials and essential teaching skills than traditional classroom staff, especially in certain geographic and subjectshortage areas.

Access to quality online teaching can result in improved student academic performance and increased course completion rates. Quality online teaching reflects the attributes of any effective teaching, whether in the traditional classroom or online. Both traditional classroom teachers and online teachers need to know their subjects and how to teach them. They also must know their students, stay up to date in their subject areas, and manage and monitor students' academic progress to ensure success.

But in the 10 years since Web-based courses were first made available to students, the understanding of what is required to be a successful online teacher has increased significantly. The technology used to access and provide Web-based courses effectively also has improved. Now it is important to re-examine what qualifications are needed to be an effective online teacher. Equally important is an understanding of the attributes of today's students, who have access to and can use technology to pursue opportunities and information never before available to them. For many students, this access has changed the way they see the world and the way they work and play. Consideration of these student issues is critical for a teacher to be effective.

Another often overlooked but important issue for online teachers: Delivery of Web-based courses is not restricted to a specific time or schedule. Because instruction does not start and stop at the same time for all students, time-management skills are extremely important, not only for the online teacher but also for students. The lack of these skills is a major reason why some students drop their online courses. Effective online teachers also must possess the ability to prepare quality written communications.

Appropriate and effective writing not only conveys information—it encourages and supports students. Words and body language that traditional classroom teachers use must be translated to the online environment for online teachers to be successful. All of these issues must be factored into setting appropriate standards for quality online teaching.

THE STANDARDS

The standards for quality online teaching in this report were developed by knowledgeable, experienced resource persons from K-12 and postsecondary education, drawn from national and regional organizations, SREB state departments of education, and colleges and universities.

Through extensive collaboration and sharing with SREB staff over many months, their work culminated in specific standards that SREB states can use to define and implement quality online teaching. Through broad acceptance of these standards, SREB states will be able to provide more students with the courses they need, regardless of where students and teachers reside.

These standards have been supported by practice over time, as well as substantiated by research. In fact, research at both the K-12 and postsecondary levels is creating a growing body of evidence that quality online teaching is not only as good as traditional teaching—in many ways it can be superior

ACADEMIC PREPARATION

- *Standard*: The teacher meets the professional teaching standards established by a state licensing agency or the teacher has academic credentials in the field in which he or she is teaching.
- *Indicators*:
  - The teacher:
    a. Meets the state's professional teaching

standards or has academic credentials in the field in which he or she is teaching;

b. Provides evidence that he or she has credentials in the field of study to be taught;
c. Knows the content of the subject to be taught and understands how to teach the content to students;
d. Facilitates the construction of knowledge through an understanding of how students learn in specific subject areas; and
e. Continues to update academic knowledge and skills.

SKILLS AND TEMPERAMENT FOR INSTRUCTIONAL TECHNOLOGY

- *Standard*: The teacher has the prerequisite technology skills to teach online.
- *Indicators*:
  - *The teacher*:
    a. Demonstrates the ability to effectively use word-processing, spreadsheet and presentation software;
    b. Demonstrates effective use of Internet browsers, e-mail applications and appropriate online etiquette;
    c. Demonstrates the ability to modify and add content and assessment, using an online Learning Management System;
    d. Incorporates multimedia and visual resources into an online module;
    e. Utilizes synchronous and asynchronous tools effectively;
    f. Troubleshoots typical software and hardware problems;
    g. Demonstrates the ability to effectively use and incorporate subject-specific and developmentally appropriate software in an online learning module; and

h. Demonstrates growth in technology knowledge and skills in order to stay current with emerging technologies.

METHODOLOGY, MANAGEMENT, KNOWLEDGE, SKILLS AND DELIVERY

- *Standard*: The teacher plans, designs and incorporates strategies to encourage active learning, interaction, participation and collaboration in the online environment.
- *Indicators*:
  - *The teacher*:
    a. demonstrates effective strategies and techniques that actively engage students in the learning process;
    b. facilitates and monitors appropriate interaction among students;
    c. builds and maintains a community of learners by creating a relationship of trust, demonstrating effective facilitation skills, establishing consistent and reliable expectations, and supporting and encouraging independence and creativity;
    d. promotes learning through group interaction;
    e. leads online instruction groups that are goal-oriented, focused, project-based and inquiry-oriented;
    f. demonstrates knowledge and responds appropriately to the cultural background and learning needs of non-native English speakers;
    g. differentiates instruction based on students' learning styles and needs and assists students in assimilating information to gain understanding and knowledge; and
    h. demonstrates growth in teaching strategies in order to benefit from current research and practice.

- *Standard*: The teacher provides online leadership in a manner that promotes student success through regular feedback, prompt response and clear expectations.
- *Indicators*:
  - *The teacher*:
    a. Consistently models effective communication skills and maintains records of applicable communications with students;
    b. Encourages interaction and cooperation among students, encourages active learning, provides prompt feedback, communicates high expectations, and respects diverse talents and learning styles;
    c. Persists, in a consistent and reasonable manner, until students are successful; z establishes and maintains ongoing and frequent teacher-student interaction, student-student interaction and teacher-parent interaction;
    d. Provides an online syllabus that details the terms of class interaction for both teacher and students, defines clear expectations for both teacher and students, defines the grading criteria, establishes inappropriate behaviour criteria for both teacher and students, and explains the course organization to students;
    e. Provides a syllabus with objectives, concepts and learning outcomes in a clearly written, concise format;
    f. Uses student data to inform instruction, guides and monitors students' management of their time, monitors learner progress with available tools and develops an intervention plan for unsuccessful learners;
    g. Provides timely, constructive feedback to students about assignments and questions; and

   h. Gives students clear expectations about teacher response time.

- *Standard*: The teacher models, guides and encourages legal, ethical, safe and healthy behaviour related to technology use.
- *Indicators*:
  - *The teacher*:
    a. Facilitates student investigations of the legal and ethical issues related to technology and society;
    b. Establishes standards for student behaviour that are designed to ensure academic integrity and appropriate uses of the Internet and written communication;
    c. Identifies the risks of academic dishonesty for students;
    d. Demonstrates an awareness of how the use of technology may impact student testing performance;
    e. Uses course content that complies with intellectual property rights policies and fair use standards;
    f. Provides students with an understanding of the importance of Acceptable Use Policies;
    g. Demonstrates knowledge of resources and techniques for dealing with issues arising from inappropriate use of electronically accessed data or information; and
    h. Informs students of their right to privacy and the conditions under which their names or online submissions may be shared with others.
- *Standard*: The teacher has experienced online learning from the perspective of a student.
- *Indicators*:
  - *The teacher*:
    a. Applies experiences as an online student to develop and implement successful strategies for online teaching;

   b. Demonstrates the ability to anticipate challenges and problems in the online classroom; and
   c. Demonstrates an understanding of the perspective of the online student through appropriate responsiveness and a supportive attitude towards students.

- *Standard*: The teacher understands and is responsive to students with special needs in the online classroom.
- *Indicators*:
  - *The teacher*:
    a. Understands that students have varied talents and skills and uses appropriate strategies designed to include all students;
    b. Provides activities, modified as necessary, that are relevant to the needs of all students;
    c. Adapts and adjusts instruction to create multiple paths to learning objectives;
    d. Encourages collaboration and interaction among all students;
    e. Exhibits the ability to assess student knowledge and instruction in a variety of ways; and
    f. Provides student-centred sessions and activities that are based on concepts of active learning and that are connected to real-world applications.
- *Standard*: The teacher demonstrates competencies in creating and implementing assessments in online learning environments in ways that assure validity and reliability of instruments and procedures.
- *Indicators*:
  - *The teacher*:
    a. Creates or selects fair, adequate and appropriate assessment instruments to measure online learning that reflect sufficient content validity, reliability and consistency over time; and

b. Implements online assessment measures and materials in ways that ensure instrument validity and reliability.

- *Standard*: The teacher develops and delivers assessments, projects and assignments that meet standards-based learning goals and assesses learning progress by measuring student achievement of learning goals.
- *Indicators*:
  - *The teacher*:
    a. Continually reviews all materials and Web resources for their alignment with course objectives and state and local standards and for their appropriateness;
    b. Creates assignments, projects and assessments that are aligned with students' different visual, auditory and hands-on ways of learning;
    c. Includes authentic assessment as part of the evaluation process;
    d. Provides continuous evaluation of students to include pre- and post-testing and student input throughout the course; and
    e. Demonstrates an understanding of the relationships between and among the assignments, assessments and standards-based learning goals.
- *Standard*: The teacher demonstrates competencies in using data and findings from assessments and other data sources to modify instructional methods and content and to guide student learning.
- *Indicators*:
  - *The teacher*:
    a. Assesses each student's background and content knowledge and uses these data to plan instruction;
    b. Reviews student responses to test items to identify issues related to test validity or instructional effectiveness;

   c. Uses observational data to monitor course progress and effectiveness; and
   d. Creates opportunities for self-reflection or assessment of teaching effectiveness within the online environment.

- *Standard*: The teacher demonstrates frequent and effective strategies that enable both teacher and students to complete self- and pre-assessments.
- *Indicators*:
  - *The teacher*:
   a. Employs ways to assess student readiness for course content and method of delivery;
   b. Employs ways for students to effectively evaluate and assess their own readiness for course content and method of delivery;
   c. Understands that student success is an important measure of teaching and course success; and
   d. Provides opportunities for student self-assessment within courses.

THE FUTURE OF ONLINE TEACHING AND LEARNING IN HIGHER EDUCATION

Institutions of higher education have increasingly embraced online education, and the number of students enrolled in distance programmes is rapidly rising in colleges and universities throughout the United States. In response to these changes in enrollment demands, many states, institutions, and organizations have been working on strategic plans to implement online education.

At the same time, misconceptions and myths related to the difficulty of teaching and learning online, technologies available to support online instruction, the support and compensation needed for high-quality instructors, and the needs of online students create challenges for such vision statements and planning documents. In part, this confusion swells as higher education explores dozens of e-learning technologies with new ones seeming to emerge each week.

Such technologies confront instructors and administrators at a time of continued budget retrenchments and rethinking. Adding to this dilemma, bored students are dropping out of online classes while pleading for richer and more engaging online learning experiences. Given the demand for online learning, the plethora of online technologies to incorporate into teaching, the budgetary problems, and the opportunities for innovation, we argue that online learning environments are facing a "perfect e-storm," linking pedagogy, technology, and learner needs.

Considering the extensive turbulence created by the perfect storm surrounding e-learning, it is not surprising that opinions are mixed about the benefits of online teaching and learning in higher education. As showed in numerous issues of the Chronicle of Higher Education during the past decade, excitement and enthusiasm for e-learning alternate with a pervasive sense of e-learning gloom, disappointment, bankruptcy and lawsuits, and myriad other contentions. Appropriately, the question arises as to where online learning is headed.

Navigating online education requires an understanding of the current state and the future direction of online teaching and learning. The study described here surveyed instructors and administrators in postsecondary institutions, mainly in the United States, to explore future trends of online education. In particular, the study makes predictions regarding the changing roles of online instructors, student expectations and needs related to online learning, pedagogical innovation, and projected technology use in online teaching and learning.

REVIEW OF LITERATURE

We began this project with a review of past studies of the issues and trends in online teaching and learning in higher education.

Online Teaching and Learning

A recent survey of higher education in the United States reported that more than 2.35 million students enrolled in online courses in fall 2004. This report also noted that online education is becoming an important long-term strategy for many postsecondary institutions. Given the rapid growth of online education and its importance for postsecondary institutions, it is imperative that institutions of higher education provide quality online programmes. The literature addresses student achievement and satisfaction as two means to assess the quality of online education. Studies focused on academic achievement have shown mixed reviews, but some researchers point out that online education can be at least as effective as traditional classroom instruction.

Several research studies on student satisfaction in online courses or programmes reported both satisfied and dissatisfied students. Faculty training and support is another critical component of quality online education. Many researchers posit that instructors play a different role from that of traditional classroom instructors when they teach online courses, as well as when they teach residential courses with Web enhancements.

Such new roles for online instructors require training and support. Some case studies of faculty development programmes indicate that such programmes can have positive impacts on instructor transitions from teaching in a face-to-face to an online setting.

Pedagogy and Technology for Online Education

Several research studies have covered effective pedagogical strategies for online teaching. Partlow and Gibbs, for instance, found from a Delphi study of experts in instructional technology and constructivism that online courses designed from constructivist principles should be relevant, interactive, project- based, and collaborative, while providing learners with some choice or control over their learning.

Additionally, Keeton investigated effective online instructional practices based on a framework of effective teaching practices in face-to-face instruction in higher education. In this study, Keeton interviewed faculty in postsecondary institutions, who rated the effectiveness of online instructional strategies. These instructors gave higher ratings to online instructional strategies that "create an environment that supports and encourages inquiry," "broaden the learner's experience of the subject matter," and "elicit active and critical reflection by learners on their growing experience base."

In another study of pedagogical practices, Bonk found that only 23–45 per cent of online instructors surveyed actually used online activities related to critical and creative thinking, handson performances, interactive labs, data analysis, and scientific simulations, although 40 per cent of the participants said those activities were highly important in online learning environments.

In effect, a significant gap separated preferred and actual online instructional practices. Technology has played and continues to play an important role in the development and expansion of online education. Many universities have reported an increase in the use of online tools. Over the past decade, countless efforts have sought to integrate emerging Internet technologies into the teaching and learning process in higher education. Several studies have reported cases related to the use of blogs to promote student collaboration and reflection.

Some researchers also have promoted the plausibility of using wikis for online student collaboration, and pod casting is beginning to garner attention from educators for its instructional use. Although some discussions in the literature relate to effective practices in the use of emerging technologies for online education, empirical evidence to support or refute the effectiveness of such technologies, or, perhaps more importantly, guidance on how to use such tools effectively based on empirical evidence, is lacking.

METHOD

This study was based on a survey of individuals believed to have relevant experience with and insights into the factors affecting the present and future state of online education.

Participants

An online survey was conducted of college instructors and administrators who were members of either the Multimedia Educational Resource for Learning and Online Teaching or the Western Cooperative for Educational Telecommunications both premier associations for online education. MERLOT is a free and open resource for higher education with membership that, at the time of this study, included more than 12,000 college professors, instructional designers, and administrators who share and peer-evaluate their Web resources and materials.

WCET is an organization with 500–600 members that provides resources and information regarding the effective use of telecommunications technology in learning. Also surveyed were those who had posted one or more course syllabi at the World Lecture Hall which has approximately 2,000 members and was developed by the University of Texas for faculty to share syllabi. This study is a part of a longitudinal effort to understand the use of technology in teaching, within both higher education and corporate training settings. The second author had previously surveyed MERLOT and WLH members on the state of online learning as well as corporate trainers on online training and blended learning.

Instrument

Using an online survey service, SurveyShare, we developed an online questionnaire as an instrument for this survey study. The questionnaire consisted of 42 questions grouped into three parts related to the current status and future trends of online education in higher education. The first part included 10 questions regarding respondents' demographic information.

The second part included seven questions about the current status of online learning at the respondents' organizations. The third part included items regarding predictions about online teaching and learning. The survey used various types of questions, including Likerttype, multiple-choice, and open-ended questions.

Data Collection and Analysis

The survey took place from late November 2003 to early January 2004. An invitation was sent by e-mail to the sample of instructors, instructional designers, and administrators described earlier. The e-mail included information about the study as well as the URL to the survey site. Of more than 12,000 who received the e-mail request, 562 completed the survey. The participants responded to the survey anonymously, and the data were stored in the hosted online survey service. Descriptive data analyses were conducted using the data analysis tool provided in the online survey site.

RESULTS

Our study confirmed some commonly held beliefs about online education, refuted others, and provided a range of predictions about the future of technology- enabled education.

Demographics of Online Instructors

Sixty-six per cent of the survey respondents held teaching positions while nearly one-fourth were administrators or instructional designers. Respondents represented institutions of various types: approximately half were employed by public, four-year colleges or universities; 23 per cent by community colleges or vocational institutes; and 16 per cent by private postsecondary institutions.

A large majority said their institutions offer online courses, and about 70 per cent of them had taught online courses. Respondents' experience with online teaching varied from none to more than 10 years. Although not every respondent had online teaching experience, more than 95 per cent had experience integrating computer or Web technology into their face-to-face teaching. Survey results show that women appear to be teaching online in far greater numbers than just a few years ago.

In fact, more than half of the respondents were women. Such findings were surprising because a similar study conducted a few years earlier was dominated by male instructors who were full professors at tier-one universities.

Perhaps female instructors had become more comfortable teaching and sharing activities online during the few years that elapsed between surveys, or perhaps support for instructors had improved on college campuses, or both.

Emerging Technology

When asked about several emerging technologies for online education, 27 per cent of respondents predicted that use of course management systems would increase most drastically in the next five years. Those surveyed also said that video streaming, online testing and exam tools, and learning object libraries would find significantly greater use on campus during this time. Between 5 and 10 per cent of respondents expected to see increases in asynchronous discussion tools, videoconferencing, synchronous presentation tools, and online testing. The survey also asked what technology would most impact the delivery of online learning during the next five years. Respondents could select one of 14 key technologies. About 18 per cent of respondents predicted that reusable content objects and wireless technologies would have the most significant impact.

Smaller percentages selected peer-to-peer collaboration, digital libraries, simulations and games, assistive technologies, and digital portfolios. In contrast, less than 5 per cent predicted that e-books, intelligent agents, Tablet PCs, virtual worlds, language support, and wearable technologies would have significant impact on the delivery of online learning. These findings seem to reflect the perceived importance of online technologies for sharing and using preexisting content. Additionally, respondents predicted that advances in Internet technology are likely to increase the use of multimedia and interactive simulations or games in online learning during the next five to 10 years.

Only about one in 10, however, predicted that advances in Internet technology would enhance videoconferencing or international collaboration, and just one in 16 thought it might offer greater chances to interact with field experts or practitioners. Again, the focus was on enhancing content and associated content delivery, not on the social interactions, cross-cultural exchanges, or new feedback channels that wider bandwidth could offer. Such responses indicate that respondents still see learning as content-driven, not based on social interactions and distributed intelligence. The emphasis remains on a knowledge-transmission approach to education, not one rich in peer feedback, online mentoring, or cognitive apprenticeship.

Enormous Learner Demands

Our study revealed a number of trends related to areas of growth in online education, future needs for online instructors, and the dominance of online versus face-to-face instruction.

Growth of Online Programmes/Degrees

Comparing current online offerings and projected future online offerings at respondents' institutions yields predictions about the areas of growth in online programmes and degrees. Most respondents expected considerable growth in online certification and recertification programmes in the next few years, as well as in associate's degrees.

Yet, our survey respondents predicted little growth in the number of institutions that offer online master's or doctoral programmes in the future. Although more than half of the respondents expected that their institutions would offer online master's or doctoral programmes in the coming years, almost the same number of respondents reported that their institutions were presently offering online master's or doctoral programmes. In contrast, respondents predicted that certification and recertification programmes would see 10–20 per cent growth from present offerings. Such responses indicate that higher education institutions might be wise to explore certificate and short programme offerings rather than full degree programmes.

Online Instructors' Readiness

Will online instructors be ready to meet the challenges

brought by the projected increases in learner demands for online education? About half of the respondents predicted that monetary support for and pedagogical competency of online instructors would most significantly affect the success of their online programmes.

In addition, instructors' technical competency was the third most pressing factor. Nevertheless, pedagogical skill was deemed more important than technological skill for effective online teaching. With regard to the needs for pedagogical competency of online instructors, a majority of the respondents expected that online instructors would typically have received some sort of training in online teaching either internally or externally by the year 2010.

The Rise of Blended Learning

The survey asked respondents for their predictions related to the growth of online education in the next few years. Respondents indicated that more emphasis is expected on blended learning—instruction that combines face-to-face with online offerings—than on fully online courses. Those surveyed predicted a distinct shift from about one quarter of classes being blended today to perhaps the vast majority of courses having some Web component by the end of the decade.

Enhanced Pedagogy

Although the use of CMSs in higher education has increased rapidly and is likely the foundation for the rapid increase in the number of online learners during the past decade, some researchers argue that CMSs are promoted as ways to manage learners rather than to promote rich, interactive experiences. As a result, enhancing pedagogy is perhaps the most important factor in navigating the perfect e-storm. In the present study, respondents made predictions about the quality of online education in the near future and about how online courses would be taught and evaluated.

The Quality of Future Online Education

Survey respondents generally agreed with recent Sloan

reports that the quality of online education will improve in the future. Sixty per cent of respondents expected that the quality of online courses would be identical to traditional instruction by the year 2006. Also, a majority of the respondents predicted that the quality of online courses would be superior to or the same as that of traditional instruction by 2013. Only 8 per cent predicted that the quality of online courses would be inferior in 2013. Similarly, a large majority of respondents predicted that learning outcomes of online students would be either the same as or superior to those of traditionally taught students by 2013.

In effect, the trend is for course quality and learner outcomes to steadily and significantly improve during the coming decade. Although we did not ask about reasons for the increase in quality, such numbers should be interesting and valuable to administrators, instructors, students, and other online learning stakeholders. In terms of factors that can improve online learners' success, respondents said that training students to self regulate their learning was needed most, followed by better measures of student readiness better evaluation of student achievement and better CMSs to track student learning.

Nine per cent said additional technology training is needed. This concern about learner self-regulation is ironic in a world dominated and driven by learning management systems that are primarily used to manage students, as alluded to earlier. Follow-up surveys might address whether learners perceive this mixed message and whether they prefer to be managed online or engage in more self-directed online environments.

As Carmean and Haefner argued, there is a need for CMS environments that foster deeper student learning and engagement. They noted that such environments might foster student choice among various activities, reflection, apprenticeship, synthesis, real-world problem solving, and rich, timely feedback. More recently, Weigel added to this argument by suggesting that the next-generation CMS should foster a more learner-centred environment that rich in critical thinking, student exploration, peer learning and knowledge construction, interdisciplinary experiences incorporating a community of educators and educational opportunities.

Online Teaching Skills

Instructors' abilities to teach online are critical to the quality of online education. Unlike our earlier study related to the state of online learning in 2001, which included many questions about online learning tools and features, the present study focused more on learning outcomes and pedagogical skills. For instance, this study found that the most important skills for an online instructor during the next few years will be how to moderate or facilitate learning and how to develop or plan for high-quality online courses.

Being a subject-matter expert was the next most important skill. In effect, the results indicate that planning and moderating skills are perhaps more important than actual "teaching" or lecturing skills in online courses. As Salmon pointed out, online instructors are moderators or facilitators of student learning.

Pedagogical Techniques

Over half of the survey respondents predicted that online collaboration, case based learning, and problem-based learning would be the preferred instructional methods for online instructors in the coming decade. In contrast, few respondents expected that instructors would rely on lectures, modeling, or Socratic instruction for their online teaching in the future. In other words, survey respondents predicted that more learner-centred techniques would be used in the future, indicating a marked shift from traditional teacher-directed approaches. Existing research indicates that online instructors tend to use easy-to implement tools, resources, and strategies rather than complex PBL, virtual teaming, cross-cultural collaboration, simulations, and other forms of rich interactive media.

If the prediction for more learner-centred pedagogies online is realised, it would be interesting to study whether those teaching online transfer such pedagogical skills to their face-to-face instructional activities. Our findings also indicated that, in general, respondents envisioned the Web in the next few years more as a tool for virtual teaming or collaboration, critical thinking, and enhanced student engagement than as an opportunity for student idea generation and expression of creativity. This is not surprising, given that most instruction in higher education is focused on consumption and evaluation of knowledge, not on the generation of it. Perhaps online training departments and units need to offer more examples of how to successfully embed creative and generative online tasks and activities.

Evaluation and Assessment of Online Courses

Evaluation is an important part of ensuring the quality of online courses and programmes. The summarizes respondents' predictions about future trends concerning the evaluation of online learning. When asked how the quality of online education will be most effectively measured during the coming decade, 44 per cent answered that a comparison of online student achievement with that of students in face-to-face classroom settings would be the most effective, followed by student performance in simulated tasks of real-world activities, calculations of return on investment, and student course evaluations.

Clearly, respondents believe that face-to-face instruction provides a valid benchmark for teaching and learning outcomes and that online performance should at least equal its effectiveness. Such views, while politically important, seem to forget that much of the learning that occurs online could not take place in a faceto- face delivery mode. It also assumes that face-to-face instruction is superior. What if institutions took the opposite stance and measured face-to-face courses based on whether they could accomplish all that online instruction can? As for the forms of evaluation that will be used during the next few years, respondents predicted that online practice quizzes and exams would be most highly used, followed by online surveying and polling, course evaluations, and online quizzes and exams.

In particular, more than 90 per cent of the respondents predicted that online surveys would be used as an important student research tool or as a teaching device in addition to student assessment and course evaluation. This finding affirms our belief that online surveys offer the chance to be learner-centred because they allow students to collect, analyse, and report on real-world data and projects.

AT THE END

As institutions of higher education continue to embrace and debate online learning, it is important to envision where the field is headed. What might the next generation of online learning environments look like? Will they move from warehousing students in online environments to engaging them in interactive and motivational activities?

What technological and pedagogical advantages will they offer? Current studies provide a glimpse of the pedagogical and technological possibilities. Clearly, we are entering a unique and exciting era in online teaching and learning. And perhaps the perfect e-storm is becoming less cloudy and ominous.

Implications of the Findings

Institutions of higher education need to consider whether they are ready to meet growing learner demands in the coming years. First of all, most respondents agreed that blended learning would have greater significance in higher education in the future. Although some institutions have already embraced blended learning, many others are slower at adopting it for various reasons.

Perhaps leadership from the institution is crucial for faculty to receive adequate support to implement changes in the teaching process. If the quality of online education is to improve as projected from this study, campuses must also look at the pedagogical issues in online learning. Collaboration, case learning, and PBL are likely to be the preferred methods of online instructors, with few relying solely on traditional methods. The data presented here also indicate that the continued explosion in online learning will bring increased attention to workshops, courses, and degree programmes in how to moderate or mentor with online learning. Given that many respondents expect to receive some sort of training and support from their institutions to be ready for online teaching, colleges and universities need to consider how they will respond to these needs.

In addition, our study indicates that postsecondary institutions are finally focusing on how online learning can develop student collaboration and evaluation skills. In fact, most now see the potential of the Web in the coming years as a tool for virtual teaming or collaboration, critical thinking, and enhanced student engagement, though not necessarily as a tool for creative and individual expression. Do current CMSs provide tools to realise the potentials of the Web for innovative teaching and learning? Perhaps recent developments in open source courseware will force CMS vendors to develop and market more pedagogically engaging tools and resources. This survey also forecasts enormous growth in online certification and recertification programmes, as well as some growth in associate's and master's degree programmes during the coming decade.

In terms of technology, the study reveals interest among online instructors in wireless technologies, simulations, digital libraries, and reusable content objects. Perhaps we are entering a world where learning objects will be at our fingertips. Learning objects on different topics will likely be something you can grab like magazines and newspapers on the way into a plane, bus, or train. In addition, as bandwidth increases with the next-generation Internet technologies and capabilities, simulation and gaming tasks that online students engage in will be more realistic and authentic.

Study Limitations and Recommendations for Research

More than two years have passed since we conducted the survey. This time gave us the opportunity to see how the predictions our survey respondents made have played out. We have continued to witness accelerating growth of learner demands for online learning as well as the potential for enhanced online pedagogy due, in part, to the recent open source movement. Predictions related to emerging technologies seem to have been inaccurate, given that only 1 per cent said that the use of blogs would increase dramatically by 2008. Given the thousands of new blogs each day, it is safe to say that this prediction did not hold.

This study did not explore actual online teaching and learning practices. It is likely that some responses were related to recent fads that may or may not be sustainable. In addition, we did not survey students for their perceptions of online learning trends and possibilities. A study of students might indicate that they deem different technologies to be important and on the cusp of significant growth. In a learner-centred world, who can better predict technology trends today—instructors or students?

This study also indicated that blended learning will perhaps be a more significant growth area than fully online learning. Follow-up studies might focus on aspects of blended learning that institutions need to address, such as types of blended learning, activities that lead to blended-learning success, and instructor training for blended-learning situations.

2

Creating an Effective Online Syllabus

INTRODUCTION

The syllabus is an important part of any course, whether delivered online or face to face. Defining syllabus broadly here, we assume the traditional syllabus should include not only a schedule of topics, readings, activities, and assignments, but also such elements as goals, objectives, or expected outcomes for the course, grading policies, procedures, and any other information necessary for students to succeed. Some instructors separate these various elements and call them "Course Information," "Course Requirements," "Grading," "Schedule," and so on.

For the purposes of this stage, however, we'll cover all these essentials with the term syllabus. Although the details of course requirements, expected outcomes, schedule, grading, and procedures are staple elements of any course syllabus, they are perhaps even more important for an online class.

Students tend to feel somewhat disoriented without the familiar first-day speeches from the instructor, and they may wonder if any of the same old rules will apply in this new online territory. It's typical for first-time online instructors to include too little detail in their syllabi. One instructor we know changed nothing in his regular on-the-ground course syllabus except to add the words "This course is delivered completely online." Unfortunately, students had a hard time even finding his syllabus, as he posted no welcome at the "entrance" to his online course, and then they were puzzled by his schedule, which still listed "class sessions" as once a week. Some students reasonably thought this phrase referred to online, real-time chat. Others wondered if the phrase meant that their asynchronous communications should be posted only once a week, on the particular day named in the schedule. As a result of this lack of clarity, the first week's discussion forum was dominated entirely by questions about where, when, and how to do the assignments, and the main topics for that week were nearly forgotten in the confusion.

Even after the instructor's hurried explanations, students continued to experience confusion about dates and times, procedures and grading. They could refer back to the first week's forum and search through the various discussion threads in which these questions had been raised, but they had no clear reference document to which they could turn. One student even had a grade dispute with the instructor that arose from an ambiguity in the syllabus. In the syllabus, the instructor had declared that all late assignments would be penalized at the rate of onequarter grade point each day, but hadn't clearly specified that the due dates for assignments were based on the instructor's time zone, not the student's.

Thus the student claimed that, when he posted an assignment at 11:00 P.M., Pacific time, on the due date, he was unfairly penalized because the server on which the course was housed, located on the East Coast of the United States, had recorded the time as 2:00 A.M. the following day. These examples, both serious and trivial, show some of the problems that can ensue if online syllabi aren't thorough and detailed. Even in hybrid courses—those that are taught face to face with an online component—clear directions are vital.

It's important, for instance, to explain to students how the mixture of different venues will be integrated. Which course activities will take place in the on-campus classroom, which in the online classroom, and what's the sequence of procedures students should follow each week? Imagine that, before the live class meeting on Wednesday, you want students to read the online lecture and post a preliminary report, but you want them to wait until after the class meeting to take part in that week's online discussion. In many cases, they won't understand that sequence unless it's carefully explained to them. There are three aspects of an online syllabus we want to emphasize in particular: the contract, the map, and the schedule.

THE CONTRACT

Increasingly, the syllabus has come to be the contract between students and instructor, laying out the terms of the class interaction— the expected responsibilities and duties, the grading criteria, the musts and don'ts of behaviour. Let's look at some features of the contract that are especially important for an online course.

CLASS PARTICIPATION AND GRADING CRITERIA

What's meant by "participation" in the online setting won't be obvious to students. Participation should be defined. For example, is it posting, that is, sending messages to the classroom discussion board? Or is it just logging on and reading? Perhaps participation includes taking part in an online group presentation or showing up for a real-time chat? If you're going to count participation towards the final grade, you should define how that will be calculated. We recommend, in fact, that you always give a grade for active participation in the class, that is, for contributing to discussions and asking or answering questions.

The plain fact is that, if students aren't graded, the great majority won't actively participate. Besides judging the quality of students' contributions, you may want to set a minimum level for quantity of participation. Another consideration in asynchronous discussion is the degree of self-pacing allowed. Must students follow a chronological order of topics in their participation, or can they go back and respond to previous weeks' topics? Can they do assignments at different times during the course? The answers really depend on the nature of your course. For example, if your course has a set number of tasks, which can be completed at any time within the ten weeks of the session, then you may not be concerned about students' skipping about or restarting conversations about previous weeks' topics. If you're going to allow some measure of self-paced activity, then you must make this clear to students in your syllabus.

The danger in this sort of arrangement is that students may get confused about the progress of the course, and they may feel that they must continually look back at earlier weeks to see if some new discussion has been posted. However, there are course management platforms and standalone forms of discussion software that alert students entering the classroom to the fact that they have new, unread messages in a particular discussion forum. In this case, students will easily discover that there are discussions going on in any of the various units of the course. If students don't have this sort of alert, you should remind them via announcements or in your syllabus instructions to check the previous weeks' discussions.

MANAGING STUDENT EXPECTATIONS

The task of managing student expectations is very important in the online classroom. Some students enroll in an online course expecting it to be much easier than a regular course. Others imagine that the course will be something like independent study. Still others think the instructor should be available for twenty-four real-time hours a day. Your syllabus as well as your introductory comments can help manage such expectations, correct false impressions, and set the stage for the smooth unfolding of your course.

It's also helpful if your institution has a general student orientation that explains how the online course will work, how much student-instructor interaction can be expected, and so forth. If your institution doesn't have such an orientation, you may need to supply some of this information in your own syllabus. A continuing education instructor we know, who has a busy professional practice, complained after a few weeks of her online class that students had "unrealistic expectations." When pressed to explain this remark, she commented that, if she didn't reply to each and every student comment in the discussion forum or if she appeared not to be in the online classroom every day, she would receive plaintive e-mail queries or even classroom postings inquiring about whether she had read a particular message. She further explained that she had expected students to work on their own during the first part of each week and only then to post their thoughts in the discussion forum. Unfortunately, neither her syllabus nor her introductory comments ever mentioned these teacher expectations.

This case shows that managing student expectations can also require an instructor to communicate his or her expectations of the students. This type of problem can be handled by a simple statement in the syllabus to the effect that the instructor will look in frequently during the week but may not be in the classroom every day, or that students should work on the week's assignments during the first part of the week and then post their responses later in the week.

Other information of a "contractual" nature that you might want to incorporate in your syllabus includes the following:

- Your policy on late assignments
- Whether due dates are calculated by your time zone or the student's
- Your availability for real-time chat appointments
- Specifications for writing assignments
- Your institution's policy on plagiarism and cheating

THE MAP

In this new territory of the online classroom, students will seize upon your syllabus as if it were a map. Students will want to know how to proceed and where everything is located. So, one of the first things you must do, whether through the syllabus or in an introductory message, is to explain the geography of the course. In fact, if the syllabus isn't visible on the first level of the course, but instead can be arrived at only by one or two clicks of the mouse, then this introductory set of directions must be given in an announcement area or even delivered prior to the course, by e-mail. An example of an announcement area with explicit directions to the syllabus. What else does "explaining the geography" mean? If your course consists of various web pages plus a discussion forum, you'll need to let the students know where to find the component parts of the course and under what headings: "Lectures will be on the page whose link says 'Lectures,' and these are arranged by weeks."

If the discussion forum is hosted on an outside site, students need to be told that this link will take them off the university server, that they must use a password given to them, and so on. If you've created a discussion forum dedicated to casual communications and socializing for students, let them know that the area you have imaginatively labeled "Café Luna" is intended to be the online equivalent of a student lounge. This is particularly important when using course management software that has its own unique and not customizable category headings.

Students will need to know what you have stored behind each of these generic headings. For example, to students taking courses within the course management system Web Course in a Box, it may not be obvious that the main page heading "Learning Links" is where they will find the threaded discussion forum. Similarly, the "Water-Cooler" forum created by the instructor in Blackboard CourseInfo, might remain a mystery without explicit directions. In a hybrid course that combines face-to-face and online components, it's essential that you specify where to do each activity. For example, in Lonnie Yandell's Cognitive Psychology class for Belmont University, his syllabus gave clear instructions for combining face-to-face and online procedures.

Here's an excerpt from the "Course Requirements" part of his syllabus:

- This course will include a major computer Internet component. Assignments, lectures, practice tests, simulations, and discussion will be held online. Time spent in class will be on computer lab simulations, in-class discussion, group work, and textbook stage tests.

And this excerpt from his assignment schedule explains the procedures:

- The course is divided into 24 modules. Each stage has from 2 to 4 modules. Each module has a related textbook reading, online lecture, online discussion question, and online self-test.
- You should read the textbook part first, then review the online lecture. The lectures will be summaries, elaborations of the textbook material, and links to related information on the Web.
- After you have completed reviewing the lecture, you should then log into "TopClass" and post answers to the lecture discussion question.You can also read other students' posts and respond to them if you like.You can receive extra credit for the discussion grade by making appropriate responses to others' posts. Discussion posts must be made by the date on the schedule to receive full credit.
- You should also complete the short self-test. The self-tests are designed to help you make sure you understand the material.

Other procedural and geographical issues you might want to cover in the syllabus include these:

- The URL for your home page
- How e-mailed assignments are to be labeled in the subject line
- Which file formats you'll accept for attached documents
- Any contact information for technical and administrative Support
- The proper sequence for accomplishing weekly activities and assignments

THE SCHEDULE

The course should be laid out by weeks for students, because this is commonly the unit by which students gauge their own participation and work. If your class starts on a Wednesday, then Tuesday will become the last day of your week unless you state otherwise. We recommend that you think in terms of subdivisions of twoor three-day spreads. For example, if you post your lecture on Monday, allow students through Wednesday to read and comment on it, rather than asking them to do so by Tuesday.

Students can be told to log on every single day, but it is perhaps wiser to take advantage of the asynchronous flexibility of the online environment. Assume that some students will log on and read on Monday night, some on Tuesday morning, and others at midnight. The Monday reader may return on Tuesday night to reread and post. The Tuesday reader may respond with comments at once. This scheduling flexibility is even more important for those who have students in different time zones or in foreign countries.

It's also good to gauge your students' access to computers and their probable work schedules. If your students are accessing the course web site from a campus lab, the dorms, or branch campus libraries, then they'll follow a different pattern than will continuing education students, who may want to use the weekends to do most of the time-intensive assignments. A Monday or Tuesday due date for assignments will allow working adults to make the most of their study time out of the office.

USING SPECIFIC DATES

Instead of simply listing the course schedule for "Week One" and "Week Two," your schedule should include the specific dates for each unit, week, or topic area covered. This is particularly important for asynchronous courses in which students may be logging on at diverse times and days during the week. It's quite common for students to lose track of the weeks in the term when following an asynchronous online schedule.

If you don't want to include dates on the main syllabus web page because you want to reuse it for subsequent terms, then send students an e-mail version of the syllabus or post a downloadable document version with the relevant dates inserted. Some course management software includes a calendar feature that you may use to reinforce the dates for each segment of the course.

SUPPLYING INFORMATION MORE THAN ONCE

It's easy to lose track of where and when something was said in threaded discussions or via e-mail. When you give directions, it may not be possible for students to simply link back to them at a later date.

For that reason, you should provide important instructions in more than one location. Although students in some course management platforms may be able to use a search function to find your instructions, in most cases students will have to waste energy and time to sift through materials before they can locate that one crucial sentence of direction. Therefore, even if you intend to explain assignments and procedures later in the course, it's best to state them up front in the syllabus as well.

Then, if your course is laid out entirely in web pages, make sure that each page permits students to link back easily to essential information in the syllabus.

A CHECKLIST FOR YOUR ONLINE SYLLABUS

Here, in summary form, is a checklist for creating your online syllabus. You needn't include all of these items nor do you have to include them all in one document called a "syllabus." You can distribute this information among several documents if desired.

- Course title, authors' and instructor's names, registration number, and term information; syllabus web pages should bear creation or "last revised" dates if the term date isn't included at the top
- Course instructor's contact information, plus contact information for technical support
- Course description, perhaps the same as the description used for a course catalog listing, but probably more detailed; should list any prerequisites or special technical requirements for the course
- Course objectives or expected outcomes; what

students can expect to learn by completion of the course

- Required texts or materials: any books or other materials, such as software, not made available in the course but required for the course
- Explanation of grading criteria and components of total grade: a list of all quizzes, exams, graded assignments, and forms of class participation, with grade percentages or points; criteria for a passing grade; policies on late assignments
- Participation standard: minimum number of postings per week in discussion and any standards for quality of participation
- Explanation of course geography and procedures: how the online classroom is organized; how students should proceed each week for class activities; how to label assignments sent by e-mail; where to post materials in the classroom; any special instructions
- Week-by-week schedule: topics, assignments, readings, quizzes, activities, and web resources for each week, with specific dates
- Any relevant institutional policies, procedures.

Sometimes it's difficult to anticipate every issue that may arise during the class and to include that in your syllabus. There's obviously a balance between readable brevity and a syllabus so voluminous as to be intimidating.

Whatever you don't include in your initial documents may still be introduced by means of announcement areas, weekly e-mail sent to all students, or postings in an appropriate forum. You will also want to use these means to reinforce important elements of your syllabus as the course progresses.

3

Analysing Online Teaching and Learning Systems

INTRODUCTION

The online learning phenomenon has become more widespread in recent years with many learning institutions adapting ways of incorporating modern technology into learning skills and objectives to facilitate students learning. Online Learning is becoming an ever-increasing way of facilitating education to students who are unable to attend a traditional on-campus university as well as supporting on-campus teaching. The most common systems used by educational establishments are asynchronous learning systems. Online learning does not just denote how learning is conducted but is "an educational philosophy for designing interactive, responsive and valid information and learning opportunities to be delivered to learners at a time, place and in appropriate forms convenient to the learners" or, even more simplistically put, learning conducted using the web and a personal computer.

Clark suggested that teaching and studying at a distance can be as effective as traditional instruction provided:

- The methods and technologies used are appropriate to the instructional tasks,
- There is student-to-student interaction, and
- There is timely teacherto- student feedback.

After a review of relevant educational literature it was found that there is no one specific method for the analysis of online teaching and learning systems. Also often the strategies presented are not student driven, hence the requirement of an alternate student focused method.

BACKGROUND TO SSM

SSM is a method that has been used by many and applied in different aspects of business and beyond. It is often not referred to as a methodology but a problem solving tool, which makes it suitable for a variety of situations. Checkland's SSM focuses on organisational problems by considering the organisation as a whole, not just looking at one particular problem and not attempting to make an early decision on a solution to a problem. SSM works through a number of stages that are showed in There are a total of seven stages in the standard SSM methodology.

Gencoglu, Altmann, Smith, and Mackay applied SSM to the study of supply chain management on the premise that SCM is affected by cultural, political, and social issues and that SSM would be an effective tool to deal with these "soft" problems. The research centred on workshops where the participants in the SCM made use of the techniques of SSM. It was concluded that the use of SSM gave the participants a greater understanding of the problem situation, and they could identify issues and conflicts more effectively.

This research highlights the effectiveness of SSM to be used in many situations and be useful in situations without easy solutions. SSM was used by Patel to analyse the teaching and learning process in a higher education institution. The standard stages of SSM were followed and the "area of concern" was wide ranging. The results produced fifteen recommendations, some of which were previously unrecognized by the lecturers.

DEVELOPMENT OF MEAD

It was decided to use SSM as a basis for the method for the analysis and design of online teaching and learning systems for a number of reasons:

- SSM is a well known, internationally used methodology and has been used in a variety of settings since its development in the early 1980s;

- SSM allows for flexibility in its application to suit the discipline and area under investigation;
- SSM encourages ownership of the problem situation by involving stakeholders in the process;
- The organisational aspects of the situation can be addressed. This may be especially important in regards to online teaching and learning systems, as it is not an isolated system, but governed by policies, procedures and structure of its environment;
- The use of rich pictures will be a communication tool with students and will present the issues in a non-threatening and easy understandable fashion. They will also aid in the participation aspect of the method.

The user participation aspect of SSM was one of the most important features when deciding to use SSM as the basis of the method. It allows the inclusion of the different perceptions and opinions of stakeholders within the problem situation. As this method is a student driven approach it is the opinions and values of that group that will formulate the analysis and design, not the perception of the designers or teaching staff. Initially a conceptual model was created identifying from the literature the most important features that should be included in the method.

These were separated into three main categories:

- *Concept and Content*: The theories and methods to be used to undertake the analysis and design;
- *Participation*: The different types and level of participation that will take place;
- *Development and Structure*: How the content and participation will be included in the development process.

These features were then incorporated into the framework of SSM to produce a new method–MEAD. As well as the seven main stages of this method there is participation that takes place at numerous stages of the method.

- *Stage Two*: In stage two a participant survey and focus

group session are both used. The survey provides the initial data for stage two and the focus group session provides validation of SSM conceptual, real world models and updating.

- *Stage Five*: In stage five the real world models that are developed are discussed with an online designer expert to assess their validity.
- *Stage Seven*: The completed design and implemented changes are presented to a focus group of online teaching and learning system users for their assessment and comments.

THE STAGES AND IMPLEMENTATION OF MEAD

The method was implemented in Deakin University, a tertiary institution located in Victoria, Australia. Deakin University is one of Australia's largest universities, with five campuses located in Melbourne, Geelong, and Warrnambool. It was established in 1974 with one campus located in Geelong. Deakin University was one of the first Australian universities to introduce off-campus learning, first through traditional paper methods and then through Internet technologies.

Since 2004, all new undergraduate students have been required to undertake at least one wholly online unit as a part of their degree and most units have an online teaching and learning presence. Deakin University currently uses software called Deakin Studies Online a part of the WebCT brand of software. This software is used in almost every unit at Deakin University with a "required" amount of information to be provided to students however most units have a much wider DSO presence, supplying various learning materials, lectures, tutorials, discussions etc. The application involved participation from an online teaching and learning expert as well as users of online teaching and learning systems.

STAGE 1 - RECOGNISE POSSIBLE ONLINE LEARNING ISSUES

Stage 1 requires the recognition that there is an issue with the current online teaching and learning system and, therefore, some action is required to improve the situation. Usually there is at least one person that recognises the possible problem situation and takes action to improve it. In the case of the online teaching and learning system, this is likely to be an academic staff member who has been informed by students as to problems or limitations of the current system, or has noted through their own teaching problems with the current system in terms of its design or lack of content and functionality.

In this case of this practical application, informal student comments and the staff member's awareness of issues and limitations were the initiation for an investigation into the situation. The work completed in stage 1 of the method was a combined effort guided by the designer with a large amount of input and consensus by the focus group participants.

STAGE 2 - ANALYSE CURRENT ONLINE LEARNING ISSUES

Stage 2 focuses upon analysing the current online learning issues; this stage has a key focus of data elicitation. Data was collected through a survey, gauging students' opinions and attitudes to numerous areas of teaching and learning online at Deakin University. The responses were collated and used to form a consensus opinion as to their attitudes towards these elements. These opinions were then used to create the initial rich picture and problem themes.

The stage also involved the use of a focus group. The first focus group was conducted with a group of students from Deakin University, Australia, who indicated in the returned questionnaire that they were willing to be interviewed. From this list a sample of students were selected. The first was a group discussion of students' attitudes, experiences, and opinions of Online Teaching and Learning systems. Discussion on the positive and negative aspects of online learning systems layout, content, and design took place. The final major part of the focus group session involved the presentation of a Rich Picture and the associated Problem themes and were offered up for discussion. Stu dents were asked to comment on each theme and identify any other problems that had not been identified. The outcome of the first focus group session was to be able to validate and update the rich picture and problem themes that were developed from the survey responses.

STAGE 3 - ROOT DEFINITIONS OF RELEVANT ONLINE LEARNING SYSTEMS

These outcomes allowed the researchers to proceed to stage 3 of the method and formulate the root definitions formulated from the earlier stages.

STAGE 4 - MODEL IDEAL ONLINE LEARNING SITUATION

Stage 4 focuses upon encapsulating the fluid information into a conceptual model that reflects the ideal online teaching and learning situation.

STAGE 5 - COMPARISON OF IDEAL LEARNING SITUATION WITH CURRENT SITUATION

When reaching stage 5 of the method an e-learning expert from Deakin University was approached and an interview was conducted, during which the researchers' models were discussed and feedback was given by the expert. This feedback was then included in the models before the comparison was conducted.

STAGE 6 - IDENTIFY FEASIBLE AND DESIRABLE CHANGES TO THE ONLINE LEARNING SYSTEM

From the research that has been conducted in the application of this method there are a number of changes to online teaching and learning system at Deakin University that have been discussed and proposed by the researcher, the participants, and the e-learning expert.

These include:

- Implement a social networking and interaction aspect to online teaching and learning;
- Provide more useful information resources;
- Provide varied resources for students that include both audio, visual, and interactive mediums;

- Larger Internet download limit for student to access materials suggested by staff on DSO for students to access;
- Wholly online units to be removed from the curriculum and online teaching and learning to be used as a supplemental resource to traditional face-to-face teaching;
- Online questions posed by students to be replied to by a staff member within twenty-four hours;
- Lecture theatres to be fitted with adequate power outlets for students to be able to use laptops to take notes during classes;
- Users of online teaching and learning systems should have input into the design of said system.

Within this stage another area to be assessed was the limitations of Technology involved. The limitations of the online teaching and learning software used by Deakin University had to be addressed.

WebCT the development company that produced DSO provides a generic standardised package, which is then adapted for use at individual institutions. Even with Deakin Univer sity, different templates and styles are used within different Faculties.

Some of the limitations faced when developing the DSO example site included:

- Limited selection of integrated communication tools
- No standard method for social interaction
- Database style of DSO Overall style of DSO site

These limitations along with the scope of this study and changes that would need to be implemented at a University level meant that a number of the desirable changes were not feasible. The following part outlines those changes which are considered feasible. From the desirable changes and applying the limitations explained, the feasible changes were identified.

They are:

- Implement a social networking and interaction aspect to online teaching and learning;
- Provide more useful information resources;

- Provide varied resources for students that include both audio, visual, and interactive mediums;

These changes were used as the basis for the creation of example DSO site to be presented to and validated by the second focus group participants.

STAGE 7 - CREATE AND IMPLEMENT A PLAN FOR CHANGES TO ONLINE TEACHING SYSTEM

The feasible changes that were identified through the SSM analysis were then applied to the specific online teaching and learning system that is used at Deakin University. Along with these feasible changes the specific opinions of the focus group participants were also applied to the design and the content inclusions. A second focus group session was conducted; the participants were presented with the example online teaching and learning system that was produced from the "feasible and desirable changes" that were identified in stage six of the method. This part was presented in the style of a walkthrough, showing the participants the different elements and features that had been included.

This included content ideas as well as some different layouts. A discussion regarding the changes that had been made was undertaken. The results of focus group two and the walkthrough of the example DSO site were very positive. Students reacted well to the change in design and layout and were particularly enthusiastic about the changes in content, especially the use of new software and the unique and varied information that was supplied to them.

CONCLUSION

The research has provided a new practical method called MEAD developed for the development of on-line teaching and learning systems based upon user participational approach. The MEAD method has adapted the traditional SSM methodology to be more applicable within the area of online teaching and learning system design. This adaptation included adding participation in the form of a survey, focus groups, and a walkthrough with an online teaching and learning expert to create a new method. It contains a high level of user participation in numerous stages of the method allowing online teaching and learning systems to be responsive to the student users. MEAD has filled a gap in the knowledge in the area of development methods for the analysis and design of online teaching and learning systems by producing a formal method that is student-user focused. This online teaching and learning method has been developed as an alternate way of developing online learning systems. The approach allows for high levels of user involvement at specific stages of the method.

This is to endeavour to improve the planning and analysis of online learning systems and try to achieve a system that works for the user. The application of this method took place in a tertiary institution in Australia and the participants were all current students at this university. The outcome of the application of this method has been a more user friendly, acceptable format for online teaching with an improved content and more interesting through the use of different mediums. Future research could be focused upon implementing the MEAD method in a number of different countries to determine cultural differences.

4

Best Practices in Online Teaching Strategies

OVERVIEW OF THE PRINCIPLES, GUIDELINES, AND BENCHMARKS FOR ONLINE EDUCATION

Numerous educational agencies, from those that focus solely on online education, such as the Sloan Consortium, to the Institute for Higher Education Policy, have provided general guidelines and benchmarks for online education. In particular, the Sloan Consortium is nationally recognized as a resource for online education through its annual Sloan-C awards for programmes and instructors that have made outstanding contributions to the field of online learning.

As a beginning to our discussion of best practice online teaching strategies, we profile one of the winners of the Sloan Consortium'S Award for Excellence in Online Teaching as a case study example of recommended teaching strategies in action. In 2003, the Consortium presented Bill Pelz, a Professor of Psychology at Herkimer County Community College, with the award. Pelz shared his three "Principles of Effective Online Pedagogy" in a 2004 report. Pelz's first principle is to "let the students do the work." As he asserts, "the more quality time students spend engaged in content, the more of that content they learn."

Pelz provides specific examples of activities for which the students do the work while the professor provides support:

- Student Led Discussions
- Students Find and Discuss Web Resources

- Students Help Each Other Learn
- Students Grade Their Own Homework Assignments
- Case Study Analysis

The second principle is that "[i]nteractivity is the heart and soul of effective asynchronous learning," but Pelz stresses that interaction must stretch beyond simple student discussion:

- Students can be required to interact with one another, with the professor, with the text, with the Internet, with the entire class, in small groups or teams, one-on-one with a partner, etc. In addition to discussing the course content, students can interact regarding assignments, problems to solve, case studies, lab activities, etc. Any course can be designed with required interactivity.

Pelz's final principle is to "strive for presence". Pelz, there are three forms of presence for which to strive in online learning environments: Social Presence, Cognitive Presence, or Teaching Presence.

These ideas are described in detail in Pelz's report:

- *Social Presence*: When participants in an online course help establish a community of learning by projecting their personal characteristics into the discussion—they present themselves as "real people." There are at least three forms of social presence:
  - *Affective*: The expression of emotion, feelings, and mood.
  - *Interactive*: Evidence of reading, attending, understanding, thinking about others' responses.
  - *Cohesive*: Responses that build and sustain a sense of belongingness,' group commitment, or common goals and objectives
- *Cognitive Presence*: The extent to which the professor and the students are able to construct and confirm meaning through sustained discourse in a community of inquiry.
  - Cognitive presence can be demonstrated by introducing factual, conceptual, and theoretical knowledge into the discussion.

   - The value of such a response will depend upon the source, clarity, accuracy and comprehensiveness of the knowledge.
- *Teaching Presence*: Teaching presence is the facilitation and direction of cognitive and social process for the realization of personally meaningful and educationally worthwhile learning outcomes. There are two ways that the professor and the students can add teaching presence to a discussion.

Interestingly, these three principles:

1. Engage student in content,
2. Promote student-teacher and student-student interaction, and
3. Strive for presence, are also found in literature regarding benchmarks and recommendations for successful online teaching.

For instance, the Institute for Higher Education Policy's 2000 report of benchmarks for successful online education emphasizes interaction and engagement in its best practices for online teaching/learning and course development:

- *Online Teaching/Learning Benchmarks*:
   - Student interaction with faculty and other students is an essential characteristic and is facilitated through a variety of ways, including voice-mail and/or e-mail.
   - Feedback to student assignments and questions is constructive and provided in a timely manner.
   - Students are instructed in the proper methods of effective research, including assessment of the validity of resources.
- *Course Development Benchmarks*:
   - Guidelines regarding minimum standards are used for course development, design, and delivery, while learning outcomes–not the availability of existing technology–determine the technology being used to deliver course content.
   - Instructional materials are reviewed periodically to ensure they meet programme standards.

- Courses are designed to require students to engage themselves in analysis, synthesis, and evaluation as part of their course and programme requirements.

Similarly, the Online Journal of Distance Learning Administration's "Checklist for Online Interactive Learning", a best practice guideline for online faculty evaluation, emphasizes the importance of Pelz's principles of engagement, interaction, and presence, particularly in Categories Two and Four. Finally, Pelz's principles for online teaching are complimented by recommendations for the key characteristics used in effective online teaching, encapsulated in the acronym VOCAL. Based on ten years of teaching experience in web-enhanced, blended learning, and entirely online classrooms, VOCAL integrates the existing foundation of best practices with the design of learning environments that foster student ownership.

The components of VOCAL are:

- *Visible*: The online classroom differs from the traditional classroom in that text largely replaces in-person, face-to-face, verbal communication. This different dynamic makes it easier for students to feel as if the instructor is not participating in learning, thus making it more likely that students take a passive role as well. A lack of visibility may lead to students' critical attitudes of the instructor's effectiveness and lower levels of affective learning. Visibility can be demonstrated through public and private communication channels, such as:
  - A part of the course website with personal and professional information about the instructor.
  - Timely return of assignments and feedback.
  - Regular course website updates and postings, and well as regular updates to a shared assignment calendar.
  - Mass and personal e-mail communications with all students.
- *Organized*: Because online learners generally choose

to take an online course because they assume it will provide more flexibility for their busy schedules, they also need to know what is expected of them so that they can organize their time to meet course requirements. This increased time management responsibility of the learner also means that there is an increased organization responsibility on the instructor.

In order to meet the needs of students, it is suggested that online instructors:

- Require students to take an online self-assessment and report what they think are the characteristics of a successful online student.
- Prepare syllabus and assignment due dates carefully and well in advance so that students know what to expect and when.
- Prepare a documents of "Do's and Don'ts" for the course, including the rules of web etiquette, posting comments in discussion forums, and communicating concerns to the instructor.
- Anticipate the need for a non-instructional venue for online discussions.
- Use different formats for online resources and label each clearly so that students can select a format that is most useful to them.
- Fully use the capabilities of the available educational technology to enhance student learning.

- *Compassionate*: Online environments can be surprisingly intimate, especially since e-mail provides a combination of privacy and distance that does not exist in traditional classrooms. This intimacy increases the need for instructors to be compassionate of students' feelings and needs. This can be accomplished through:
  - Permission for students to communicate directly with the instructor.
  - Discussion forums in which students introduce

themselves and provide personal information, or use "ice-breaker" techniques to get students to share personal information with each other.

- Reminding, if necessary, student of the class expectations of conduct, participation, and the instructor's response to unanticipated problems.

• *Analytical*: Instructors need to manage the online learning assignment to ensure that students are completing assignments and achieving learning outcomes.

  This includes the timely return of assignments as well as the analysis of student data. While many course management systems provide tools for assessment and analysis, it is the instructor's responsibility to determine if the assessment if appropriate to the subject.

  Suggested strategies include:

  - The use of smaller and more frequent assignments throughout the course to reduce test anxiety and provide learners with opportunities to process course concepts and content.
  - The use of satellite offices, if possible, to administer face-to-face exams.
  - Specify the format and file naming conventions for assignments submitted online to help easily organize and alphabetize assignments.
  - Provide opportunities for students to provide feedback on the course.
  - Provide clear expectations and guidelines for assessing participation.

• *Leader-by-Example*: The online instructor sets the tone for student performance through teacher-student interactions. Consequently, instructors should attempt to model best practice strategies to assist student learning.

  Ways in which instructors can model good online learning and behaviour include:

  - Introductions in which the instructors shares

personal information with students both formally and informally.
- Model responsibility by returning assignments within the communicated established time period.
- Model the right way students should communicate online.
- Use public and private communication to ensure visibility.
- Plan for and implement an activity at the end of the course that brings closure to the class, reinforces what was learning, and acknowledges the contributions of students.

Not only are variations on these three best practice principles of online teaching highlighted in current recommendations–they are also integrated into projections of pedagogical techniques in online teaching which will be used in the coming decade.

For instance, a survey of instructors and administrators in postsecondary institutions primarily belonging to the Multimedia Educational Resource for Learning and Online Teaching and the Western Cooperative for Educational Telecommunications estimated that the following teaching strategies, in order of importance, will play a significant role in the future of online teaching. It is interesting to note the continued importance of interactivity in online instruction, as seen in elements such as group problem-solving and collaborative tasks, coaching or mentoring, and discussion.

- Group problem-solving and collaborative tasks;
- Problem-based learning;
- Discussion;
- Case-based strategies;
- Simulations or role play;
- Student-generated content;
- Coaching or mentoring;
- Guided learning;
- Exploratory or discovery;
- Lecturing or teacher-directed activities;

- Modeling of the solution process; and
- Socratic questioning.

PRACTICES IN ONLINE TEACHING STRATEGIES

The literature regarding best practices in online teaching strategies can be organized into three major components of the instructional process:

- Planning and development,
- Teaching in action, and
- Student assessment and data evaluation.

Together, these three components significantly influence the effectiveness of the online environment, making it especially important that instructors are aware of best practice teaching strategies.

BEST PRACTICES IN PLANNING AND DEVELOPMENT

One of the most important elements of planning and managing online courses is instructors' recognition of the fact that although there are a wide array of educational technologies and course management tools available for online teaching, not all of these technologies are appropriate matches to the subject taught and the teacher's pedagogical style and strategies. As such, it is very important that instructors ensure that pedagogical principles drive the use of technology rather than the other way around. Instructors must strive to achieve certain learning standards, regardless of the medium through which they are teaching. Because of this, course planning should take place before instructors select the technology and course management system that will be used for the course.

The first step in the planning process involves the development of learning objectives. The importance of learning objective development and communication is highlighted throughout the literature, including Park University's guidelines for the creation of learning objectives:

- *Behaviour*: Learning objectives should be written in terms of observable behavioural outcomes. Clear, targeted verbs should be used to communicate with students the expected outcomes of learning activities.

- *Student-Centred*: All learning objectives should focus on the student. Effective objectives explain expectation for student behaviour, performance, and understanding.
- *Conditions*: Learning objectives should be specific and should target one aspect of understanding. The conditions of the objective include the tools, references, and/or aids that will be provided to the student.
- *Standards*: Each learning objective should be measurable and should include the criteria for student assessment. Standards are important because they both inform students of performance expectations while providing insight as to how these expectations will be measured.

Following the development of clearly defined learning objectives and the special needs of students, instructors may begin to select the technological option best-suited for the course. It is important to note, however, that although there is tremendous variety in the educational technologies available to online instructors, the field of distance learning technology is changing quickly, and it is therefore necessary for instructors and administrators to keep a close eye on emerging trends and associated best practices.

For example, the annual Horizon Report, a long-running qualitative research project that seeks to identify and describe emerging education technologies, projects that mobile technologies, cloud computing, geocoded data, personal web programmes, semantic-aware applications, and smart objects will significantly impact the choices of educational institutions within the next five years.

While these six technologies in online education are still emerging as educational tools, online technologies such as web-pages, discussion forums, course management systems, audio tools, and video tools are well-entrenched in the field of online instruction. However, with each technology comes a number of planning considerations that are important for online instructors to reflect upon as they develop their courses and choose the most appropriate technologies. The University of Washington's "Learning and Scholarly Technologies," a website that provides a help centre for online instructors, addresses a number of these technological considerations.

One final yet very important factor that should be taken into consideration in the planning and development component of online teaching strategy is the need for the online courses to be delivered in such a way as to create a learning community among students and the instructor. Research shows that many of the instances in which distance education courses fail to promote student learning, the cause is students' sense of isolation or low level of self-directedness.

In order to combat this isolation factor, successful online courses develop established protocols for building, maintaining, and evaluating student-to-student and student-to-faculty interactions. Teaching methods including training in technology for distance learning students, interactive teaching that fosters critical dialogue, mentoring, cooperative peer learning, group out-of-class activities, and the use of e-mail or web announcements to inform students about opportunities for interaction should be designed into the online course to enhance student learning.

PRACTICES IN TEACHING-IN-ACTION

As discussed earlier in this report, the level of interaction among students and between students and the instructor is particularly important in online instruction. Distance education provides many opportunities to foster an interactive "classroom," including two of the most commonly used pedagogical techniques to promote interactivity:

- Online discussion forums and
- Student collaboration on assignments.

Online discussion forums are one of the best ways to facilitate interaction and learning in the online classroom, in part due to their ability to promote constructivist thinking, critical thinking, and higher-order thinking, all while distributing knowledge among all the students in the class. Additionally, discussion is a relatively simple way to encourage interaction in the online environment. For example, interactive learning can be promoted through the use of e-mail or electronic discussion tools, such as the University of Washington's Catalyst GoPost tool, a web-based discussion board where students can compare notes, discuss assignments, post attachments, or work together, and the Google platform, Wiki, a tool which allows individuals to create websites which can be viewed and edited by site members.

However, regardless of the technologies used, online discussion forums lose effectiveness without the development of thoughtful and relevant questions and instructor's moderation of responses.

The following guidelines are recommended to promote the important element, constructivist thinking, in the online discussion and pedagogy:

- Pose a stimulating question,
- Brainstorm answers to the question,
- Compare ideas, and
- Fuse to the curriculum.

The first step in this process, "Pose a stimulating question," deserves special focus due to its important role in determining the direction of online discussion. As such, it is recommended that instructors consider the cognitive levels of the questions, the educational situation, the goals and objectives of the instruction, and the needs of the students when designing online discussion questions. A survey of the types of discussion questions used by online instructors revealed that the questions could be grouped into the following categories:

- *Interest-getting and attention-getting questions:*
  - *Example*: "If you awakened in the year 2399, what is the first thing you would notice?"
- *Diagnosing and checking questions*:
  - Example: "Does anyone know Senge's five principles of a learning organization?"
- *Recall of specific facts or information questions*:
  - *Example*: "Who can name the main characters in Moby Dick?"

- *Managerial questions*:
  - *Example*: "Did you request an extension on the assignment due date?
- *Structure and redirect learning questions*:
  - *Example*: "Now that we have discussed the advantages of, and limitations to, formative evaluation, who can do the same for summative evaluation?"
- *Allow expression of affect questions*:
  - *Example*: "How did you feel about our online guest's list of ten things trainers do to shoot themselves in the foot?"
- *Encourage higher level thought processes questions*:
  - Example: "Considering what you have read, and what was discussed in the posts this past week, can you summarize all the ways there are to overcome obstacles to effective teamwork?"

During the discussion process, it is important that instructors continuously manage students' ideas and further facilitate interactions. However, if the online discussion is going well without instructor feedback, it is often best for teachers to wait to jump into the discussion until the students' responses are waning. At that point, it is recommended that instructors summarize key points or ask prompting questions to recharge the discussion. The second strategy to facilitate interactivity: "encourage student collaboration," relies on the use of educational technologies to simulate face-to-face meetings when students work together on assignments. However, it should be noted that a review of the literature identified one study that found that while instructors perceive the learner-instructor and learner-learner interactions as key factors in quality online instruction, students' varied regarding their opinion on whether interaction is important.

The authors of the study suggest that this variance in student opinion is related to differences in learning style and personality, as well as students' lowered expectations of the quality of interaction in online instruction. While these findings emphasize that instructors need to identify the needs of their students in online instruction, they also suggest that interaction is considered by both teachers and students to influence the effectiveness of instruction in a primarily positive way. Beyond these two major pedagogical strategies for enhancing the success of online teaching, Pennsylvania State University's World Campus, which offers more than 50 degree and certificate programmes through distance and online education, provides a detailed guide of best practices strategies and pedagogical advice for online teaching. This is a set of best practice recommendations and related strategies for the process of teaching, the majority of which directly compliment the literature asserting the need for interactivity, instructor presence, student collaboration, and the creation of a learning community.

Prepare Your Students for Learning Online

Online instructors need to provide sufficient orientation for students regarding the technology and instructional methods used in the course.

This can be accomplished by:

- Posting a welcome message to help students get started.
- Include a brief orientation for students to get familiar with the terminology and tools used in the course management system.
- Provide contact information for technical help in a variety of places, as well as personal contact information, standard response times, and preferred communication methods.
- Remind students to set up e-mail forwarding to their preferred accounts. However, faculty and students should keep all course-related communications within the course management system to maintain confidentiality.
- Provide online office hours as needed.
- Structure the course by providing guidelines for participation and other policies to help students learn more effectively.

- Provide resources and strategies for online learning and explain how online learning is different from classroom learning.
- Include a Student FAQ with common questions about courses, registration, tuition, financial aid, course materials and software.

Specify Course Goals, Expectations, and Policies

It is important to provide course goals, expectations, structure, and related course/departmental/institutional policies at the beginning of the course. These elements are commonly included in course syllabus, although they may be placed elsewhere.

Important information includes:

- Course goals and learning objectives, including a description of course structure.
- Required and optional course materials or textbooks.
- Clear and specific grading policies and academic integrity policies.
- The guidelines for student participation and collaboration, including any recommendations for online communication, policies for assignment submission and grading, and web etiquette guidelines for online courses.

Create a Warm and Inviting Atmosphere to Build a Learning Community

A variety of literature asserts the need for online instructors to build learning communities that engage students.

Learning communities can be built by:

- Welcoming students before the course begins via e-mail or course announcement. This welcome should be resent after the add/drop period ends.
- Posting a personal introduction with an informal tone.
- Providing lots of encouragement and support, particularly in the beginning of the course. This

includes positive feedback administered to students privately by e-mail.

- Encouraging students to create their own homepage, or post a short self-introduction to the discussion forum. Alternatively students can be encouraged to develop a social space by creating a group inside or outside of the course site.
- Uploading any relevant pictures to the course site, and encouraging students to do so as well.

Promote Active Learning

The online teaching strategy should foster students' active, constructive participation in learning.

This can be accomplished by instructors that:

- Emphasize to students the importance of learning by playing an active role in the learning process, a role which differs from the direct instruction or lecture in traditional classrooms.
- Provide opportunities for students to critique and reflect upon certain course topics.
- Encourage students to use the Internet for researching course topics, but remind them to be critical about the information they find and share.
- Encourage students to be proactive learners by regularly logging into the course site, submitting assignments on-time, participating in discussions, and cooperating with teammates.
- Provide opportunities for active problem solving and for team work.
- Encourage the active participation in online discussion by designing provocative questions, encouraging students to respond to questions at a deeper level, and by pointing out any opposing perspectives.
- Use multiple discussion formats, including small group discussions, "buzz groups", case studies, team debates, "jigsaw groups" where subgroups discuss parts of a topic and then collaborate on their findings, and role play.

Model Effective Online Interaction

- *Instructors can model effective interaction through frequent interactions with students that:*
  - Respond to student comments and questions within time frames set at the beginning of the course. Instructors make sure to notify students if these time frames change, or if they will be unavailable for some period during the semester.
  - Provide general feedback to the entire class on specific assignments or discussions, while at the same time providing individual encouragement and comments to students. Feedback on graded assignments should recognize good work and make suggestions for improvement.
  - Provide a weekly "wrap up" before the next session, and introduce each new week with an overview of the session plan and deadlines.

Monitor Student Progress and Encourage Lagging Students

Because students have different learning styles, instructors should monitor students and identify those who are lagging. Important points to aid the monitoring process include:

- Instructors' awareness that students who fall behind are in jeopardy of not completing the course, which may endanger their financial aid.
- Use of available educational technology tools, such as course management systems, to track student progress in course activities.
- Contact students who haven't logged in for over a week to inquire whether they're experiencing technical difficulties or problems with course content/ activities. If students can't participate due to technical problems, connect them immediately to technical help.
- Contact students who have not completed assignments by e-mail or phone.
- Include flexibility in grading if possible

Assess Students' Messages in Online Discussion

Instructors should assess students' messages in online discussion forums through a set a specific criteria. These assessment criteria for online discussion should be included in the course syllabus, a course announcement, or within the instructions for the discussion task.

Criteria should:

- Make sure the assessment criteria measure both the quantity and quality of the online message.
- Consider assigning points to messages that encourage additional posting.
- Make use of recommended rubrics from the literature.

  Examples of good rubrics include:

  – Edelstein and Edwards' Assessing Effectiveness of Student Participation in Online Discussions. This rubric considers five categories that are important for building a learning community: promptness and initiative, delivery of post, relevance of post, expression within the post, and contribution to the learning community.

  – Garrison's, *et al.* Cognitive Processing Categories. *May be useful when assessing the quality of postings*:

    1. Triggering;
    2. Exploration,
    3. Integration, and
    4. Solution.

  – Kleinman's Grading Rubric for Online Discussion Participation. Provides detailed grading criteria.

Sustain Students' Motivation and Provide Feedback and Support

There are a variety of teaching strategies to support, guide, and motivate students to learn actively in the online environment, including:

- Provide opportunities for student collaboration and facilitate collaborative learning processes and tools such as Breeze.

- Choose a conversational tone that makes students feel comfortable in the online learning environment and that establishes trust in communication while building a learning community.
- Provide meaningful feedback to all assignments and comments.
- Provide a weekly summary of discussion topics to demonstrate your participation, and assess messages for both quantity and quality.

Similarly, it helps to provide feedback and support to students through the:

- Encouragement of students to articulate their confusion or difficulty with course content, projects, requirements, or instructions for activities.
- Quick response to students' concerns or technical difficulties.
- Use of peer assessment to provide additional feedback to students while reducing faculty workload.
- Participation in online discussion by encouraging openness in online discussions, diagnosing misconceptions immediately to avoid confusion, providing additional resources, and encouraging student to use examples, case studies, or literature to support their arguments.

Encourage Students to Regulate Their Own Learning

In order to succeed, students must be encouraged to become "self-regulated learners."

Strategies to accomplish this self-regulation include:

- Allowing students to become "process managers" in the online course by giving up some of the traditional power of teachers. For example, students may be directed to take turns leading online learning experiences.
- Encouraging students' reflection and feedback through the inclusion of an introductory survey with questions on student expectations for the course and

engagement in students' course evaluations.

- Allowing students to take responsibility for their peers' learning as well as their own through discussion forums.
- Provide opportunities for peer review.

Understand the Impact of Multiculturalism

It is important that online instructors understand and are aware of cultural-based differences in online classrooms, and that they cultivate cultural sensitivity in e-learning through the appropriate use of technology.

This can be accomplished by:

- Using non-discriminatory language and being aware that cultural diversity exists both in nationality/ ethnicity as well as in generation, religion, political beliefs, or socioeconomic status.
- For difficult, emotional, or controversial topics, use chats or threaded discussions, or make discussion optional. At the same time, threaded discussions can be used to invite feedback and reflection on the topic.
- If possible, by creating teams of students from diverse backgrounds to encourage cross-cultural facilitation.
- Providing high-quality resources to explain conflicting perspectives.
- Providing appropriate supports if it is suspected that a culturally related factor may negatively affect an online learning experience.
- Joining professional teaching communities or conferences to gain exposure and connections to our global society.

Deal with Conflicts Promptly

Conflicts should be dealt with promptly to minimize student distractions.

Conflict management strategies include:

- The provision of web etiquette guidelines.
- Intervention only when conflicts intensify to a point where students can no longer work through the issue

on their own. Otherwise, conflict should be welcomed as a sign that the learning community is developing.

- Private communication with students who are posting inappropriately, and contacting the appropriate department if you suspect that a student has violated academic integrity policies.
- Provide a regular peer evaluation function so that students can communicate their impressions on how the group is functioning.

PRACTICES IN STUDENT ASSESSMENT AND DATA EVALUATION

Best practice recommendations for the assessment of student learning in an online environment include:

- Assessment through an evaluation process that uses several methods and applies specific standards for student learning.
- The regular review of intended learning outcomes to ensure clarity, utility, and appropriateness.
- Timely evaluations at regular intervals to increase course flexibility for students.
- The assurance that monitoring/proctoring policies are in place during assessments of student learning.
- The integration of some sort of verification method to ensure academic integrity.
- Assessment strategies are integral to the learning experience, enabling learners to assess their progress, identify areas for review, and re-establish immediate learning or sessions goals.
- Strategies are varied and aligned to instructional goals.
- Assessment criteria are clearly articulated.

Pennsylvania State University's World Campus' guide of best practice online teaching strategies also emphasizes the need for instructors to gather and analysis student evaluation data to improve course content and pedagogy. Student data can be collected and used through many methods, including the use of a discussion board for anonymous course feedback, the encouragement and rewarding of students who report significant errors in course content, and through the review of faculty evaluations to provide feedback for future course redesign.

Finally, best practices in online teaching assert that instructors should be careful to follow intellectual property guidelines, participate in an online teaching community to learn from peers, and learn to manage time effectively. Instructors' ability to manage time and workload effectively is especially important because there are no set hours to online instruction, making it easy for online teachers to become overwhelmed. In order to manage time effectively, it is suggested that instructors use the following guidelines:

- Set limits,
- Do not always be available to learners,
- Establish clear priorities for dealing with messages,
- Put time limits on discussion,
- Provide learners with predetermined answers to frequently asked questions,
- Encourage learners to find local tutors and mentors,
- If possible, hire a TA to respond to students,
- Try to immediately acknowledge the receipt of a student's question, and set a period of time in which feedback will be returned.

AN EXEMPLARY PROGRAMME AND EXAMPLES OF EFFECTIVE PRACTICES

There are a number of programmes that have successfully instituted the online teaching strategies discussed in this report. As a beginning to our review of example programmes, we first provide a description of the University of Central Florida's online education programme.

This programme is profiled in order to provide a comprehensive example of the use of exemplary online pedagogical strategies as well as the necessary institutional and technological supports for effective online teaching. We then re-focus on effective teaching strategies with a review of the online instruction practices of three professors awarded the Sloan Consortium's "Effective Practice Awards."

REVIEW OF THE UNIVERSITY OF CENTRAL FLORIDA'S ONLINE EDUCATION PROGRAMME

A winner of the Sloan Consortium's 2008 Ralph E. Gomory Award for Quality Online Education, the university states that its online education programmes adhere to the "Principles of Good Practice" established by the Southern Regional Educational Board. Many of the Southern Regional Educational Board's principles emphasize curriculum and instruction, institutional context, and programme evaluation elements that can be used to support and compliment the best practice teaching strategies promoted by the university.

For example, the University of Central Florida's "Faculty Centre" site promotes and provides resources for best practice teaching pedagogies including collaborative learning, discussion boards, web-streaming techniques and the use of wikis. The following paragraphs discuss the institutional and technological supports necessary for faculty to enact these pedagogies.

Faculty Development and Support for Online Instruction

The university states on its website that "[w]ell-trained, prepared and supported faculty members are critical to the delivery of quality distributed learning courses and student success." UCF offers several courses to its faculty members in order to develop their skills in online instruction. The first of these courses, "Interactive Distributed Learning for Technology "Mediated Course Delivery," "models how to teach online using a combination of seminars, labs, consultations, and Web-based instruction." The second course, "Advanced Distributed Learning for Technology–Mediated Course Delivery," deals with "the important pedagogical, logistical, and technological issues involved in delivering effective online courses." Lastly, the university offers a course entitled "Essentials," which is "a self-paced faculty development workshop" that instills professors with "the foundational knowledge required to develop and deliver a web-enhanced course."

Course Development and Web Services

The university's CDWS department "has developed conventions for online courses as well as a support system for faculty teaching in the online environment."

The department comprises several teams, which are described below:

- *The Instructional Design Team*: The Instructional Design Team facilitates the development and design of online courses through a combination of face-to-face interaction, just-in-time training and ongoing professional development. The Instructional Design Team's award-winning faculty development course, IDL6543, continuously improves through the commitment, research and integration of instructional best practices and emerging technology.
- *TechrangersSM Team*: The Techrangers primarily provide the Tech Support for online courses that utilize WebCT. Techrangers are also responsible for coding the pages on Reach and WebCT.
- *Digital Media Team*: Graphic Designers, Artists and Photographers...working behind the scenes to make the visual content of all CDWS projects aesthetically pleasing.
- *New Media Team*: New Media's mission is the research and development of emerging technologies for instructional innovations and resources towards enterprise applications for UCF and beyond.
- *Video Convergence Team*: The Video Convergence team strives to develop training, services and media components that benefit anyone involved in educational endeavors. We begin by sharing our knowledge and research with the faculty and staff at UCF, empowering them to create educationally sound components for their online courses, face-to-face courses or whatever their specific needs may be.

The CDWS department strives to create "courses that are easy to maintain by both faculty and CDWS," and offers "professional development programmes" in order to help faculty do so. CDWS has also developed two websites–"Teaching OnlineWeb" and "Learning OnlineWeb"–which contain resources for teachers and students to engage with online education more effectively.

Web-based Courses

The university's web-based courses are "are delivered through the Internet and are accessible anywhere, anytime." It offers two distinct forms of web-based courses, as described below:

- World Wide Web courses are conducted fully via Web-based instruction and collaboration. Courses may require proctored examinations, and may include opportunities for face-to-face orientations, but there will be no class attendance requirements.
- ReduceSeatTime/Mixed Mode courses include both required classroom attendance and online instruction. These classes have substantial content delivered over the Internet, which will substitute for some classroom meetings.

The university provides specific details regarding the different modalities used for its web-based courses:

- *WW World Wide Web*: Courses conducted fully via Web-based instruction and collaboration. Courses may require proctored examinations, and may include opportunities for face-to-face orientations, but there will be no class attendance requirements.
- *M ReduceSeatTime/Mixed Mode*: Courses include both required classroom attendance and online instruction. All M classes have substantial activity conducted over the Web, which will substitute for some classroom meetings.
- *MT ReduceSeatTime/Mixed/ITV Recv*: An M class with class meetings conducted via 2-way interactive television. Class meetings are at a remote site from the instructor.
- *ML ReduceSeatTime/Mixed/ITV-LO*: An M class with class meetings conducted via 2-way interactive

television. Class meetings are at the origination site with the instructor.

Video Streaming Courses

Additionally, the university makes "extensive use of video streaming" in some classes:

- Video Streaming courses are delivered over the Web via streaming digital video and may be supplemented by additional Web activity, projects or exams.
- Reduced Seat Time/Video Stream courses include some or all of the following elements: face-to-face lecture, web, video streaming, and labs.

Videos are made available "for on-demand streaming" over the web. The university provides specific details regarding the different modalities used for its video streaming courses:

- *V Video Streaming*: Courses delivered over the Web via streaming digital video and may be supplemented by additional Web activity, projects or exams.
- *LV Face to Face/VS-Origination*: Class meetings are recorded for subsequent video streaming over the Web.
- *RV ReducedSeatTime/Video Stream*: Courses include streaming video delivered over the Web that substitutes for some classroom meetings.

Interactive Television Delivery Courses

The integration of interactive television into courses has occurred across a number of UCF campuses and instructional centres. These courses are synchronous, live televised courses delivered via 2-way compressed video on T1 lines, in which the faculty member teaches to a face-to-face student group in the live part and to remote parts at area campuses and instructional centres. Students at the remote sites can interact with the faculty member and students at the other sites via the interactive two-way audio and video system.

The university provides specific details regarding the different modalities used for its video streaming courses:

- *T 2-Way Interactive TV*: Courses delivered via live two-way interactive television to selected locations. Class meetings are at a remote site from the instructor.
- *L Face to Face/ITV-Origination*: Courses delivered via live two-way interactive television to selected locations. Class meetings are at the origination site with the instructor.
- *MT ReduceSeatTime/Mixed/ITV Recv*: An M class with class meetings conducted via 2-way interactive television. Class meetings are at a remote site from the instructor.
- *ML ReduceSeatTime/Mixed/ITV-LO*: An M class with class meetings conducted via 2-way interactive television. Class meetings are at the origination site with the instructor.

5

Expectations for Classroom Setup and Online Teaching

BEFORE THE START OF THE TERM

The following are visible to students in the WebTycho classroom, starting a month before classes begin, so faculty are encouraged to post these required items as soon as possible:

- An accurate e-mail address
- An up-to-date biography
- A welcoming initial class announcement that tells students where to find materials, how to begin, and asks students to introduce themselves during the first week

Although no teaching will take place before the formal start date of the course, the following are visible to students in the WebTycho classroom starting one week before classes begin and should be ready by that date, if not mandated earlier by the school or programme. If faculty must revise the syllabus after it has been made visible to students, they should announce that updates have been made.

- A detailed course syllabus in accordance with departmental guidelines that includes:
  - Faculty contact information, including where, when, and how students may contact the instructor and the timeframe for responding to them
  - Course goals and objectives, if not already provided
  - Required text and other course materials, if not already provided

  - Grading criteria, including explicit expectations for participation and policy on late submissions
  - A brief description or listing of project assignments and any extra credit opportunities
  - Course schedule
  - Overall accuracy and attention to detail, free of grammatical and spelling errors, and with all dates and information updated when re-using material from an earlier class
- An introductory announcement, welcoming students, detailing any necessary explanations about the layout of the classroom, and giving them directions about how to get started in the course.
- Classroom management/"housekeeping" information that includes:
  - The instructor's preferred file formats and labeling conventions for assignment submission, as well as the method for submission
  - A short introductory document about the course as well as any required departmental information
- The first week's complete content and activities, including faculty presentation material, reading or other content, and all assignments
- Introductory and first week's conferences:
  - A conference where the instructor and students can introduce themselves during the first days of the course or the first course of a cohort-based programme like the MBA. The faculty member should post an introductory thread, introducing himself/herself and asking a few questions that will help students to get to know each other Please note that the uploading of student photos should always be optional.
  - A conference for casual conversation or off-topic issues
  - A faculty-monitored conference for student questions related to the course as a whole—this can be a separate conference such as Admini-

strative Questions or can be included in the Cybercafé-type conference

When creating content and assignments for the online classroom, the following principles should be kept in mind:

- Learning activities should be closely aligned with all course learning objectives, particularly those stated in the syllabus, and adequate practice should be provided to master them. Be explicit with students about the objectives for each assignment and also explain how the assignments are inter-related and build upon each other.
- Pacing and sequencing of course activity as well as clear deadlines are essential to help students manage their course workload.
- A variety of learning approaches should be used, including whenever appropriate, small group and peer-to-peer activities, project-based assignments, case studies, role playing exercises and debates, problem-based learning, and multimedia-enriched presentations and resources. Through the use of collaborative work or public presentation of some assignments in the classroom, students are also able to develop a sense of a learning community. When using Study Groups, faculty shouldn't assume that students know how to organize themselves or work collaboratively. Give detailed directions, guidelines, and due dates. Let students know ahead of time that you are monitoring the activity and that you are ready to jump in to assist if needed.
- Online students expect opportunities to explore beyond the assigned textbook(s), including faculty commentary, web resources, and multimedia. It's important to integrate web, textbook, and library resources into the course so that students feel these are intrinsically valuable and relevant to the course. Faculty should provide guidance as to the appropriate use and purpose of all course content.
- Incorporate adult learning principles into assignments

and discussions, such as allowing students to apply their real-world experience to the course content.

- Emphasize discussion questions and assignments that require critical thinking skills. Promote active learning strategies.

DURING THE TERM

The following are essential practices for running a successful online classroom:

- Post materials and conference topic threads on a pre-announced and consistent schedule, for example, each Sunday before the Monday on which each week of the course begins. This helps busy adult students manage their time.
- Create at least one focused conference for each week or unit of the course. Provide deadlines and clear guidelines for conference participation so that students are able to participate as a unified group. Faculty may even want to make the conference "read-only" after the due dates. When appropriate, use conferences for presenting individual student projects, group work, weekly summaries by students, demonstrations of problem solving, or for other activities beyond "discussion."
- Start initial conference topic threads for each weekly or unit-based conference.
- Facilitate but don't dominate the discussions. Ask follow-up questions and redirect to elicit responses from classmates. Faculty should be "visible" in each week's conference to let students know that they are "listening."
- Participate actively in the class conferences a minimum of three, but preferably four times or more per week.
- Provide dated class announcements at least weekly in the online classroom. Previous announcements should also remain available somewhere in the classroom. If faculty remove announcements, they

should always archive them in a conference for reference and to maintain a complete record of the course. Announcements can be used to remind students of due dates, to let students know that a new conference or lecture has been posted, provide encouragement and positive feedback, etc. Use e-mails primarily to repeat or reinforce class announcements.

- Respond to all student inquiries within 48 hours, even if it is just to let the student know that the instructor is working on the issue and will get back to the student in due time. If the instructor will be absent for any period of time, she or he should indicate the duration to the students.
- Organize class activities so that they take place primarily in the online classroom, rather than by e-mail, phone, or mail.
- Send a personal e-mail as a friendly reminder to students who are not actively participating in the class.
- Provide resources and referrals as a way to offer personalized support and demonstrate concern. Examples include referrals to services such as the Effective Writing Centre, Information and Library Services, Advising, as well as appropriate books or Web resources.

The following are essential practices related to effective feedback and grading in the online classroom:

- Provide adequate feedback on all assignments and pay special attention to providing adequate feedback on the first major assignment. Instructor feedback will help set expectations for students about future assignments.
- Assignments on which future assignments depend should be returned as quickly as possible so students have plenty of time to make corrections based on your feedback that will carry over into the next assignment

- Provide feedback that suggests areas for improvement and growth as well as reinforcement and acknowledgement, pointing students to possible use of what's learned in forthcoming assignments.
- Clearly state the criteria or create rubrics to manage student expectations on grading.
- Comments and grades for individual work should be placed in the Gradebook in a timely manner. On major assignments, students should receive their graded assignments back within 10 days.
- For group projects, students should be graded in some measure on individual contribution as well as for the group as a whole
- Make participation in the online classroom a significant portion of the grade and ensure that part of the participation grade is for responses and interaction with classmates, not just with the instructor. Discussion should be focused and task-oriented. Faculty should clearly communicate their precise guidelines and explain what constitutes participation.
- Use a framework in which grades are distributed over a variety of assignments rather than establish grades that are heavily weighted in favour of just one or two exams or deliverables, especially when these are due only late in the term.

AFTER THE TERM ENDS

- Final grades must be submitted within 72 hours after the official course end date or within 72 hours of a proctored exam packet to the Faculty Portal, My UMUC.
- Any students receiving a grade of incomplete who need continued access to the classroom after the archiving period will need to be manually rostered in by the faculty. Faculty are still responsible after the term ends for any students who receive a grade of incomplete.

- Make regular self-assessments of teaching methods and style.
- Set an example for your students of commitment to life-long learning—participate in faculty development workshops to improve your teaching and technology skills and in professional development activities to keep current in your field.

6

Leadership: Capacity Building in Online Teaching and Learning

INTRODUCTION

The leadership in online teaching and learning involving capacity building, so that leadership occurs at multiple levels in order to sustain and transform learning. Literature conceptualising leadership as capacity building is examined. The document considers practical examples of leadership as capacity building in online teaching and learning, and poses questions for further investigation.

Effective leadership in online teaching and learning must involve a significant element of capacity building, so that leadership occurs at multiple levels in an organization in order to sustain, renew and transform teaching and learning for the future. As Lambert points out, "increasing leadership capacity over time is the most productive way to bring about improvements that can be sustained". Building leadership capacity in online teaching and learning is an issue because it does not always happen.

Individuals who have taught online may leave the organization and capacity is thereby lost. Online learning and teaching is affected, as finding staff to teach in online papers can be a challenge. Paradoxically, online teaching and learning may hold the solution to its own dilemma, as the key to learning to learn and lead in online teaching and learning lies within the online settings: one builds capacity for leadership in online teaching and learning by engaging in learning and leading with a mentor or team within these settings. Leadership obligations in online teaching and learning therefore include the need for those who teach and learn online to work together, ensuring benefits to students, reciprocal learning for teachers involved, as well as a measure of accountability, and ultimately building of leadership capacity.

WHAT IS LEADERSHIP AS CAPACITY BUILDING

There are various strands of literature around the notion of leadership as building capacity among a wider group of people. Related terminology and concepts include notions of leadership density through expansion of leadership capital; distributed leadership, systemic leadership; teacher leadership; relational or post-heroic leadership; shared leadership, dispersed leadership, collective leadership, parallel leadership, or a leader-rich culture. Raelin also refers to "creating leaderful organizations".

The salient idea shared by these notions of leadership is that leadership is no longer purely an individual matter, but is spread throughout an organization with leadership roles and functions being performed by various people who do not necessarily hold formal leadership positions. The work of Lambert redefines leadership as constructivist learning. Constructivist learning entails actively creating knowledge. In particular, social constructivism emphasises that learning occurs when people interact in order to construct knowledge, within collaborative learning environments.

When leadership is viewed as constructivist learning, "leadership is about contributing to, learning from, and influencing the learning of others". Leadership is about creating opportunities for others to learn. Leadership is about learning together towards a shared purpose or aim. "Learning and leading are deeply intertwined... Indeed, leadership can be understood as reciprocal, purposeful learning in a community". By defining leadership as constructivist learning, Lambert emphasises that "The key notion in this definition is that leadership is about learning together, and constructing meaning and knowledge collectively and collaboratively. It involves opportunities to surface and mediate perceptions, values, beliefs, information, and assumptions through continuing conversations; to inquire about and generate ideas together; to seek to reflect upon and make sense of work in the light of shared beliefs and new information; and to create actions that grow out of these new understandings. Such is the core of leadership".

A number of other well known writers in the field of leadership also make close links between leadership and learning, particularly as it occurs collectively and within a community. For example, Senge regards leadership as collective learning, and leaders as responsible for learning. He argues that organizations in the knowledge era should be "communities of leaders and learners". In a similar vein, Sergiovanni also takes a constructivist view of leadership and learning, asserting "In communities, leadership and learning go together. So does leadership and sense-making".

This is further supported by Harris who suggests "that leadership is part of the interactive process of sense-making and creation of meaning that is continuously engaged in by organisational members.... Taking this view, leadership is about learning together and constructing meaning and knowledge collectively and collaboratively". Fullan argues that learning in context helps to produce leaders at many levels within the organization. There is strong support for the notion therefore that leaders must be learners. In accordance with Lambert's definition, "leadership capacity" refers to broadbased, skilful involvement in the work of leadership." In order for leadership involvement to be broad-based, there must be many parties involved in leading.

This means that a significant number of teacher-leaders are present within the organization. In addition to the teacher-leaders, leadership is the domain of students. This view of leading as a shared endeavour aligns capacity building with democratic ideals, involving shared purpose, action and responsibility, and a realignment of power and authority. In Senge's terms "leadership in the future will be distributed among diverse individuals and teams who share responsibility for creating the organization's future". Similarly, Harris concurs that "school leadership is a function that needs to be distributed throughout the school community", so that it is "devolved across the whole school rather than located in a single individual". With leading redefined as learning, it follows that there must be broad-based involvement in constructivist learning processes. Both teachers and students, as leaders, should be involved in learning together within a professional community, engaging in practices such as inquiry-based decision making and practice, collaboration, and reflection. Again, there is a great deal of support for these elements of constructivist learning within the leadership literature.

The importance of inquiry as a basis for decision-making is widely emphasised. Collaboration is seen as crucial for learning and for organisational improvement. Reflection is also viewed as essential. The three elements of inquiry, collaboration and reflection can be combined in reflective practice that seeks to inquire about the most fundamental assumptions behind our practices. Reflective practice occurs not only individually, but also in concert with others so that we subject our assumptions to the review of others, and participate in collaborative reflection. Leadership as capacity building can thus be regarded as a form of distributed leadership, which is closely aligned with distributed learning. There is more than just one source of both leadership and learning.

Just as the teacher is not the holder of all knowledge, so are there many avenues of leadership. Building leadership capacity involves creating conditions and opportunities that are conducive to this collective, reciprocal learning. This entails bringing people together so that they can construct and negotiate meanings, and arrive at shared purpose. The goal of building leadership capacity is to enable more individuals to build their own informal authority and demonstrate leadership behaviours. On this account, therefore, leadership is not focused on one person in a position of formal authority, and neither is it about leadership traits, charismatic or heroic leadership. Such traditional conceptualisations of leadership are regarded by commentators like Lambert as limiting, as they allow some people to abstain from the work of leadership, abdicating both responsibility and opportunity. "When we equate the powerful concept of leadership with the behaviours of one person, we are limiting the achievement of broad-based participation by a community or society".

Instead, just as to Harris "a new model of leadership is emerging, one that recognises the limitations of an approach to organisational change and development premised upon the efforts of just one person". Building leadership capacity is regarded as a worthwhile endeavour because it is a way for an organization to achieve and maintain "a momentum for self-renewal". That is, with this type of leadership the organization or community can keep moving when current leaders leave, and improvement within the school can be sustained. In Senge's terms, this would constitute an organization in which continuous learning occurs, or a "learning organization".

Sustainability is therefore a key advantage of this approach to leadership and "sustainability depends on many leaders–thus, the qualities of leadership must be attainable by many, not just a few". "The commitment necessary for sustainable improvement must be nurtured up close in the dailyness of organizational behaviour, and for that to happen there needs to be many leaders around us. There needs to be leaders at many levels".

In terms of current practice, there are a number of encouraging initiatives that can be interpreted as embodying notions of leadership as capacity building in online learning and teaching. Examples to be outlined briefly here are the University of Waikato's Mixed Media Programme, the FLLinNZ project, the Interim Tertiary e-Learning Framework, and the Ministry of Education's e-Learning Fellowships. The University of Waikato's Mixed Media Programme began in 1997 as an alternative way of teaching the three year Bachelor of Teaching and was initially designed to meet pre-service needs in the more distant areas of the University's region. Over the years it has extended to include students throughout the North Island. The programme is designed to cater for students whose commitments prevent them from participating in a traditional on-campus programme. MMP entails multiple levels of capacity building because offering a Bachelor of Teaching programme online requires tertiary teaching staff to learn to teach online. This is accomplished by encouraging staff with online experience to mentor other staff who are new to teaching online.

Professional development programmes offered at the time of the inception of MMP aimed to "facilitate the participants' activity, inquiry and problem-solving" and helped lecturers to establish both formal and informal networks for sharing information about online teaching and learning. Campbell's study of the process of building capacity in online learning and teaching within the MMP at Waikato "highlighted the need for changes in values, strong leadership and vision, and a commitment to academic staff support structures in tertiary education". Since those early days, the MMP has strengthened the practice of capacity building. From 13 staff involved in 1997 there are now over 40 teaching a range of papers. In 2002 MMP was recognised by the Tertiary Teaching Excellence Awards, for excellence in innovation.

While the contribution of MMP to the local community in terms of building capacity is striking, there has been a parallel contribution to building capacity within the academic community involved in teaching in the MMP. As a new lecturer joining the MMP team to learn to teach within the programme, MMP has been a training ground for the development of expertise in online learning, teaching and leading. MMP has offered the opportunity to team-teach online with experienced staff, and to be continuously involved in inquiry, collaboration and reflection within the online context itself. While teaching online with experienced lecturers within MMP, I have engaged in continuing conversations about learning and teaching online. These conversations have taken place within shared spaces within the online forum itself, and face-to-face, both formally and informally. I have been able to inquire about and generate ideas together with colleagues and students, and we have sought to reflect upon and make sense of our work together online in light of shared beliefs and understandings.

The beliefs and understandings have further evolved during our work together online. We have then endeavoured to act on these new understandings. Through these processes, my experiences have closely corresponded to Lambert's conception of leadership as "purposeful learning in a community". Flexible Learning Leaders in New Zealand or FLLinNZ is a national project focused on building leadership capacity in online learning and teaching, throughout a variety of tertiary education organizations in New Zealand. FLLinNZ embodies leadership as capacity building because the project aims to fund, guide and support the "leadership and professional development" of the participants, and thereby "enhance the capability of a significant group of people who have the potential to make a difference in the tertiary e-learning landscape in New Zealand".

The project aims to establish a national mentoring network, to provide access to opportunities for research and inquiry, and to provide opportunities for leaders to visit other institutions in order to share a range of different models of e-learning innovation. Overall, FLLinNZ is focused on "the creation of a pool of leaders in the field who are committed to sharing their expertise nationally". It is readily apparent therefore, that FLLinNZ is about leadership as capacity building in online teaching and learning.

The Interim Tertiary e-Learning Framework is intended to provide a national direction for tertiary e-learning. It is intended that this framework be eventually superseded by a pan-sector e-learning strategy encompassing early childhood, school and tertiary sectors. In the meantime, the Interim Tertiary e-Learning Framework embodies leadership as capacity building because the principles of the framework are focused on learning, sharing of good practice, and collaboration. Once again, the recurring theme of communities through which "practitioners are able to share e-learning information and experiences in a collegial manner" is evident. The framework emphasises research and professional development, just as MMP and FLLinNZ do. Finally, the e-learning fellowships are aimed at helping teachers to expand their teaching and learning through ICT. Some $4.02 million has been earmarked for these year-long fellowships over the next four years.

The e-learning fellowships embody leadership as capacity building because they are intended to lead to focused inquiry or research opportunities, and to the development and sharing of new approaches to teaching and learning through ICT. Once again, the support from an online learning community is an inherent part of the fellowships, as is professional development and mentoring. All four examples outlined here–MMP, FLLinNZ, the Interim Tertiary e-Learning Framework, and the e-Learning Fellowships–are working examples of leadership as capacity building in online teaching and learning. This is because, in each case, the initiatives described satisfy a number of conditions.

These conditions are outlined below:

- In each case, learning is seen as the central purpose, and the content of leadership generated by the initiative;
- All of the initiatives support research and inquiry in the field, especially action research;
- In each case there is an emphasis on the importance of building networks for information sharing and community. For example, interactive online communities of learners are integral to the endeavours; as is the belief that one learns to learn and to teach online by working through the medium;
- In each instance, there is an emphasis on professional development and reflective practice.

Taken together, the literature conceptualising leadership as capacity building, along with the examples of capacity building in online teaching and learning, imply that there is an observable trend towards distributing leadership in order to sustain improvement in e-learning. With this in mind, key leadership obligations in online teaching and learning are likely to focus on learning and creating opportunities for others to learn; to emphasise inquiry and research, in terms of continuous experimentation, feedback and improvement; and to involve essential collaboration between members of online learning communities. There are a number of leadership questions that arise however. These are worthy of further investigation and research, within and between institutions.

Leadership questions include:

- How can we ensure there are leaders at many levels in online learning and teaching?
- How are opportunities for others to learn created in relation to teaching and learning online? What are the structures and processes for participation and opportunities to become skilful participants?
- To what extent do teachers share ideas and know what is going on in each other's classes online?
- Do we have a shared vision about our online learning and teaching? What are our underlying beliefs, values and norms?
- How did we arrive at these and how do we re-examine them?
- How does our instructional practice connect to our vision?
- How do we make time for inquiry, collaboration, dialogue and reflection? What "feedback loops" are in place?
- To what extent is decision making within our organization shared?
- How are students included in the development of leadership capacity? What student acts of leadership are evident?
- To what extent do wider policies and practices support leadership capacity building?

Questions like these will require continuous reassessment if we are serious about increasing leadership capacity in online teaching and learning, in order to sustain improvements over time.

7

Online Teaching in Online World

AN OVERVIEW

Welcome to the first of at least two reports related to instruction on the Internet. The aim of this particular report, "Online Teaching in an Online World," is to understand the online learning experiences, obstacles, supports, and preferences of college instructors across a variety of institutional settings and disciplines.

Whereas this initial report focuses on the online learning needs and supports of higher education faculty, the second study, "Online Training in an Online World," addresses similar issues in the corporate training world. After detailing the survey results and conclusions, a set of recommendations are proposed related to online learning in higher education settings.

Perhaps no technology has so swiftly assumed prominence in both educational and commercial settings as the Web. In educational arenas, those who previously found higher education too expensive or physically inaccessible can now access a myriad of online information resources and materials.

Ideas and feedback from online expert guests, mentors, and peers are now available in college classes. Finnish instructors and students can collaborate with those in the United States and Korea. Online student mentoring can come from practitioners in the field, experts at the North Pole, or graduate students and colleagues down the hall. Collaborative teaming in online college settings knows no bounds, and, not surprisingly, higher education administrators have taken notice. As a result, new instructional expectations for college faculty are emerging. This survey targeted instructors who were likely to have greater experience with these new teaching methods and tools than others. This final report is intended to provide insights into the future directions of online teaching as well as to identify the gaps in tool and courseware development efforts.

PREVIOUS REPORTS

A report from the Web-based Education Commission indicates that Web technologies are increasingly used in both online and traditional classroom-based courses. This report also notes that distance learning course offerings are expected to increase from 62 per cent of four-year colleges offering some courses online in 1998 to 84 per cent of such colleges offering such online course experiences in 2002. As a result, the Commission notes that many higher education institutions are forming consortia and collaborative groups to share course materials and resources in an effort to enhance college teaching and learning.

In terms of specific Web tools, the commission reports a dramatic increase in college faculty utilizing e-mail, Web resources, course homepages, and online discussions within their courses. In fact, they report a 25 per cent increase from 1996 to 1999 in college faculty utilizing Web resources in their class syllabi.

This report also acknowledges the additional time and risk on the part of faculty who attempt to take advantage of online learning tools and activities in their courses. But why is there a risk? Higher education institutions simply do not yet have the teaching rewards, expectations, or support structures in place for promoting faculty teaching in an online world. As e-learning environments take centre stage in college programmes around the world, it is vital to determine the tools and tasks that facilitate student learning in this new context as well as to establish quality standards for such courses. A recent report from the Institute for Higher Education Policy that was commissioned by the National Education Association and Blackboard, Inc. identified 24 key benchmarks for online learning quality.

These benchmarks addressed course development guidelines, instructional material reviews, student feedback and interaction, access to library resources, technical support, student advising procedures, and the evaluation of intended learning outcomes. There are a number of other summary reports attempting to describe and evaluate the use of distance education technology in education.

Some reports speak to the challenges of teaching in an online world, including issues of compensation, time, ownership, profitability, training, technology infrastructure, and university policies. Jaffee for instance, discusses the costs of online instruction as well as the forms of resistance to such courses and programmes at both the institutional and individual level. Others point to new economic markets and opportunities. Such reports document key trends, social demographics, stakeholders, policy makers, major players, and workplace needs. Still other reports detail newly formed and tenuous partnerships and consortia. What about the instructional, psychological, and social aspects of online learning? At least one report has been commissioned to develop guidelines or benchmarks—including many instructional design guidelines—to ensure quality distance education practices.

On the social and psychological side of online learning, Joseph Walther and his colleagues point to the social issues embedded in online environments such as student social isolation and shared knowledge. In a more recent report, Bonk and Wisher summarize the research related to online collaborative tools, e-learning, the role of the instructor, and the increasing importance of learner-centred approaches to instruction.

They also suggest more than two dozen psychologically-based research opportunities in online collaboration related to principles of cognition, motivation, social interaction, and individual differences. Within the plethora of distance education reports and prophecies, the TeleLearning Network Centres of Excellence of Canada have assumed a leadership role related to online learning research. One of their key reports compares eight key post-secondary institutions offering e-learning. In this report, Massey and Curry provide a preliminary analysis of universities emerging in this field such as Stanford University, Nova Southeastern, Western Governors University, Indiana University, the University of Illinois, Open University UK, University of Phoenix Online, and California Virtual University.

They offer a competitive analysis of the courses/ programmes, pedagogy, and learner support structures in place at each of these institutions. In addition, they address expansion plans, marketing, faculty, learners/clients, and course production and delivery mechanisms at each institution. As such, this particular report offers useful insights into the direction of online technologies and course delivery.

While the TeleLearning NCE is a source for online learning reports from Canada, UCLA has recently published an inaugural report on the impact of the Internet on social, political, cultural, and economic behaviour and ideas across the United States. While that research investigates Internet usage across the general population of the United States, the data in the present study focus on evaluations of Internet usage in college courses among college instructors likely to use it.

CURRENT TENSION

There is no doubt that the Internet has brought about a new forum for learning and instruction. Higher education faculty and administrators must not only understand the new technologies that present themselves, but they also must grapple with how best to utilize them for student learning. Or as Steven Gilbert recently noted, "Acquiring the knowledge and skill necessary to improve teaching and learning with technology requires faculty, support professionals, and administrators to think and behave in new ways—deep learning." The challenge, he argues, is for early adopters of technology to push at the educational frontiers in ways that help transform themselves as well as their colleagues with new insights and lifelong learning, while staying within the educational missions and resources of their respective institutions.

But on college campuses there is tension and uncertainty surrounding the use of the Internet in teaching and learning. There is also a lot of hype. Free classes mentioned one day are delayed by downturns in the economy the next. Standards and guidelines are encouraged, but too often not established. Distance learning policies created one year are revamped in the years that follow. Moreover, too many reports speak from an administrator, politician, or corporate executive viewpoint. What is often lacking is a sense of what the faculty member or instructor thinks about the online experience. As a result, few reports reflect on the pedagogical practices that lead to online learning success.

It is as if the technology alone is sufficient to build an effective environment for learning. And this, we know, is not the case. Few can doubt that Web-based teaching and learning is a growing field with rapid changes. In part, it has emerged to fill the void in training as technical skills quickly fall into obsolescence. Reskilling simply is a fact of life. Online reskilling may be a necessity as the age of learners increases and the time available for one's studies is curtailed by job and family responsibilities. Web-based courses may simply be the only viable option for many learners.

The present study attempts to determine the supports and resources that college faculty have available to meet those needs. Whereas other surveys of online learning in higher education have explored areas such as technological resource availability, instructor skills and attitudes, or institutional policies, this particular study is more comprehensive by attempting to understand instructor attitudes, experiences, preferences, and online support structures, as well as prevalent pedagogical tools and practices. Given this focus, the results of this survey can perhaps help educators design more powerful e-learning environments as well as methods to teach within them. Hopefully, it will serve as a barometer for higher education institutions considering online courses and programmes as well as a guidepost for instructors first encountering online teaching in this online world.

FOCUS ON PEDAGOGICAL PRACTICES

There is no doubt that Web-based instruction offers new ways for students to collaborate and for instructors to share pedagogical ideas and practices. It is also a way to expand the resources available to students and build permanent course archives. With the emergence of the Web, it is now possible to involve practitioners, experts, and peers as online learning guides or mentors. Case-based learning can take on a new sense of authenticity as business students chat with company executives, counseling students reflect online about crisis situations faced during internships, preservice teachers peek in on the classroom management strategies of expert teachers, and medical students virtually view sophisticated operations in action.

There seem to be limitless opportunities to exploit the Web in college teaching and learning. As online learning resources accumulate and become archived, there is even a new sense of course history and legacy. Events that were delivered or that unfolded a decade or more ago can be replayed, modified, salvaged, contemplated, and debated at any time. As a result of all these new instructional opportunities, the decisions confronting the online college instructors are multiplied. Part of this is due to the complexity of these environments that often beg for quick managerial decision making one minute, technological expertise the next, and social or pedagogical intervention just a few moments later.

This survey will help document some of the early pedagogical practices of those deciding to teach online, or, at least, those beginning to utilize online resources somewhere in their teaching practices.

PURPOSE OF THE STUDY

This report is based on a survey of 222 college faculty members, most of whom have been early adopters of

Webbased technology in their instruction. Unlike some of the previous studies, online course quality is just one aspect of this particular report. In addition, this survey report is intended to inform administrators and courseware designers of the benefits and challenges of using Web-based learning tools in higher education settings.

It also provides suggestions about the types of tools, activities, resources, and support structures that might enhance online learning in college settings. This survey report provides descriptive information about the types of college instructors and institutions involved in typical online environments.

It has five primary goals:

- To identify the resources, tools, and activities that college instructors desire in their Web-based teaching efforts;
- To document the gaps between online teaching practices and preferences;
- To understand some of the key obstacles as well as support structures for Web-based teaching in college settings;
- To point to online learning tools and communities that might be developed to enhance teaching and learning in higher education settings; and,
- To determine who is responsible for making online learning decisions in higher education.

In effect, this study intends to document how faculty educators are being trained, supported, and rewarded for online instruction. It also seeks to determine the types of online tools and activities that faculty prefer. Additionally, this survey explores college instructor attitudes related to online learning obstacles and support.

It addresses their perceptions of controversial online learning issues such as course ownership and quality, online programme accreditation, online teaching and learning opportunities, and the general utility of the Web as a teaching and learning resource. The conclusions are intended to help those teaching in online environments as well as those developing policies and funding new online initiatives. The findings may also be useful to companies developing and evaluating online tools for distance teaching and learning.

METHODS AND DATA

METHODOLOGICAL OVERVIEW

As distance learning tensions rise in response to concerns about online pedagogy and policy, we need to understand more from faculty who have crossed some of the first hurdles. Where can one go to look for the early adopters or at least those who are less resistant to incorporating the Web in their teaching? Who are the ones to ask about online teaching practices? While previous research indicates that college instructors too often are not utilizing the most sophisticated technologies and interaction opportunities, nevertheless, faculty members were considered ideal sources for providing information on Web-based teaching policies, experiences, training, and incentives in higher education. In this report, we sampled college instructors who had a history of sharing resources on the Web.

SAMPLING PROCEDURES

Our sampling of instructors employing the Web for teaching and learning purposes comes from two separate sources. First, we selected a random sample of names from The World Lecture Hall. The WLH is an international site first created in 1994 at the University of Texas at Austin to post college syllabi for courses within a variety of academic disciplines. The developers have received national praise and recognition for offering this service.

When beginning to select that sample, however, we noticed the emergence of another resource for faculty and students in higher education. MERLOT was created in 1997 by the California State University Centre for Distributed Learning. It has since expanded to consortia of other institutions and state systems. MERLOT is now a fast growing and free resource intended as an online community of shared knowledge and ideas. In contrast to the WLH, the MERLOT site was originally designed for sharing a wide variety of online learning materials, including assignments, reviews, and member profiles across many academic disciplines within higher education. The capability for peer instructors to review online learning materials was the key feature that distinguished MERLOT from other online resource sharing sites at the time of this study. Even though the WLH and MERLOT members are not representative of all college faculty members, they provide richer online learning backgrounds and experiences than most other available populations. Over 2000 syllabi reflecting more than 80 disciplines and subdisciplines have been posted to the WLH.

Those posting syllabi to the WLH include faculty from religious studies, sociology, theater and dance, accounting, philosophy, marketing, zoology, history, neuroscience, astronomy, nutrition, anthropology, rhetoric, law, and electrical engineering.

At the time of this study, MERLOT contained over 2000 members representing more than 120 different disciplines. Members of MERLOT include faculty from such disciplines as nursing, teacher education, business information systems, geology, arts, computer science, political science, evolution, and theoretical mathematics. The combined sample population, therefore, included a variety of disciplines, degree programmes, and types and sizes of institutions. It also included a wide range of Web expertise.

All these people, however, either had experience posting syllabi online or posting online profiles, critiques, or learning materials. For some in the sample, however, this may have been just a one-time post or brief comment. While the WLH and MERLOT were perhaps the most well known Web sites for resource sharing within higher education at the time of this study, we were not aware of surveys of college faculty representing either or both of these sites. Our random sample during November and early December 2000 included 415 instructors from MERLOT and 286 from the WLH, or a total of 701 instructors from a wide spectrum of disciplines at both sites.1 From e-mail solicitations to this sample, we collected

222 completed surveys; the vast majority were faculty or administrators with additional college teaching responsibilities. While our 32 per cent response rate was generally lower than direct mail or phone surveys, online survey research suggests that this rate is quite good. However, at this time, no expected response rate for online surveys has been firmly established. Nearly fifty different disciplines and subdisciplines were represented in our final sample. Most responses were received from instructors from across the United States, though around 5 per cent of the respondents came from other countries including Hong Kong, Australia, Canada, and the United Kingdom.

LIMITATIONS OF THE STUDY

As with most online surveys, the present project had several limitations that may have constrained the results and generalizability of the study:

- There are few available resources for faculty online course-sharing, thereby limiting the selection to two of the more popular sites, the WLH and MERLOT. These two Web sites were possibly not representative of all college faculty members who use the Web in their teaching.
- Since users created these sites over long periods of time, many of the collected online faculty member names and e-mail addresses were outdated, incorrect, or changed, especially those in the World Lecture Hall.
- Many of the faculty respondents here were Web savvy and could be described as early adopters of Web technology, thereby inflating any optimistic results regarding online learning experiences and felt need for additional online collaborative tools compared to college faculty in general.
- Tools for teaching and learning on the Web are constantly changing. As a result, it is difficult to generalize many of the findings of this survey related to the utility of particular Web-based instructional tools.

- The online survey instrument was relatively lengthy, effectively lowering the response rate and perhaps causing some inaccurate or skipped responses.
- This survey report labels respondents as college or post-secondary instructors, even though a few of the respondents were in administrative positions with only part-time faculty or teaching responsibilities.
- In an effort to keep the survey at a manageable length, the online survey failed to address key issues such as how courseware tools are funded, the per cent of respondents with tenure, the perceived quality of online certificates or institutes, the forms of online training for instructors, the types of technical support provided for students and faculty working online, how costs are determined for online courses, and perceived learning and motivational factors in online learning. It is hoped that future studies will address such issues.

Despite these limitations, the response rate for this online survey was higher than expected for an e-mail solicited Web survey. In fact, only 7 per cent of those solicited in this particular survey explicitly refused to participate.

FINDINGS

RESPONDENT BACKGROUND

Description of Survey Respondents

Nearly 64 per cent of our sample came from MERLOT, while 36 per cent were from the WLH. In addition, the response rate was slightly higher for MERLOT participants as compared to WLH participants. These differences in response rate are due, in part, to MERLOT being a recent phenomenon with a more current faculty listing.

Type and Size of Respondent Institution

National studies indicate that distance education is more prevalent in public than private institutions and in 4-year rather than 2- year institutions. Not surprisingly, then, it appears that college instructors who are active in posting resources to the Web are from those types of institutions. In this particular study, over two-thirds of our respondents were from public institutions. Only 1 per cent came from 2-year private institutions and 20 per cent from 4-year private institutions.

Nine per cent of the respondents were employed in other types of instructional situations or indicated that they were in a public or private college setting but without noting whether it was a 2-year or 4-year institution. Respondents were three times more likely to be from 4-year than 2-year institutions. The type and size of institutions ranged from large Research I institutions such as the University of Texas at Austin, Arizona State University, the University of Illinois, and the University of Maryland College Park to more modestly-sized state colleges such as Indiana State University, Northern Michigan University, the University of Wisconsin Whitewater, and the University of Akron, to small private institutions such as St. Norbert College, Oberlin College, Nazareth College, and Belmont Abbey College.

As indicated by reports from the National Centre for Education Statistics and the National Educational Association, distance education is often linked to institutional size. In those previous studies, distance learning faculty members were more likely to work at larger institutions. Additionally, distance education courses were more likely to be taught at the larger institutions. In this study, more than 50 per cent of the survey participants were from large institutions. In contrast, approximately 20 per cent were from small institutions that had enrollments of less than 3,000. Slightly more than onefourth of the respondents were from medium-sized institutions.

Years of College Teaching Experience

In addition to the institution the participants represented, we also were interested in their teaching experiences. Unlike the NEA study which found that distance learning faculty members tended to be younger and have fewer years of teaching experience, the present study found that college instructors who are willing to share resources online tended to be older and more established. While 30 per cent had 10 or fewer years of experience teaching college, 34 per cent had 11 to 20 years of experience, and around 36 per cent had more than 20 years of experience.

This is an important finding since it reveals that Web-based instructional role models can be found across generations of faculty. It also indicates that there are many established college instructors who can mentor incoming faculty in Web-based practices and experiences. As will be pointed out later in this report, established faculty may have more time available to explore online teaching methods and do so at significantly lower risk.

Age of Respondents

Based on the research mentioned previously from the NEA, it was expected that younger faculty members would be sharing resources online more often than older instructors. Surprisingly, nearly half of our respondents were over age 51. Fewer than 7 per cent were under age 36. These data are somewhat surprising given the conventional wisdom that the Internet is dominated by younger age groups and that older faculty members tend to be more reluctant to use technologies in their instruction. This finding is in contrast to a UCLA report that computer use is nearly double a source of stress for faculty over the age of 45 than for those younger than 35. Nevertheless, the more recent survey on Internet usage from UCLA also indicated all age groups now utilize the Internet. Even the 2 per cent of Web users over age 65 in the present study is quite heartening.

Gender of Respondents

Nearly 60 per cent of the WLH or MERLOT respondents were male. Given the gender-related trends of the past few decades related to both computer experience and use favouring boys and higher education employment figures favouring males, this is not too surprising. The gender representation in this sample is reflective of commonly cited gender patterns of higher education faculty.

Faculty Rank

The recent NEA study revealed that distance education and traditional faculty have similar educational backgrounds, professorial ranks or positions and tenure status. In the NEA study, 36 per cent of those teaching distance education courses were lecturers and another 7 per cent were unranked, or about 43 per cent of the total. In contrast, in the present study, lecturers represented fewer than 5 per cent of those posting to the WLH or MERLOT and adjunct professors accounted for another 8 per cent. In effect, the WLH and MERLOT seem to attract very few lecturers and adjunct instructors. Ten per cent of the respondents in this study were classified as "other". So while the NEA data clearly indicated that lecturers and unranked faculty members are involved in Web-based instruction, they are not typically sharing their work electronically with other college faculty in two of the most prominent course-sharing sites—the WLH and MERLOT. And, in contrast to the large unranked or lecturer population in the NEA study, most respondents here were in professorial ranks.

Educational Background

Our sample also differed from the NEA study in terms of educational backgrounds of the participants. In the NEA study, about half of the respondents had master's degrees but only 30 per cent had a Ph.D. or Ed.D. In our study, in contrast, 70 per cent of the sample had a Ph.D. or Ed.D. and another 6 per cent were ABD, while just 22 per cent had a master's as their highest degree held. Thus, college faculty members involved in sharing course resources online appear to have more extensive educational backgrounds than other distance education faculty. The determinants of these differences are unknown.

Level of Courses Taught

It was also deemed useful to find out what type of courses

these instructors taught. Given the amount of negative press about the lack of undergraduate level involvement of college faculty from Research I institutions, it was encouraging that almost all respondents had undergraduate teaching experience. Still, more than 60 per cent had taught at the graduate level. Perhaps most interestingly, over forty per cent had taught non-credit or other types of courses such as workshops, enrichment programmes, or training courses.

PARTICIPATION IN ONLINE COURSE SHARING

When Do They Share

The emergence of online course sharing is a relatively new phenomenon. In fact, 54 per cent of respondents first posted to one these two Web sites— the WLH and MERLOT—within the past year, and an additional 17 per cent within the past two years. The remaining 29 per cent indicated that they posted more than two years ago. While these numbers are reflective of how long these sites have been available, a culture of sharing online resources seems to be emerging.

It might be the case that sites such as the WLH and MERLOT have simply become more popular among faculty during the year leading up to this study. Or, perhaps, sufficient Internet access and speed finally exists for college faculty to share resources online.

How Did They Discover Sharing Resources

We were interested in finding out how the college faculty members discovered sites for sharing resources online. Thus, we inquired as to how they heard about the WLH or MERLOT resources. Fewer than 5 per cent had heard about them through advertisements, and, surprisingly, none listed a friend as an important source. More typically, they had learned about these resources through their institution, a colleague, an Internet link, or through other means such as mailing lists, journal objects, special interest groups, or conferences. Thus, the most effective communication channels were professional contracts or electronic communications.

Why Share

In addition to asking how the faculty respondents in our study were informed of these resources for online course sharing, we asked why they posted to these sites. Around 8 per cent responded that their institution or department required them to do so. Approximately twice as many respondents claimed to have posted to these sites as a means of marketing themselves to other colleagues. About the same number indicated that they posted to one of these sites as a pedagogical experiment, while another 16 per cent became active in the site for fun.

Thirty-eight per cent of those posting simply wanted to share pedagogical theories or strategies with their colleagues. Slightly more were active in one or more of these sites in order to grow as professionals. The most frequently selected response was that they simply believed in the importance of course sharing. Around 18 per cent gave other reasons for their affiliations to the WLH or MERLOT. For instance, several respondents noted that they were asked by Merlot officials to join, while a few others indicated that someone else posted their name or information.

Type and Number of Resulting Contacts

We also inquired about the type and number of contacts that these faculty respondents received as a result of posting resources or information to one of these two Web sites. Of the faculty completing this item, sixty-one per cent were contacted by others after sharing their syllabus or profile on the Web. The data here are varied and interesting.

Twelve per cent of the respondents had been contacted by researchers, while nearly three times as many were contacted by other instructors. In addition, more then 30 per cent had been contacted by students not in their courses. Interestingly, 14 per cent had been contacted by publishers and 12 per cent by other companies and institutions. Such findings reveal the marketing and networking potential of online resource sharing. Not only are students attracted to one's class after reading an online syllabus, but textbook publishers, researchers, and other institutions are also knocking on one's door. We were interested in determining the average number of contacts for each group described previously. Whereas contacts by publishers, institutions, and other companies were relatively infrequent, a number of people indicated that they had been contacted by students or instructors more than ten times as a result of their online resource contribution or membership.

Perhaps it is the course marketing and enhanced collegiality that instructors find most appealing about these course-sharing resources. In fact, more than ninety per cent indicated that comments from colleagues on their syllabus or other posted course resources would be helpful.

ATTITUDES ABOUT ONLINE LEARNING

Course Material Ownership

No matter what the motive, there are a myriad of issues confronting those teaching online. Some of these issues relate to costs and benefits, copyright, ownership, quality, and compensation. One issue, ownership of course materials, is a particularly sensitive topic since course materials are now more mobile than in the past. Policy recommendations here are not simple since faculty might own course materials but not the courses. In recapping discussion from an invited symposium of higher education leaders, Carol Twigg details a range of potential situations and issues surrounding ownership of online courses and materials.

Her report recommended, "that the default policy position for all institutions should be that the faculty member own the course materials he or she has created." She points out that institutions could have mechanisms in place that spell out situations or conditions wherein a secondary policy would come into play. Faculty in the present study held similar views. Only 16 per cent of faculty members completing this survey agreed that online courses were the property of an institution; 63 per cent disagreed. Keep in mind that this particular survey question concerned courses, not course materials. It is likely that the attitudes would be even stronger in regards to specific course materials. In part, to the fact that only 31 per cent of those responding to the survey indicated that their institution had clear policies regarding ownership of course material. In addition, more than a quarter of those responding to this question were unsure.

As Twigg's report indicated, this is a complex area that higher education institutions need to start addressing more fully so that both faculty and administrators have a clear understanding of university policy on this issue. Despite the lack of clarity regarding ownership of the rights to online courses, more than three-fourths of the faculty members completing this survey indicated that they planned to abide by the ownership guidelines of their home institution, while 19 per cent were unsure if they would. Such responses make it imperative that institutions of higher education clearly state their policies regarding course ownership.

Course Quality

Another commonly debated issue is online course quality. When asked about whether the quality of learning is improved in online environments compared to traditional learning, faculty member opinions were fairly divided. Nearly 40 per cent of the respondents reported that they were unsure, while 32 per cent noted that course quality was, in fact, improved, and another 29 per cent said that it was not.

Such division among early Web adopters is a clear indication that additional research on learning outcomes is needed. As the NEA study points out, those teaching traditionally hold a less positive view of Web-based courses than those actually teaching via distance education. But even among those teaching online, there are some distinct differences of opinion.

Quality of Degrees

As another indicator of faculty views about online course quality, these faculty members were asked about whether they were opposed to bachelor's, master's, and doctoral degrees earned entirely online. Not surprisingly, the responses were less favourable for online doctoral degrees than bachelor's and master's degrees. While around 45 per cent thought that online bachelor's or master's degrees were legitimate, only 29 per cent agreed that doctoral degrees should be available entirely online. For all degrees, the per cent of respondents strongly supporting degrees earned entirely online was under 20 per cent.

Accreditation

Sally Johnstone recently pointed out that many new organizations are emerging to accredit online programmes. However, she also noted that "there are about 100 accrediting bodies that are unrecognized by both the U.S. Secretary of Education and/or the Council for Higher Education Accreditation". Johnstone argues that online education requires speedier responses in terms of accreditation than has been the norm.

As a result, many regional accrediting associations are rethinking and reorganizing their accrediting processes and procedures. In terms of quality, our faculty respondents were believers in the importance of distance education accreditation. In fact, 80 per cent agreed or strongly agreed that accreditation for online distance education is necessary for ensuring academic quality for students.

Perhaps this is not too surprising given the high number of respondents that came from large four-year institutions. We suggest some caution in interpreting these findings, however, since faculty members teaching online at small private universities or at virtual universities may have answered this question quite differently.

Instructor Compensation for Online Teaching

Another major issue, of course, is rewarding faculty who teach online. The traditional publish or perish focus of research-intensive universities forces many young faculty members to avoid pedagogical innovations with technology. Perhaps this accounts for the fact that our sample was older and at higher professorial levels than expected. As cited in Dukart, Lucio Teles argues, "Universities do not have the infrastructure to support online teaching as they do for face-to-face teaching." In terms of compensation, the NEA report showed that distance learning faculty members tend to make comparable wages to those teaching in more traditional settings.

Yet, both sets of faculty members were concerned that they would not be compensated for intellectual property and that they would encounter more work for the same pay. In that study, only 22 per cent of college educators teaching via distance learning received a reduction of course load. Despite these additional burdens, most of those teaching distance learning courses do so voluntarily.

In the present study, instructors were asked how those teaching online should be compensated. One-third indicated that additional salary would be the method of choice. Other answers were fairly equally represented including stipends to spend how they wished, course royalties, and release time. Release time was a common write-in response and would likely have been much higher had it been among the listed options. Awards or recognition was selected by only 4 per cent of the faculty.

Across these answers, some type of monetary commitment is preferred with 63 per cent choosing stipends, royalties, or additional pay. Still, nearly 20 per cent responded that instructors should receive no additional compensation for teaching online courses beyond their normal course pay.

CURRENT ONLINE TEACHING SITUATION

Online Experience

While the vast majority of our survey respondents had been active in posting course resources, syllabi, or personal information on the Web, not all had previous experience in Web-based instruction. Nearly a quarter of the respondents had never taught even a portion of a course online. On the other hand, nearly 4 in 10 respondents had taught courses partially online; among this group, the average number of partially online courses taught was about four. Another 18 per cent had experience teaching fully online courses, with an average of five such courses. In addition, 19 per cent had done both—partial and completely online courses—with an average of 10 such online course experiences.

Calculations across these responses indicated that nearly 4 in 10 early Web adopters had taught completely online courses, while nearly 6 in 10 had taught at least part of a course online. Given these data, the respondents in this study certainly had extensive online teaching experiences on which to base their survey answers.

Respondent's Web-Related Skills

An instructor's degree of comfort in using different Web technologies has a direct bearing on classroom practices as well as the decision to teach even part of a course online. When instructors are hesitant or lacking in confidence, there is less likelihood for innovation and risk taking.

Therefore, we asked these early Web adopters about their degree of comfort with the following Web skills:

- Creating HTML pages,
- Hosting an online chat,
- Sending and receiving file attachments,
- Using Web-based courseware systems, and
- Moderating a Web-based asynchronous discussion.

The responses were interesting. For instance, over 90 per cent of these faculty members felt a high degree of comfort sending and receiving file attachments in e-mail. Fewer than one per cent of respondents were uncomfortable with this skill. Somewhat surprisingly, 62 per cent were highly comfortable with creating HTML pages and another 20 per cent had a medium level of comfort.

However, this acknowledged degree of comfort likely includes a range of skills from using standard software options such as "save as HTML" to actually being facile with HTML and other programming code. The degree of expertise with HTML remains a question for future surveys. These early adopting faculty were somewhat less comfortable moderating a Web-based asynchronous discussion forum or bulletin board. Still, nearly 50 per cent rated their degree of comfort as high, while another quarter of them reported a medium level of comfort. Similarly, 44 per cent were highly comfortable with Web-based courseware systems and another 34 per cent felt moderately comfortable.

On the low end was comfort with hosting an online chat session. Perceptions of online chat tools were roughly split across low, medium, and high comfort categories. These results indicate that these faculty members possessed at least some basic technology skills. Perhaps, as the NEA survey of traditional and distance learning higher education members revealed, workshops and training sessions on teaching via distance learning are now readily available.

While such a skill base and comfort level may be expected of these early Web adopters, many of these faculty members are either taking advantage of university training and support or are engaged in a heavy amount of self-teaching in regard to Web-based teaching tools. Or perhaps they are overstating their skills. In fact, latter parts of this report reveal a somewhat different picture.

Time Commitments

In terms of overall time investment, these college instructors almost unilaterally agreed that teaching online is more time-consuming than traditional classroom-based instruction. More than 4 in 5 faculty agreed that teaching online courses requires more time than traditional courses.

Fewer than 10 per cent disagreed with that statement. Once again, this is consistent with the NEA report finding that more than half of college faculty teaching via distance learning spent more time on their online courses than their traditional ones regardless of the number of students or times they had previously taught the course.

Such findings point to a need for greater course support and incentives that could ease time pressures felt by instructors involved in online teaching.

Attrition

Some reports and media releases contend that students are more likely to drop online courses than traditional ones. Those utilizing a mixed mode or blended approach—traditional and online in the same course—were less likely to experience significant student attrition than those teaching completely online courses.

In fact, only 29 per cent of those utilizing a blended approach experienced more than 10 per cent drop the their courses, whereas 44 per cent of those teaching completely online courses had more than 10 per cent drop their course. Perhaps more strikingly, only 2 per cent of blended courses experienced more than a 50 per cent attrition rate compared to 10 per cent of the completely online courses with such huge attrition rates.

Internet Access

Computer access does not appear to be a problem for these early adopters of Web technologies. Seventy-eight per cent of these college instructors had Internet access in their current or most recent classroom. Computer lab accessibility was even higher with 93 per cent indicating that they had access to an Internet-connected computer lab for class use. Even more, 97 per cent, had Web access from home.

This is more than double the 47 per cent of Americans who are users of the Internet at home as reported in a recent UCLA study. Such high level of technology access is not too surprising given that the majority of the respondents were early Web adopters who had a high level of education.2 In effect, these findings indicate that access to computers and Internet resources is no longer an obstacle for many college faculty.

Platform Choices and Preferences

The delivery platform for online courses is a significant factor in faculty online teaching experiences. Eighty-three per cent of the respondents to this survey indicated that their institution provided a Web-based platform or courseware system for developing online courses or enhancing on-campus courses with online features. Our survey data also indicated that many institutions are utilizing more than one courseware package. In fact, 22 per cent of the respondents worked at institutions that provided access to more than one Web courseware or conferencing platform; when excluding those having yet to adopt a Web courseware system, this increases to 27 per cent. Moreover, 10 per cent provided access to three courseware systems or conferencing tools, and 5 per cent had four or more systems or tools available. When asked what is missing from the courseware tools that they use, slightly over half of the respondents at institutions supporting at least one courseware platform offered some ideas.

The specific features mentioned in their open-ended responses included:

- Ability to annotate documents and visuals in real-time,
- Better grade reporting systems,
- Collaborative white boards,
- Collaborative working tools,
- Drawing software,
- Easy ways to create animations,
- Effective drop box tools,
- Efficient ways to display mathematical notation,
- Electronic library resources,
- Good real-time chat tools,
- Improved quizzes,
- Options for chatting and using PowerPoint at the same time,
- Private asynchronous rooms for group work,
- Proctored testing,
  Streaming video,
- Three-dimensional concept visualization tools,
- Tools for tracking student statistics, and,
- 24/7 support.

Of course, many of the tools already exist in the common courseware platforms used in higher education. Other features, such as "options for chatting and using PowerPoint at the same time" are available in various synchronous presentation and collaboration tools often found in corporate training settings. Some general design features requested by these respondents included simplicity, ease of use, user friendliness, enhanced speed, less ugly designs, less cumbersome interfaces, customizability, integration across areas of campus, and flexibility to organize content. In general, there appeared to be a call for more professional appearance, easy to use features, and functional or usable tools. When asked what they liked about their present courseware tools or system, 56 per cent of the respondents offered ideas.

Instructors preferred:

- Ability to link in lectures with PowerPoint presentations,
- Assignment parts for students to pick up homework,
- Chatrooms,
- Comprehensive tools,
- Consistent course appearance,
- Customizability,
- Data and course security,
- Detailed statistics on bulletin board use,
- Ease of use,
- Flexibility,
- Good online help,
- Internal e-mail systems.
- Online discussion boards,
- Password access,
- Posting of assignments on the Web,
- Posting of deadlines and due dates,
- Randomized test banks,
- Reliability,
- Student drop boxes, and,
- Versatility in quiz types.

FUTURE ONLINE TEACHING SITUATION

Predicted Instructional Time Online

Given that many of those surveyed were likely among the technology leaders at their respective institutions, it was important to ask about the per cent of time they anticipated teaching online in the next 1, 2, 5, and 10 years. Interestingly, while just under a third of these faculty members anticipated teaching more than one-fourth of their teaching load online one year from now, this increased to 43 per cent of the respondents in two years, 61 per cent in five years, and 59 per cent in 10 years. The reason there was a drop-off in the 10 year data was due to a dramatic increase in those not anticipating to be teaching a decade from now. Once again, the age and experience level of these instructors would indicate that many of them plan to retire before the decade is out. When excluding the data related to those retiring or not teaching, the predictions regarding online teaching commitments were even more striking.

The per cent of respondents who anticipate devoting more than one-fourth of their teaching load to online activities increased as follows: 27 per cent in one year, 44 per cent in two years, 64 per cent in five years, and 73 per cent in ten years. Those predicting that at least half their teaching load would be online increased from 13 per cent in one year to nearly 50 per cent in ten years. And those expecting 75 to 100 per cent of their teaching to be online increased from 5 per cent a year in 2001 to 17 per cent at the end of the decade.

Hence, the college instructors responding to this survey expect the Web to become an even more vital instructional tool during the upcoming decade. Though most respondents do not view it as a replacement for all of their teaching activities and requirements, this finding indicates that Web-based teaching expectations will soon be common.

Freelance Instruction

In addition to predictions of increased online teaching loads within university settings, many college faculty members will likely encounter a myriad of new opportunities to teach for other institutions online. Whether "star" faculty members will be hired guns within the online teaching world is not yet known. Instead, what is occurring already is the use of college instructors as freelance instructors in online institutions. These faculty members might work for multiple institutions, teach online during breaks or in the summer, or perhaps even take a leave from their institution to attempt to earn an income teaching online. Other freelance instructors might include practitioners in the field wanting to keep one foot in academia, recently minted Ph.D.'s struggling to find tenure-track positions, and graduate students seeking relevant teaching experiences. Fueling such freelance needs, many institutions are offering new online courses or programmes without expanding their faculty lines, thereby forcing them to find adjunct faculty or add to present faculty teaching loads.

The scenarios leading to freelance instruction are certainly complex. The 16 per cent of the faculty respondents in this study had experience as freelance or adjunct online instructors. However, in the next five years, 75 per cent of these respondents indicated that they believed that they would be interested in teaching as freelance or adjunct online instructors. There definitely is potential here for someone to help coordinate and manage freelance instructor services.

Perhaps pending retirements of our respondents factor into these predictions, but other considerations may include additional online course opportunities and expected increases in Web tool availability and reliability

INSTITUTIONAL MOTIVES AND DECISION MAKING

Primary Institutional Motives for Online Education

As Ron Owston pointed out, during the past few years, perhaps nothing has captivated and excited the minds of administrators and educators more than the notion of teaching courses on the World Wide Web. He then argued "Before we introduce any new technology into our classrooms we must be able to justify its contribution".

The three key areas wherein Owston suggested that Web-based learning might be evaluated were improved access to education, student learning, and cost efficiency. While he detailed many improvements to educational access as a result of online technologies, documenting learning outcomes and costs proved much more difficult.3 In order to establish the level of college instructor agreement with Owston's key areas, our study participants were asked whether profit, improved learning, or access to education were among the primary motives behind the development of online education across institutions of higher education.

They could select all three. As Owston had documented, there appears to be more support among these early Web adopters for the use of Internet technology to increase access to education than for improving profit or learning. Of our respondents, 93 per cent agreed that access was a primary motive for developing online education. Only one person strongly disagreed with that statement. Additionally, 61 per cent agreed that improved learning was a primary motive. In contrast, only 41 per cent felt that profit was a primary motive.

Hence, those in the Web-based learning trenches put the emphasis on access and learning over profits. When asked the same questions about their own institutions, these general patterns hold. However, these instructors were slightly less likely to agree that each of the three motives were applicable to their particular institution; only 29 per cent agreed or strongly agreed that profit was a motive while 53 per cent agreed that learning was a motive and 81 per cent felt that their own institution was concerned about access. The reasons for the lower agreement levels were unclear.

Reasons for Institutional Investment

These early Web adopters were asked to rate the level of importance of five key reasons why colleges and universities, in general, might be interested in investing in Web-based teaching and learning. Access to an external universe of libraries, information resources, and databases was the most important reason cited by respondents to explain university investment in Web-based teaching and learning. The second most important reason, just as to these faculty members, was to support improved efficiency and effectiveness in teaching and research. Offering distance education to a potentially unlimited audience was rated third, while fostering closer inter-institutional cooperation, consortia relationships, and resource sharing within the higher education community was rated fourth. Finally, some respondents felt that building partnerships with private businesses and the government was a critical reason for investing in Web-based teaching and learning. Fewer than 10 per cent of the respondents offered additional reasons why higher education institutions should invest in Web-based teaching and learning.

Most of these reasons concerned student recruitment, student access to education, student skill development, contributing to the economy of the state, revenue enhancement, and staying up to date. Quotes from some respondents included, "to offer equal opportunity of high quality education to students in more rural areas," "we are under a mandate to increase the number of students we serve. We cannot do it on campus, so we are trying distance learning...," "to recruit and retain tech-savvy students," "It's a new revenue source, that's #1," and "because Web-based activities are becoming ubiquitous in ALL workplaces." One person simply stated, "Students will demand Web-based courses or go somewhere else."

Web-Based Teaching Technology Decision-Makers

We also asked about the organizational level in which decisions regarding Web-based teaching, including system purchases and policies, were made. Surprisingly, faculty governance also appears to play a key role in these institutions as 40 per cent of our respondents indicated that technology decisions regarding Web-based teaching were made at the faculty level. Similarly, 39 per cent indicated that it was a departmental responsibility or decision.

There were other key players here. For instance, 36 per cent of respondents thought that the technology support unit on campus made these decisions, while 27 per cent considered it a function of the Chief Technology Officer. Twenty-two per cent selected the teaching and learning centre director level as responsible for these decisions. Four per cent listed others as responsible including the office of distance education, grant administrator, board of regents, or college provost. Finally, only 5 per cent did not know who made these decisions. There were no statistically significant differences in instructional technology decisions across size and type of institution. However, there were some interesting trends. For instance, in institutions with fewer than 3,000 students, facultylevel decisions are made regarding courseware slightly over 50 per cent of the time, whereas this drops to 32 per cent in medium sized institutions and 41 per cent in large institutions. In comparisons of public and private institutions, we found that college instructors have a role in instructional technology decisions in nearly half of the 45 private institutions, whereas in this survey just 34 per cent of the faculty members in the 151 public institutions in this study helped formulate such decisions.

Besides asking for faculty input, smaller institutions also seem to rely on campus technology support units and the chief technology officer slightly more often than medium and large institutions. Larger institutions have a slight preference for learning centre and departmental-level decisions compared to smaller institutions. Still, most institutions appear to rely on highlevel administrators to make the technology decisions that impact Web-based teaching and learning. Next, we looked at differences in the organizational level at which instructional technology decisions are made between institutions with fewer than 10,000 students and those with 10,000 or more students. At the larger institutions, the department or school is more involved in these instructional technology decisions than in smaller institutions.

Teaching and learning centre directors are also more involved in making these decisions in the larger colleges and universities than in smaller ones. This is not unexpected since larger institutions are more likely to have campus teaching and learning centres. Administrators are involved in Web-based teaching technology decisions at roughly the same rate at both types of institutions. None of these comparisons were statistically significant, however. That differences in the organizational level of technology decisions between public and private were minimal. Public institutions more often involved teaching and learning centre directors in their decision-making about the use and support of instructional technology than private institutions whereas private institutions more often involved faculty members in these decisions than public institutions. Administrative-level decisions were made at over 60 per cent of both public and private institutions. Once again, none of these differences were statistically significant.

USEFULNESS OF WEB-BASED TOOLS FOR TEACHING AND LEARNING

Usefulness of Web-Based Tools for Teaching and Learning

We were also interested in the attitudes of these college instructors about Web-based instructional tools, resources, and activities. As a result, the respondents were asked to rate the degree of usefulness for items categories:

- Online Class Tools.
- Collaboration and Sharing Tools.
- Instructional Activities.
- Web Resources.

After rating each item as low, medium, or high usefulness for online teaching and learning, the instructors were also asked whether they in fact used that item in their courses.

Useful Online Class Tools

In general, these college educators perceived high utility for most of the online class tools considered in this part of the survey. Perhaps more importantly, at least one-third of the respondents actually used each of the items in this category. Not surprisingly, respondents tended to rate the tools that they actually used as more useful.

The highest rated tool was for posting syllabi online. Not only did 72 per cent of the faculty respondents report this feature as highly useful, 85 per cent actually used such a tool in their courses. These findings also match the Web-based Education Commission report, which documented the increased posting of course syllabi to the Web and incorporation of Web resources within college instructor syllabi. Of course, many of our survey respondents were selected for this survey because they had already posted their syllabus online.

The fact that more use this type of tool than rate it as highly useful indicates it is relatively easy to do. The large number of respondents using tools to post their syllabi online reveals an initial area of penetration for the Web in college teaching and learning. For example, the University of Michigan School of Information has compiled a list of faculty course syllabi and placed it online. Similarly, the UCLA Humanities Department created the E-Campus for syllabi, assignment announcements, and other course related links. However, as indicated earlier, the most complete listing of college syllabi to date is located at the World Lecture Hall. This site hosts syllabi across disciplines for college instructors worldwide. A tool for posting cases, questions, or problems corresponding to course material on the Web was the next most valuable courseware feature of these early Web adopters.

Not only did 70 per cent rate this survey item as highly useful, but nearly 70 per cent also had engaged in such online activities. In fact, only 4 per cent rated this item as low in perceived usefulness. These college instructors also valued file uploading and downloading tools. Sixty-five per cent of the respondents felt they were highly useful, and 71 per cent had used such tools in their teaching. The next highest rated item in terms of usefulness was an online lecture notes utility, which was rated as highly useful by 57 per cent of the respondents and actually used by 69 per cent of them.

Once again, this indicates that while faculty members might view different tools as more useful, they generally rely on readily accessible tools that perform a useful function. Such findings also signify that online tools for posting lecture notes, cases, and syllabi are among the first wave of Web-based instruction courseware. In contrast, online databases received high ratings for usefulness from 51 per cent of the respondents but only 44 per cent were using such a tool. Perhaps such tools are not yet available to the degree that college instructors would like. Once a course is on the Web, there must be some student evaluation and assessment. Indeed, some scholars advocate the use of the Web for online testing and evaluation as a means for reducing costs and increasing speed.

In addition to quick and cost effective feedback, online evaluations provide more organized, individualized, and plentiful course feedback. Despite these benefits, Hmieleski and Champagne report that 98 per cent of the most wired schools still use pen and paper course evaluations. Among the early Web-adopting faculty members of this study, however, 52 per cent rated student online evaluation tools as highly useful and 48 per cent were actually using such tools. Online quizzes or tests were deemed highly useful by 47 per cent of respondents and nearly the same per cent were actually using online exams in their teaching. One in five respondents gave a low usefulness rating to such tools, however.

Receiving even lower support was online student evaluations of course materials. Only 41 per cent rated these as highly useful, while just 36 per cent used such tools. Most of the findings are consistent with the research from Peffers and Bloom which found that online instructors tend to rely on common software such as e-mail, file uploading and downloading, and asynchronous conferencing as well as simple tools for posting static or dynamic syllabi, Web links to course material, and lecture notes. Significantly fewer instructors used chatrooms, multimedia lectures, online examinations, animation, and video streaming.

However, this research also revealed that the instructional impact of Internet media tools in college settings is expected to dramatically increase in the next few years. Firdyiwek's review of courseware tools indicates that few such tools support pedagogy in an integrated fashion. As tool development proliferates, so, too, does resulting confusion about how to effectively use these online tools. Interestingly, in this study, only 49 per cent of respondents were highly supportive of tools to place their entire courses on the Web and 47 per cent were using such tools. Could such modest numbers among early Web adopters be due to the lack of pedagogical support in these tools? Or does it reflect a lack of time or training? Perhaps these early Web adopters simply do not want to give up traditional instruction. Or perhaps they rely on customised courseware tools. Whatever the answer, this seems a ripe area for additional research.

Useful Collaboration and Sharing Tools

There are decades of research studies detailing the clear advantages of cooperative and collaborative learning over more individual and competitive formats. Fortunately, many collaborative pedagogical strategies have relevance in Web-based instruction. In fact, a proliferation of collaborative learning technologies have recently emerged for both work and educational environments. In higher education, technologies are becoming more interactive and distributed, enabling learners and instructors to participate in an incredible array of information, resources, and instructional experiences.

The blending of technological and pedagogical advancements presents new opportunities for both research and teaching focused on online dialogue, information sharing, and facilitating learning. In part, such collaborative tools have come on the scene to meet the needs of an older and more diverse student population than in the past. Perhaps this survey will help educators design more powerful e-learning environments for Web-based collaboration and sharing. Collaborative Web-based learning tools offer unique ways for learners, instructors, and experts to interact.

There are now Web tools for student collaborative inquiry, problem-based learning, articulation and dialogue, debate, and personal reflection. Some research indicates that effective use of these new tools can actually foster communities of practice. To create a learning community, the tool or system must bring people together for some initial common interest or quest. There not only is a need for a common reference point or issue for the online group, but members also need multiple ways to become informed about events of that community. Sharing information online often involves conferencing and computer-supported collaborative learning tools. Fortunately, such tools have begun to infiltrate online learning courseware. In addition, communities such as the World Lecture Hall, MERLOT are now available for visitors to locate and share learning materials within specific discipline or interest areas. But what were the views about such resources and tools among the respondents to this particular survey who already had been involved in online information and resource sharing?

Surely, they would understand and promote collaboration and sharing tools more than the rest of the population. As research from Peffers and Bloom predicts, the respondents to this survey perceived less utility for collaborative and online sharing tools than for test, lecture note, and syllabus tools. For instance, when asked about the utility of tools to share success or failure stories with other instructors, only 27 per cent had done so and only 30 per cent listed this as a highly useful item. Another 51 per cent, however, rated the degree of usefulness as medium.

Hence, more than 80 per cent would find some use for such tools; perhaps they simply are not yet available. Similarly, only 26 per cent used online tools to collaborate and form partnerships with other instructors. Still, 40 per cent saw this as a highly useful idea. Another 44 per cent saw it as of medium utility. Slightly more college instructors used Web-based tools in their courses for students to share success or failure stories with other students.

Forty-one per cent listed this as highly useful and another 45 per cent felt that it was of medium utility. Slightly higher, 46 per cent of the respondents used tools for students to collaborate and form partnerships with other students. In fact, 56 per cent felt that this was a highly useful endeavor and another 34 per cent found it of medium usefulness. The fact that 90 per cent perceived value in student online collaboration is of significance. Asynchronous discussion forums, synchronous chats, and annotation or feedback tools are common means for electronic collaboration. Sixty-one per cent of faculty members in this study utilized bulletin board or asynchronous types of discussion in their courses. While 60 per cent rated this type of tool as highly useful, another 31 per cent saw it as having medium utility. There was a significant drop in perceived utility and actual use in terms of synchronous collaborative environments compared to asynchronous environments.

Only 32 per cent of the instructors in this survey had used real-time chats, and only 37 per cent rated this item highly. In fact, 28 per cent of the respondents rated this item low in utility. In contrast, tools for interactive feedback, commenting, and annotations fared much better in terms of usefulness among these respondents. Forty-six per cent of the faculty respondents had used interactive feedback or annotation tools in their classes. Even more, 56 per cent perceived them as highly useful, while only 6 per cent rated this type of collaborative tool as low in utility. Perhaps software developers might want to target annotation and feedback tools; they are highly valued and yet not everyone is using them.

Personal profile tools are another means to share information online with peers and other instructors. Whereas 52 per cent claimed to use instructor profile tools in their courses, only 34 per cent utilized student profile tools. Such a finding seems odd. Perhaps there was misinterpretation on this item or perhaps it is easier to reflect on tools one is personally using. Only 30 per cent considered instructor profiles important, indicating that they are using such a tool simply because it is there and it is easy to use. Even less, just 25 per cent, found student profile tools useful.

In fact, 35 per cent rated the degree of usefulness of student profile tools as low. Online guestbooks were even less appealing. Only 6 per cent used them and just 7 per cent rated them highly. In fact, 66 per cent of the respondents—the largest of any item—rated this type of tool as low in usefulness. Related to our findings about online evaluation and testing, only 7 per cent used the Internet for collaborating with other instructors for test-making. Still 22 per cent rated this as a highly useful item, while another 40 per cent felt it was of medium utility. Similarly, few instructors collaborated with other instructors on class tasks, activities, and discussion. Only

18 per cent had engaged in such collegial activities, while 34 per cent rated this as highly useful and another 41 per cent consider it of medium utility. Perhaps these are two immediate areas wherein universities and software development companies might partner together to develop and test new Web-based teaching and learning tools. Finally, online technology demonstrations received fairly favourable reactions from our respondents.

Thirty-one per cent of the faculty members had used this type of tool in their classes. In addition, 42 per cent rated this item as highly usable in their classes, while 38 per cent rated it of medium utility. Despite these findings, college instructors perceived a need for more collaborative tools. Tools with more than a 10 per cent gap between actual use and perceived high utility included tools for instructors to form collaborations with other instructors, tools for students to share stories with other students, tools for interactive feedback and annotations on student work, tools for instructor test-making collaboration, tools for instructor task collaboration, and tools for online technology demonstrations.

These large gaps between teaching practice and perceived utility indicate a need for more collaborative tools in e-learning environments. They may also point to the current direction of Web-based teaching and learning practices.

Useful Online Instructional Activities

Instructional activities that these instructors found useful were also of interest in this study.

The first four online activities asked about were:

1. Scientific simulations;
2. Data analysis;
3. Lab activities; and
4. Performance activities.

Examples of the latter activities might include band or music tasks as well as online decision making in any discipline including counseling, finance, or teaching. These four activities were all infrequently used by the survey respondents. The actual use of these tools ranged from 23 to 26 per cent, with lab and performance being used slightly more often than scientific simulations and data analysis. All of these types of activities were deemed highly useful by approximately 45 per cent of the respondents. Such are interesting since the percentage of respondents who rated these items as highly useful was nearly double the percentage of who actually used them. When combining those who rated activities moderately or highly useful, more than 75 per cent of the respondents indicated utility for each of the four tools. Such data clearly indicate that there is a market for such tools, but college faculty members currently do not have access to them. A fifth and final instructional activity was online critical and creative thinking activities. This item was rated more favourably than the other four.

Forty-five per cent of these faculty members used such activities in their online teaching, and even more impressively, 62 per cent rated them as highly useful for their teaching discipline. An additional 28 per cent rated them of medium usefulness. Only 10 per cent considered their degree of usefulness low. Such results are further indication of the need for better pedagogical tools in online learning environments.

Useful Web Resources

The Web is highly touted as an online resource. Some suggest that it is a gigantic library sprawling in front of students and instructors alike. But in what ways do early Web adopters actually view it as a resource for teaching? Questions were asked about the utility of such Web resources as search engines, glossaries with links to examples, Web link suggestions, article and journal links, book recommendations, newsgroups, collegial Web sites, and general and discipline-specific online resources.

Given that research has revealed that college instructors tend to rely on easy to use tools, it is not surprising that search engines were the most commonly used Web resource with 83 per cent of these faculty members utilizing search engines in their teaching. Equally impressive, 70 per cent ranked search engines such as Yahoo or Lycos as highly useful and only 6 per cent ranked them low. The next most favourable ranking was for online article and journal links. Seventy-four per cent of the respondents used such tools and 70 per cent rated them as highly usable. Only 3 per cent rated this item low. Sixty-one per cent of these college educators used discipline specific resources in their teaching and 63 per cent found them highly useful. Along these same lines, 59 per cent had used Web sites created by colleagues in their teaching. Such collegial Web site use included syllabi and lecture notes. This is not surprising given where the sample was derived. In fact, only 8 per cent rated the utility of this item as low. Similarly, 58 per cent had used general teaching and learning resources or instructional strategies that had been posted online. Once again, only 8 per cent viewed this item as low in utility.

Online glossaries are another emerging Web-based teaching resource. In fact, 57 per cent of the survey respondents had used online glossaries with links to examples on the Web in their teaching. Similarly, 55 per cent viewed this Web resource as highly usable, while another 35 per cent gave it a medium rating. In effect, the use of online glossaries, colleague Web sites, and general as well as discipline-specific online teaching and learning resources indicates that the Internet has spawned a new type of teaching—one that is reliant on the Web for a significant part of college instruction. Online teaching in an online world is different, and new faculty, as well as experienced ones, need to be prepared for it.

The three lowest rated areas, which were the only items used by less than 50 per cent of the respondents, were student Web link suggestions, online book reviews, and newsgroups. Slightly under half of the faculty members in this survey had used tools where students made Web link suggestions. Still, 45 per cent of the survey participants viewed this item as having high utility, while another 42 per cent rated it as medium in degree of usefulness. Book recommendations received roughly the same ratings; 47 per cent had used such a tool and 44 per cent deemed it as highly useful. In contrast, newsgroups were used by only 18 per cent of these faculty members, while just 17 per cent rated them as highly useful.

Our findings suggest a relatively high and diverse use of Web resources in teaching. Web resources are highly valued by college educators since they can augment lecture notes with visual depictions of concepts, replace the need for textbooks with online articles and glossaries, and provide more current research and professional news. Tools to search, share, and evaluate online course materials are vital parts of one's Web-based teaching arsenal.

When asked to share URLs of Web resources they found particularly useful in their teaching, 15 per cent of these college instructors responded with extremely diverse suggestions. For instance, they listed course-sharing Web sites such as MERLOT, professional organization sites such as the American Psychological Association, textbook publisher Web sites, locations for instructional design models, and university teaching and learning centre resource listings. Only MERLOT was listed more than once.

The findings denote many areas wherein improvements in online teaching and learning could occur. The numbers reveal that tools for collaboration and resource sharing are highly valued by college faculty members but are not yet part of their typical online teaching life. Tools for annotation and feedback, article or journal linking, and online discussion were considered highly valuable. Additionally, activities for student labs, simulations, and critical and creative thinking have not been as prevalent as college faculty desire. Nevertheless, the number of tools and activities that were of substantial use already, as well as the high usefulness ratings that many additional tools received, was striking. Such ratings are signs that online teaching and learning is not going away in higher education settings, but, instead, is about to be enhanced, extended, and perhaps even transformed.

OBSTACLES AND SUPPORT MECHANISMS

Obstacles to Web-Based Teaching

There certainly are a myriad of obstacles to utilizing the Web in higher education instruction. Issues of time, training, experience, ownership, costs, confidence, technological infrastructure, administrative support, and interest are often mentioned. In this study, the main obstacle to effective use of the Web was time; more specifically, the amount of preparation time required for Web-based course development and delivery. Sixty per cent of the college instructors in this survey reported that preparation time was a major issue. What other obstacles did our respondents face? Contrary to findings from the NEA study, nearly 4 in 10 found the lack of technical support to be a major deterrent.

Slightly fewer, 37 per cent, indicated that a lack of time to learn to use the Web was an obstacle. Along these same lines, a quarter of the respondents lacked training on how to use the Web. And even if they did receive proper training or time allocation, nearly 30 per cent felt that they lacked the equipment or software to display the Web in the classroom. Of course, such findings contrast with what was reported earlier about fairly abundant technology access. Perhaps it indicates that technology is available in their buildings for utilizing the Web in instruction, but it is not yet found in their particular classroom settings.

What were not viewed as major obstacles? Fewer than 20 per cent of the faculty respondents cited lack of hardware or outdated equipment in their office as a barrier. Even fewer, 15 per cent, indicated that the lack of software or outdated software was a problem. And amazingly, fewer than 2 per cent had no interest in using the Web in their teaching. Keep in mind, once again, that the respondents were generally early Webbased teaching adopters who would be expected to be interested in using the Web in their instruction. Still, the nearly unanimous interest in using the Web indicates that this is a technology with the potential for transforming higher education. Around 17 per cent of the respondents remarked on other problems holding up their adoption of the Web in their teaching. In open-ended responses, these early Web adopters focused on issues of administrative support, time, student interest, pedagogy, vision, funding, incentives, utility, reliability, motivation, and bandwidth.

Administrative support comments included:

- "Lack of administrative vision."
- "Lack of incentive from administration and the fact that they do not understand the time needed."
- "Lack of system support."
- "Little recognition that this is valuable."
- "Rapacious U intellectual property policy."
- "Unclear university policies concerning intellectual property."

Pedagogical comments included:

- "Difficulty in performing laboratory experiments online."
- "Impossible to teach drawing and lithography."
- "Lack of appropriate models for pedagogy in content-based instruction."

Time-related comments included:

- "Lack of incentive."
- "More ideas than time to implement."
- "Not enough time to correct online assignments."
- "People need sleep; Web spins forever."
- "Time to grade/interact."

Cost also appears to be an issue as the following comment notes, "Institution supports because it is the cheapest...is too hard for students and faculty to learn." The following comment from one respondent summarizes many of these issues:

- "...(the) lack of time to develop materials and add to what is already developed. Little recognition that this is valuable and thus hurts promotion and tenure decisions which seem to be primarily based on publications in juried journals not on stuff on the Web."

When comparing obstacles encountered at private and public institutions, two important differences emerged,

1. The perceived lack of time to learn to use the Web and
2. Other obstacles faced by faculty at private institutions.

First, faculty members from public institutions were significantly more likely to indicate that time to learn to use the Web was a problem than those from private institutions. It is unclear, however, whether this is due to differing teaching and research expectations, support structures, or Web-based learning initiatives at their institutions.

Second, 30 per cent of the faculty respondents from private universities noted that they faced other obstacles not listed as compared to just 14 per cent of respondents from public institutions. On several other items, faculty members from public institutions were more likely to indicate problems than those from private ones. For instance, faculty respondents from public institutions were slightly more likely to complain that Web-based learning required too much preparation time and that they lacked the proper equipment to display the Web in their classrooms.

An interesting finding emerged when comparing differences in the number and type of obstacles by the size of the institution. While faculty respondents from smaller institutions perceived a lack of Web training, computer hardware, and technology support compared to those from larger institutions, only the perceived lack of support for technical problems and courseware development was significantly different.

More specifically, 47 per cent of those from institutions under 3,000 students viewed this as a problem, 53 per cent of those from institutions between 3,000 and 9,999 noted it as a major obstacle, and only 31 per cent from institutions over 10,000 indicated that this was an obstacle. When combining the responses for those in institutions under 10,000 students, the differences remained significant with 51 per cent of those in the smaller institutions indicating a need for such technical and courseware support versus only 31 per cent in larger institutions.

There were also some modest indications that the lack of Web training and inadequate technology in the classroom and office were also obstacles in the smaller colleges and universities. We also explored obstacles to Web-based teaching as reported by gender. The only item that approached a significant difference here was a lack of software or outdated software that was noted by 19 per cent of the males compared to only 9 per cent of the females. However, females pointed to such obstacles as time to learn to use the Web, lack of classroom equipment to display the Web, too much preparation time, and a lack of technical and courseware development support. Apparently, there are more perceived barriers for female instructors in college settings than for males.

While male instructors might recognize outdated software tools, females seem to be seeking additional training and support. Overall, time for course preparation and delivery as well as technical and administrative support are among the major obstacles for college instructors attempting to teach online. Equipment and software tools are less significant factors. All findings vary, however, by type and size of institution.

Support for Web-Based Teaching and Research

The survey also addressed the type of support required by college educators to utilize the Web in their teaching, research, and administrative duties. Given the previous answers regarding online teaching obstacles, it was not surprising that release time was the most popular form of support selected here.

In addition, each of the following three forms of support were desired by nearly 7 in 10 respondents:

1. Recognition for use of the Web in tenure, promotion, and salary review decisions;
2. Technical support staff to assist with online course development and associated technical problems; and
3. Instructional development grants or stipends.

Given the lack of differentiation in responses, universities may want to embed aspects of a few of these key support preferences in their distance education policies and initiatives. For instance, they might offe options between release time, instructional development grants and stipends, additional salary, and designated technical support. They might also adopt policies and practices wherein online teaching and research activities would be more fully recognized in college professor tenure and promotion cases. Nearly 60 per cent of respondents felt that it would be valuable for instructional designers to assist faculty members when needed. The same per cent asked for time to learn about and utilize the Web. In addition, 45 per cent thought that additional training on how to use the Web in teaching would be beneficial.

Around thirty per cent of these faculty respondents suggested that greater student access to computers as well as online resources would also be helpful, while slightly over one fourth of them considered e-mail notification of technology changes or updates to be valuable. In contrast, a mere 13 per cent thought that chat room help for Web-related problems was a support they needed for effectively using the Web in teaching, research, or administrative duties.

A few respondents suggested additional ideas for online teaching support. Among the advice was for "better equipped classrooms for demos," "really specific examples of 'good courses' so we have some idea what we are trying to achieve," "more money," and "assistance with routine office tasks, grading objective tests, etc., to free up my time to create Web lectures and other course materials." Others argued for outcome data and useful learning research, clearer royalty definitions, and administrators who believed in the priorities of student learning and could articulate the importance of Web teaching.

These support needs correspond closely with the perceived obstacles including the need for greater technical support. Given these findings, it appears that a multi-pronged approach to online instructor support and training is warranted. Respondents at public and private institutions expressed some significant differences in the types of support they needed.

Those in public institutions were significantly more likely to ask for online resources to use the Web effectively in their teaching, research, and administrative duties compared to those in private institutions. They were also significantly more likely to suggest that they needed instructional development grants or stipends to support their online teaching efforts than those at private institutions. Along these same lines, they were significantly more inclined to ask for release time than those in private institutions. Perhaps faculty members at public institutions are simply more demanding.

For instance, other areas wherein faculty members in public institutions indicated that they needed more support to effectively use the Web in their scholarly pursuits than those in private institutions included the need for instructional design help, time to learn about and utilize the Web, greater training regarding how to use the Web in teaching, greater access to computers for students, and recognition for tenure, promotion, and salary review decisions.

Technical support staff was identified as necessary by about 68 per cent of both public and private institution respondents. It is clear that those in public institutions have higher expectations of the support structures required before adopting the Web in their teaching and other duties. Whether they have differing instructional standards, course loads, or support histories and experiences is not known and is an open question for further investigation. In exploring the data by size of institution, there were no significant differences in Webbased teaching support.

However, from a descriptive standpoint, faculty members at institutions with enrollments under 3,000 students pointed to the need for instructional design support and training on how to use the Web in teaching. Instructors in medium-sized institutions were more likely to select time to utilize the Web and student access to computers. Instructors at the medium and large institutions favoured recognition for tenure, promotion, and salary review decisions, development grants and stipends, and release time.

While none of these differences were significant, they do provide an interesting picture of Web-based teaching support needs at different sized institutions. When comparing those in institutions larger and smaller than 10,000 students, respondents at the smaller colleges and universities were more likely to select technical support and student access to computers as important issues, whereas instructors at the large institutions were focused on having more online resources, recognition, and development grants or stipends. Gender differences in terms of perceived supports were minimal.

ONLINE COMMUNITIES, SERVICES, AND RESOURCES NEEDED

Online Communities for Resource Sharing

As indicated throughout this report, the Web offers new opportunities to share resources with colleagues online. The survey participants were asked whether they would be interested in becoming part of a no-cost community for sharing of course resources and teaching ideas. Given the present sample was derived from the WLH and MERLOT Web sites, it was anticipated that they would be interested in such a course-sharing resource.

In fact, 82 per cent of the respondents expressed interest in joining such a community. When asked what components or features of such a community would make it more likely that they would regularly participate, one feature, sharing "pedagogical ideas," was clearly preferred among these instructors. In fact, more than three-fourths of the respondents selected this item. As with their earlier responses to survey items about instructional activities for online critical and creative thinking, these early Web adopters remain hopeful that an online community will provide this.

Similarly, more than 60 per cent of the respondents wanted any free course-sharing resource community to offer expert advice as well as answers to teaching problems. Somewhat surprisingly, well over half of the respondents indicated that online classroom management tips or advice would benefit their teaching.

The next most frequent response for participating online was professional recognition, selected by slightly more than 4 in 10 instructors. Several items were less important than anticipated. For instance, only a quarter of the respondents indicated that they would participate in a free online community as a result of an online newsletter. Even fewer, less than one in five, would regularly participate in order to engage in online storytelling. This is similar to earlier responses that only one fourth of respondents wanted courseware tools for sharing stories with other instructors. A few respondents listed other reasons to participate such as access to session plans, simulations, laboratory experiments, collaborative projects, discipline specific issues, legal counsel on intellectual property issues, and time-saving tools.

Some offered to make their resources available to others. Still others thought that such a resource would help them get paid for their knowledge and expertise. What is apparent is that those teaching in college settings wanted online instructional help and communities of people with similar interests. Instead of simply sharing war stories, they preferred access to useful information, advice, and pedagogical ideas. Naturally, some members also would like some reciprocity for that information sharing, while others want to use the online community as a means of professional recognition.

Useful Web-Based Services, Resources, and Information

Finally, we asked about the types of Web-based services, resources, and information to which they would like to have access as instructors. There were 18 choices including online bookstores, course listings, mentoring services, papers, survey tools, conference information, library resources, and downloadable freeware. With all the possible choices, the most vital services to which these instructors wanted access were online course design and development help, which 73 per cent selected. Such help might entail guides, courses, workshops, newsletters, tutorials, and conferences. The need for other teaching resources was also important to these instructors. While 71 per cent indicated that electronic papers, journals, and technical reports would be helpful to their online teaching efforts, another 70 per cent selected online teaching help. Examples of the latter included tips and guides, demonstration courses, workshops, newsletters, tutorials, and conferences.

Fifty-four per cent indicated that online library resources were worthwhile, while roughly half noted instructional value: online conference information online course listings and online workshops and institutes. Only 1 in 5 respondents, however, noted that online listings of courseware companies would be needed for their teaching. Once again, it was unclear whether they expected those services to be provided commercially or free. With the requests for online papers and journals, online library resources, conferences, course listings, and workshops or institutes, there definitely is a great need for more effective and useful Web-based information resources and services for college teaching. Other teaching or instructional services were also fairly popular among our respondents.

Online mentoring and tutoring services, for instance, were selected by 45 per cent of these college instructors, though it is unclear whether they expected such services to be free or if they felt that their institution should pay for such services. In terms of marketing themselves, 45 per cent wanted access to freelance teaching possibilities. Once again, many of these instructors predicted that their teaching futures would involve working outside their home institution. Naturally, the Web opens up such new and exciting instructional outlets and services. While faculty member entrepreneurship is on the rise due to the Web, it is also bound to raise many institutional and ethical issues and dilemmas related to hiring practices, compensation, and promotion and tenure policies.

The desire for commercial services for technology, bookstores, and instructional resources received mixed feedback. Of course, the world of higher education often struggles with budget allocations for hardware, software, and other resources compared to the corporate world. Thus, it was not too surprising that nearly 60 per cent of the respondents wanted access to downloadable freeware and shareware in their teaching.

Nearly half would find trial or demonstration software useful as instructors and would like access to specially priced computer technology and software. Roughly the same number of respondents also would like Web-based survey and evaluation tools as well as Web-based simulations and experiments. Yet, fewer than one in five would find online resources with specially priced instructional resources useful. Around half would find online bookstores valuable; however, just 35 per cent indicated that online university bookstores and merchandise would be utilized within their instruction.

FINAL COMMENTS

Some of these early Web adopters provided rather strongly worded final comments. For instance, those with reservations about Web-based teaching in higher education indicated that they were disappointed with the rush to use technology before research backs up the use. Comments about poor quality materials and unimpressive courseware were prevalent.

Others were disappointed with their home institution since it failed to support their online activities, thereby forcing them to volunteer and self-finance their Web-based teaching initiatives. Still, others viewed their institution as motivated simply by a need to save money. In fact, one person claimed, "Universities are ripping off their faculty. And, they are going to shut down participation in free-lance operations. So, it would be in your interest to get some legal challenges going to challenge the monopoly." Another respondent thought that if universities claimed ownership of online course materials, then instructors must get compensated with both royalties and recognition.

In some places this is already occurring. For instance, the University of North Texas has instituted a policy that pays instructors a 4 per cent royalty of the tuition from every student when other instructors use their online course materials. Undoubtedly, similar policies are on the way. Perhaps one respondent summarized the situation best when arguing that the key problem here is that administrators did not share the ideas or goals embedded in much of this survey. There is minimal support, money, and focus for building cohorts of competent online college instructors. Others were somewhat more positive. One instructor, in fact, was "convinced that interuniversity collaboration and pooling of resources is the way forward." This person suggested that teachers and lecturers needed time to acquire new skills and materials for the Web as well as opportunities to share programmes and interactive activities. In this way, more people with disabilities and financial hardships could access education and better society.

Another instructor viewed online course offerings as a means to teach students about effective technology use. Still another viewed it as something he or she could utilize more fully after retirement when teaching part-time courses. Others were interested "in doing freelance teaching now" and wanted ideas on how to start the process.

In touching on many of these themes, one instructor's hope for the future was extremely detailed and optimistic:

- "I have always had the vision of a virtual university, where qualified faculty could teach courses they were skilled in, to an Internet audience. A university where faculty were paid for these classes and the number of students they taught. These faculty could come from any institution or not be affiliated with an institution at all. An arena where faculty who love to teach in a virtual world, could teach their subject to students who could receive their education totally online. The faculty would not be employees of the virtual university, but would be paid for quality and quantity of courses taught and number of students enrolled in their online class. There are many faculty who are caught in the middle of traditional university life and virtual education opportunities, who would love the opportunity to teach their classes outside the traditional boundaries, and be compensated for the work they do in this arena."

Higher education institutions and corporations should find a myriad of implications from these final survey questions. For instance, college professors and lecturers want access to online information and various collaborative and interactive technology resources within their teaching. Clearly, these faculty respondents were more comfortable than most about Web-based teaching, but their overwhelming support for a diverse set of online tools and services should motivate many entrepreneurs to take a lead role here. There are numerous resources that college professors and instructors can utilize in their teaching.

First and foremost they want pedagogical tools and instructional design support. As part of such support, there is a need for sample courses as well as Web-based teaching institutes. Since these college instructors were not afraid of receiving help in their teaching no matter how long they had been teaching, more online Web-based teaching services will likely be applauded. This survey of early Web-adopting faculty members provides an interesting look at online teaching experiences, supports, obstacles, and preferences. Online teaching in an online world is not simple but it is bound to increase dramatically during the upcoming decade. The following part offers some conclusions and recommendations for those contemplating new programmes or activities in this area.

CONCLUSIONS AND RECOMMENDATIONS

CONCLUSIONS

The results of this survey paint both pessimistic and optimistic portraits of the state of Web-based teaching and learning in higher education. While a myriad of collaborative tools and institutional support mechanisms were identified as needed, many of the early adopters of the Web for college teaching already have extensive experience with both fully online and blended courses.

And they seem to enjoy online teaching despite barriers related to time, training, recognition, and overall institutional support. Moreover, new opportunities to embed the Web in instruction as well as to share the results online in an online community of peers were revealed throughout this survey report. What is the profile of the faculty member who shares information online? As expected, most of the early Web resource-sharing instructors are at large public institutions with fairly extensive teaching experience. A large percentage are males with doctoral degrees. They find out about course sharing resources through advice from colleagues or their institutions. They tend to look at online course sharing as vital to their personal growth or simply believe that sharing ideas, strategies, or courses is important.

In return, students and other instructors contact them. It is almost as if the WLH and MERLOT provide a pedagogical sharing outlet that they find lacking in traditional teaching environments. Not surprisingly, then, these Web-experienced college instructors are asking for advancements in Web-based pedagogical and collaborative tools for their teaching. What are their attitudes about these online environments? Many of these early Web adopters have strong beliefs and opinions. First of all, they believe that they own their online courses, even though their institutions have unclear guidelines about ownership.

They also believe that accreditation is needed to maintain quality within distance learning offerings. They are more likely to endorse undergraduate and master's degrees earned entirely online than doctoral degrees. They perceive that access and learning are more prevalent motives for institutions adopting online education than profit. While they recognize that teaching online is more time-consuming than teaching in traditional classrooms, they simultaneously recognize that a growing portion of their instructional load will increasing shift to online environments.

In return, they would like additional salary, royalties, course development stipends, or, at the very least, some instructional sign and technology support. What types of online experiences do these early Web adopters have? Most of these instructors have experiences teaching in Web environments, including both partially online and fully online courses. In terms of course delivery, many of their institutions offer a choice between two or more platforms. Courseware decisions are made primarily by university administrators, though departments, faculty, and technical support personnel are often consulted in such matters. Courseware tools that are appealing to early Web adopters are those that are flexible, easy to use, comprehensive, interactive, well supported, functional, and attractive.

What tools are needed? Early adopting faculty members are looking for tools to share syllabi, post cases and lecture notes, upload and download files, provide feedback, hold discussion forums, demonstrate ideas, and foster student collaboration. In addition, they would like access to online journal articles and papers, glossaries, teaching resources, and search engines. Conference information and library resources are also viewed as helpful. These professors and instructors want to utilize the Web for pedagogical ideas and expert advice or answers to their teaching problems.

And while they ask for additional technical support and instructional design aids, they are fairly savvy in their use of the most common Web tools. What are the online supports deemed necessary for effective online teaching? And what are the key obstacles or barriers common to online teaching? In terms of supports, college faculty members would like to be recognized for their efforts from their institutions including release time, stipends, or additional salary.

In regards to obstacles, preparation time and technical support were the key barriers noted by our respondents. It appears that college instructors would like technical or instructional design help as well as training in Web-based instruction. In addition, training to simply use the Web as well as reports and guidelines about teaching online were perceived as valuable. What's next? Many college faculty members anticipate teaching online more frequently in the future, especially as freelance instructors.

Before this occurs, it would be useful to develop online communities for these freelance instructors. To establish such communities, some colleges and universities might provide Web-based support mechanisms including online course development and teaching, library resources, professional information about upcoming conferences, survey and evaluation services, simulation tools, freeware, teaching advice, mentoring or tutoring help, and relevant online papers and reports. Teaching is complex. The trends towards more online teaching and learning in the upcoming decade will not simplify this.

Whereas other surveys of college instructors have focused on technological resource availability, instructor skills and attitudes, and institutional policies, what sets this particular study apart is the focus on pedagogical tools and practices. Benchmark data collected here help predict and evaluate future trends in online teaching and learning. As Web sites evolve beyond the WLH and MERLOT, we enter an era of knowledge sharing at perhaps the highest level ever attempted.

The Web already is the largest collection of instructional expertise on this globe. Hopefully, this report provides some indicators as to where these course-sharing and online teaching efforts are headed. As this survey indicates, entering the world of Web-based teaching can be complex for new instructors. Certainly, signals sent from early Web adopters and resource sharers provide brief glimpses of what is possible. They note many weaknesses as well as opportunities within this new teaching and learning arena.

They understand most of the obstacles and necessary support structures holding back other faculty. Perhaps some of them will serve as mentors for others adopting such an approach. In fact, that is one of the recommendations listed in the next part of this report.

RECOMMENDATIONS

This report detailed many online teaching findings and suggestions for college instructors, administrators, and higher education institutions. Seven recommendations based on the data from this survey.

The first three relate to instructor development including training, recognition and support, and sharing of expertise. The other four recommendations are more generally related to online learning policy, research, courseware and tool development partnerships, and pedagogy.

- *Instructor Training*: Colleges and universities need to consider how they are training faculty for teaching in an online world. For instance, instructional design support and guidelines should help instructors get acclimated to this new form of teaching. In addition, they might offer institutes, courses, online mentoring, and instructional design help. Time allocated to training is a key consideration. Early Web adopters might be utilized as mentors for new faculty members.
- *Instructor Recognition and Support*: Colleges and universities need to consider how they recognize online teaching efforts in promotion and tenure. They could also give release time, instructional development grants, stipends, and other forms of assistance.
- *Instructor Sharing of Expertise and Resource Exchange*: Higher education institutions should create ways for faculty members to share online services, expertise, and resources as well as mentor new instructors. They might also develop tools for instructor sharing of activities and resources, including tools for the sharing of reusable knowledge objects or perhaps some type of a knowledge exchange programme.
- *Online Learning Policies*: Higher education institutions need to develop clear guidelines or policies regarding the ownership of online course materials and applicable royalties. They should have policies related to freelance online instruction for other institutions. They might also attempt to clearly articulate why certain courseware tools, policies, and expectations have been adopted related to Web-based instruction.
- *Online Learning Research*: Before drafting new e-learning policies, colleges and universities should review existing research. They might also provide internal mini-grants for faculty members to research their own programme and course development

efforts. Similarly, internal research related to the perceived obstacles to online learning as well as case studies of successful faculty member adoption may be helpful. Results of such research should be made available to all professors and instructors of the institution.

- *Online Learning Courseware Development Partnerships*: Rather than every large higher education institution attempting to spend money to develop its own courseware platform or shell, colleges and universities should seek partnerships with courseware companies wherein they serve as testbeds for new tool development efforts. They might also seek to form tool development consortia with other institutions. Technology centres and research institutes within higher education could perform usability studies and help co-develop products in return for lowered courseware fees.
- *Online Learning Pedagogy*: In conjunction with the last recommendation, higher education institutions need to demand and perhaps help develop and research different types of pedagogical tools for e-learning that foster student higher-order thinking and collaboration. Once developed, tools for fostering critical and creative thinking as well as teamwork online should be showcased to faculty, students, and administrators.

There were a variety of interesting and important findings within this study. What this study clearly reveals is that while many faculty members are adopting Web technologies in their teaching, the levels and types of support structures vary tremendously. As new tools, courseware platforms, and standards are developed, there is a need for online learning leadership and exemplary models or frameworks for Web-based instruction. There also is a pressing need to openly share what we know about online learning with both the early Web adopters of this study as well as with potential Web instructors in free online learning communities. When this occurs, tools for online sharing of resources will have a major impact on college learning and instruction in this decade and beyond. As with most studies, additional research is needed to confirm and extend these findings. Other research might explore how courseware tools are paid for, the perceived quality of online certificates or institutes, the forms of online training for instructors, the types of technical support provided for students and faculty online, how costs are determined for online courses, and the perceived learning and motivational factors in online learning.

We hope to address some of these issues in our upcoming studies. There are many directions for higher education institutions to take in terms of online learning support structures and expectations. No matter what directions are decided, learning in college will never be the same. Online teaching in an online world will also guarantee that post-secondary teaching will never be the same either.

8

The e-Learning: Principles Procedures and Practices

E-LEARNING: DEFINITION, SCOPE, TRENDS, ATTRIBUTES AND OPPORTUNITIES

DEFINITION AND SCOPE

E-learning is commonly referred to the intentional use of networked information and communications technology in teaching and learning. A number of other terms are also used to describe this mode of teaching and learning. They include online learning, virtual learning, distributed learning, network and webbased learning.

Fundamentally, they all refer to educational processes that utilize information and communications technology to mediate asynchronous as well as synchronous learning and teaching activities. On closer scrutiny, however, it will be clear that these labels refer to slightly different educational processes and as such they cannot be used synonymously with the term e-learning.

The term e-learning comprises a lot more than online learning, virtual learning, distributed learning, networked or web-based learning. As the letter "e" in e-learning stands for the word "electronic", e-learning would incorporate all educational activities that are carried out by individuals or groups working online or offline, and synchronously or asynchronously via networked or standalone computers and other electronic devices.

Individualized Self-paced e-learning Online

Individualized self-paced e-learning online refers to situations where an individual learner is accessing learning resources such as a database or course content online via an Intranet or the Internet. A typical example of this is a learner studying alone or conducting some research on the Internet or a local network.

Individualized Self-paced e-learning Offline

Individualized self-paced e-learning offline refers to situations where an individual learner is using learning resources such as a database or a computer-assisted learning package offline. An example of this is a learner working alone off a hard drive, a CD or DVD.

Group-based e-learning Synchronously

Group-based e-learning synchronously refers to situations where groups of learners are working together in real time via an Intranet or the Internet. It may include text-based conferencing, and one or two-way audio and video conferencing. Examples of this include learners engaged in a real-time chat or an audio-videoconference.

Group-based e-learning Asynchronously

Group-based e-learning asynchronously refers to situations where groups of learners are working over an Intranet or the Internet where exchanges among participants occur with a time delay. Typical examples of this kind of activity include on-line discussions via electronic mailing lists and text-based conferencing within learning managements systems.

CONTEMPORARY TRENDS IN E-LEARNING

The growing interest in e-learning seems to be coming from several directions. These include organizations that have traditionally offered distance education programmes either in a single, dual or mixed mode setting. They see the incorporation of online learning in their repertoire as a logical extension of their distance education activities. The corporate sector, on the other hand, is interested in e-learning as a way of rationalizing the costs of their in-house staff training activities. E-learning is of interest to residential campus-based educational organizations as well.

They see e-learning as a way of improving access to their programmes and also as a way of tapping into growing niche markets. The growth of e-learning is directly related to the increasing access to information and communications technology, as well its decreasing cost. The capacity of information and communications technology to support multimedia resource-based learning and teaching is also relevant to the growing interest in e-learning. Growing numbers of teachers are increasingly using information and communications technology to support their teaching. The contemporary student population who have grown up using information and communications technology also expect to see it being used in their educational experiences.

Educational organizations too see advantages in making their programmes accessible via a range of distributed locations, including oncampus, home and other community learning or resource centres. Despite this level of interest in e-learning, it is not without constraints and limitations. The fundamental obstacle to the growth of e-learning is lack of access to the necessary technology infrastructure, for without it there can be no e-learning. Poor or insufficient technology infrastructure is just as bad, as it can lead to unsavory experiences that can cause more damage than good to teachers, students and the learning experience.

While the costs of the hardware and software are falling, often there are other costs that have often not been factored into the deployment of e-learning ventures. The most important of these include the costs of infrastructure support and its maintenance, and appropriate training of staff to enable them to make the most of the technology.

ATTRIBUTES OF E-LEARNING

There is a growing body of literature on e-learning

technologies. These are: a) the flexibility that information and communications technologies afford; and b) electronic access to a variety of multimedia-based material that they can enable.

THE FLEXIBILITY THAT E-LEARNING TECHNOLOGY AFFORDS

A key attribute of information and communications technology is its ability to enable flexible access to information and resources. Flexible access refers to access and use of information and resources at a time, place and pace that is suitable and convenient to individual learners rather than the teacher and/or the educational organization. The concept of distance education was founded on the principles of flexible access. It aimed to allow distance learners, who were generally adult learners in full or part-time employment to be able to study at a time, place, and pace that suited their convenience. The goal of distance education was to free these learners from the constraints of conventional residential educational settings. They would not be required to live or attend lectures in locations away from where they may be living and working. The printed distance study materials, which each distance learner received, would carry the core subject matter content they would need including all their learning activities and assessment tasks.

Students would be required to complete these tasks, submit their assignments and take their examinations within a set time frame. While these printed study materials allowed distance learners a great deal of freedom from time, place and pace of study, it had its limitations. For one thing, non-printed subject matter content and simulations etc. could not be easily represented in print form.

Access to information and communications technology changed all that as it offered a range of possibilities for capturing and delivering all types of subject matter content to learners and teachers in distributed educational settings. This meant access to subject matter content and learning resources via networked information and communications technologies across a range of settings such as conventional classrooms, workplaces, homes, and various forms of community centres. Contemporary educational institutions, including conventional distance education providers, often pride themselves in being able to meet the learning needs of their students and staff at a time, place and pace that is most convenient to them. They have been able to do this with the help of information and communications technologies which afford learners access to upto- date information as and when they need them, and also the opportunity to discuss this information with their peers and teachers at their convenience. This is becoming increasingly affordable and palatable with a wide range of software applications and computer conferencing technologies for collaborative inquiry among students and asynchronous discussion. These applications enable learners and teachers to engage in synchronous as well as asynchronous interaction across space, time, and pace.

ELECTRONIC ACCESS TO HYPERMEDIA AND MULTI-MEDIABASED RESOURCES

Information and communications technology also enables the capture and storage of information of various types including print, audio, and video. Networked information and communications technologies enable access to this content in a manner that is not possible within the spatial and temporal constraints of conventional educational settings such as the classroom or the print mode. In the context of this distributed setting, users have access to a wide variety of educational resources in a format that is amenable to individual approaches to learning and accessible at a time, place and pace that is convenient to them. Typically, these educational resources could include hyper-linked material, incorporating text, pictures, graphics, animation, multimedia elements such as videos and simulations and also links to electronic databases, search engines, and online libraries.

OPPORTUNITIES AND AFFORDANCES OF E-LEARNING

A growing body of literature on learning and teaching is suggesting that learning is greatly enhanced when it is anchored or situated in meaningful and authentic problem-solving activities. This approach to learning and teaching is founded on the principles of learning by doing and experiencing. It places or confronts learners with authentic situations and scenarios which are motivating and which require learners to carry out tasks or solve problems and reflect upon their actions. While such learning designs are suited for any learning and teaching context or media, their effectiveness and efficiency can be somewhat constrained by the fixed time, space and pace limitations of learning and teaching in conventional campus-based classroom settings. Similarly, printed study materials, while they afford transportability, are limited by their inability to capture and carry much else other than text, pictures, and illustrations.

Information and communications technologies, on the other hand, afford us a wide range of opportunities to capture, store and distribute information and resources of all types and formats. Along with text, pictures and illustrations, these include multimedia-based simulations of complex processes from all sorts of domains such as the biological and medical sciences, agriculture, engineering and educational practice which are not easily or cheaply accessible in real time and settings.

PEDAGOGICAL DESIGNS FOR E-LEARNING

The main point of this stage is to explore issues surrounding the influence of media on learning, and to examine pedagogical designs for optimizing elearning. The following are the key questions in relation to an exploration of these issues. Do media influence learning? Can we differentiate the unique influences of media on learning from the influences of instructional method? How can we optimize the influences of media on learning? Do we need different pedagogical designs for e-learning? If yes, then what are those designs that can optimize e-learning?

DO MEDIA INFLUENCE LEARNING

While it is clear that information and communications

technology offers tremendous opportunities for capturing, storing, disseminating and communicating a wide variety of information, does it influence learning, and if it does, what is the nature and extent of that influence? These questions are at the heart of a longstanding debate and discussion on the influences of media on learning. The origins of this debate and discussion on the influences of media on learning date back to the invention of radio and television.

On developing a camera that used film rolls, Thomas Edison had expected that the motion picture would revolutionize education and make schooling a lot more attractive and motivating for students. Commentators of that time had suggested that instead of wanting to stay away from school, students would rush back to school and not want to leave school. While we know that this did not actually happen, the moving image did influence our ability to represent many things in many different ways, in and outside of school. Several decades after Edison's inventions, and based on the growing influence of radio, television and other media on our lives, Marshall McLuhan claimed that the "medium is the message". With this aphorism, McLuhan was suggesting that each medium has characteristics and capabilities that have the potential to shape, direct and enhance our capabilities.

As such McLuhan saw media as "extensions of man" which is the subtitle of his classic book. The 1960s and 70s saw growing enthusiasm in the use of computers in education. This was naturally followed by similar interest in the impacts of computers on learning with many researchers concluding that while media may have some economic benefits, they did not show any benefits on learning.

Several leading researchers of the time argued that learning and any learning gain is actually caused by the way the subject matter content is presented via a medium, rather than the medium itself. A prominent contributor to this discussion on media research - Richard Clark - has in fact proclaimed that "media will never influence learning". He has in fact suggested that "media are mere vehicles that deliver instruction but do not influence student achievement any more than the truck that delivers our groceries causes changes in our nutrition". Clark concedes that media can have important influences on the cost and speed of learning, but argues that it is only the instructional method that can influence learning.

He defines instructional method as "the provision of cognitive processes or strategies that are necessary for learning but which students cannot or will not provide for themselves". Clark's argument is that media is replaceable and therefore "any teaching method can be delivered to students by many media or a variety of mixtures of media attributes with similar learning results". Based on this claim, he put forth a challenge for anyone to "find evidence, in well designed study, of any instance of a medium or media attributes that are not replaceable by a different set of media and attributes to achieve similar learning results for any given student and learning task". However, not everyone agrees with these suggestions and claims of Richard Clark.

One of these is Robert Kozma who is another prominent contributor to this discussion. Kozma reviewed relevant research on learning with media which suggests that the "capabilities of a particular medium, in conjunction with methods that take advantage of these capabilities, interact with and influence the ways learners represent and process information and may result in more or different learning when one medium is compared to another for certain learners and tasks".

The body of literature that Kozma reviewed supports a theoretical framework for learning which sees the learner as "actively collaborating with the medium to construct knowledge", where "learning is viewed as an active, constructive process whereby the learner strategically manages the available cognitive resources to create new knowledge by extracting information from the environment and integrating it with information already stored in memory". In such educational settings, the medium is not inert and it does not exist independently of the learning context and the subject matter content. In fact, when it is carefully integrated into the learning experience, the medium often interacts with the instructional method to produce the intended learning outcomes for the students in a given learning context. Therefore the media used, along with the instructional method would seem to have an influence on learning. In such educational settings, it would be difficult to disentangle the discrete and unique influences of the media and the method on learning.

WHAT IS THE ROLE OF MEDIA IN LEARNING

Therefore, it is arguable that in most contemporary technology enhanced learning environments where media is skillfully integrated with the instructional method, media can and do play a very influential and critical role in learning and teaching. Some prominent examples of such educational environments are the Jasper Woodbury Series, and Exploring the Nardoo.

In these contexts, media play a critical and a very important role in achieving the intended learning outcomes for the students. They serve to motivate students with clever use of sound, pictures and animation. They are also very useful in representing contexts and situations from the real world which are harder to bring into the classroom for live demonstrations. The majority of these learning environments such as the Jasper Woodbury Series and Exploring the Nardoo are grounded in constructivist principles of learning, and situated cognition.

These learning environments skillfully utilize the strengths of various media attributes with powerful learning strategies such as problem solving, collaborative inquiry and critical reflection to engage learners in meaningful and motivating learning tasks. In such educational settings media take on a very important role in both learning and teaching. Learning and teaching is adversely affected when media are not skillfully integrated into the learning experiences. Conversely, learning and teaching is optimized when media have been carefully selected and applied with sound instructional strategies to serve specific learning needs in different domains of learning.

OPTIMIZING THE INFLUENCE OF MEDIA IN E-TEACHING AND E-LEARNING

Skillful integration of media and instructional method is critical in the optimization of the influence of media in learning. This has to do with careful selection and matching of media attributes with learning and teaching strategies. Contemporary information and communications technologies afford a wide range and variety of opportunities to re-think and re-engineer the nature of our teaching and learning practices.

A major part of this re-engineering process includes shifts in the roles of teachers from being providers and deliverers of subject matter content to becoming moderators and facilitators of learning within the context of a learner and learning-centred approach to education. Learner and learning-centredness is regarded as a desirable trait in education and training generally. Learner and learning-centred educational environments are those where the learner and the learning process is the focus of programme design, development and delivery. In such educational settings, the learner—not the teacher, organization, or technology—is in charge of the learning experience.

Learner and learning-centred educational processes are defining characteristics of situated learning environments. The concept of situated learning is grounded in the principles of constructivist learning theory. It is based on the belief that learning is most efficient and effective when it takes place within the context of realistic educational settings which are either real or contrived. The roots of situated approaches to education and training are traceable to the concepts of experiential learning, and problem based learning.

Exemplar situated learning environments use "authentic learning tasks" to immerse learners in the total ecology and culture of the subject matter that is being taught and learned, much like an apprentice carpenter is immersed in a building site with architects and experienced builders. These so called authentic learning tasks serve to "anchor" learning and teaching activities in order to scaffold learning and cognition.

The notions of situated learning and the use of authentic learning tasks that serve to anchor and scaffold learning and teaching are heavily dependent on the use of real-world or contrived educational activities that adequately reflect real-world settings. These sorts of educational activities are inherently complex and as such time-consuming to manage. They are harder to integrate into conventional classroom settings which are limited by the opportunities they afford to engage students in authentic realworld problem-solving.

While field trips and excursions offer occasional and limited opportunities, they are not enough. Therefore many teachers and organizations refrain from engaging in situated learning activities in their classes and instead depend on approaches that are a lot more expedient and teacher and subject matter centred. Contemporary information and communications technologies offer some reprieve from the confines and constraints of conventional classrooms. They afford us opportunities to capture and/or represent real-world scenarios for use by learners within the conventional classroom.

These representations can include actual images or simulations of complex phenomena from the field which can be a lot more easily integrated into the classroom curricula. They can be used as additional resources in lieu of actual field experience, or they can form a core component of the learning experience of students as is possible in the case of goalbased or problem-based learning, case-based reasoning or scenario-based learning. The rest of this stage discusses a number of these pedagogical designs for optimizing the influence of media on learning in this manner.

PEDAGOGICAL DESIGNS FOR OPTIMIZING E-LEARNING

It is widely acknowledged that the role and influence of media on learning and teaching is optimized especially when it is skillfully integrated into the educational experience. For this to happen we need to focus our attention foremost, on the careful design of the learning experience rather than the presentation of the subject matter content or the technology. This means careful orchestration of what the learners are going to do in the learning environment. This concept of "learning by doing" has been popularized, among others, by Roger Schank and his collaborators and it is at the heart of pedagogical designs that stand to optimize e-learning.

These pedagogical designs include "scenariobased learning", "goal-based learning", "problembased learning", "case-based learning", "learning by designing", and "role-play-based learning". These pedagogical designs are grounded in the principles of constructivism and situated cognition, and in the belief that learning is most efficient and effective when it is contextualized and when it is based on realworld or similarly authentic settings.

SCENARIO-BASED LEARNING

A very good example of learning by doing is scenario-based learning. Scenario-based learning is a pedagogical design where one or more learning scenarios serve to anchor and contextualize all learning and teaching activities. The scenarios in these educational settings are usually drawn from real life situations. They may be contrived but they aim to be as authentic as possible and reflect the variety and complexity that is part of real life situations.

For the teacher and the tutor this scenario provides a meaningful context which can be used to explain abstract concepts, principles and procedures a lot more easily. For the learner, it serves to make learning relevant, meaningful and useful. Typically a good learning scenario will reflect a common occurrence from the relevant field. It may be a case, problem or incident that is commonly encountered in the workplace.

Using such cases, problems or incidences from the workplace in the education of learners serves to more adequately prepare them for the workforce as opposed to focusing their attention on the mastery of the subject matter content. The use of such scenarios is particularly relevant and meaningful in professional education. A typically good learning scenario will sound like a story or a narrative of a common occurrence. It will have a context, a plot, characters and other related parameters. It usually involves a precipitating event which places the learner or a group of learners in a role, or roles that will require them to deal with the situation or problems caused by the event. The roles that learners might be asked to assume are those that they are likely to play in real life as they enter the workforce.

Attached to these roles, will be goals that learners will be required to achieve. In order to achieve these goals they will be assigned numerous tasks and activities, some of which may require them to collaborate with their peers and other relevant groups, if these are part of the intended learning outcomes of their subject. While these activities essentially serve as learning enhancement exercises, a selection of them could be made assessable and given a mark which would contribute to the student's final grade in the subject. In order to attain the goals that learners are assigned in the scenario, and complete all the required activities, learners will have access to a wide range of relevant resources. These resources could include textbooks and other relevant reading material, multimedia content, and also experiences from the field of how expert practitioners have gone about solving or dealing with similar cases, situations, problems or incidences.

The learning scenario, its accompanying learning activities, and the assessment tasks serve as essential scaffolds for promoting and engendering meaningful learning activity. They also serve to contextualize learning and motivate learners who are turned off by too much focus on the mastery of the subject matter content and not enough on practical and generalizable skills.

The assessment tasks and learning activities which the students are assigned are critical to the achievement of the intended learning outcomes. It is therefore essential that they are congruent with the intended learning outcomes for the subject. While they are embedded within the learning scenario they must be carefully designed and skillfully applied to direct students to the core subject matter content. By successfully completing these assessment tasks and learning activities, it is expected that learners will have accomplished the intended learning outcomes of the subject.

RELATED PEDAGOGICAL DESIGNS

Other pedagogical designs that are also grounded in the concept of learning by doing include "problem-based and goal-based learning", "case-based learning", "role-play-based learning", and "learning by designing". They are different from scenario-based learning in the nature of the "precipitating event" or "trigger" in the situation. A brief discussion of each follows.

PROBLEM-BASED AND GOAL-BASED LEARNING

Of all learning by doing type pedagogical designs, these two designs are in fact most similar in orientation to scenario-based learning. In problem-based learning, a problem situation serves as the context and anchor for all learning and teaching activities. Problem-based learning begins with the presentation of a problem to students, which can be in the form of short video clip, a picture with text, or just text.

Upon encountering this problem situation, students are expected to analyse it and decide what needs to be done next. A critical feature of problem-based learning is small group problem-solving and inquiry. Students work in small groups to analyse the presenting problem, make decisions on what needs to be done next, and act upon them to resolve the problem situation satisfactorily.

In so doing they will have been expected to achieve the intended learning outcomes. While problem-solving is implicit in problem-based learning, learners are not told explicitly what is their role in the problem, or what they are supposed to do as they seek to analyse the presenting problem. In goal-based learning, on the other hand, they are told very specifically what is their role in the scenario and what they are supposed to do in order to resolve the problem satisfactorily. How they go about analysing the problem to achieve a satisfactory solution to the problem is left to their imagination and creativity. Both, problem-based and goal-based learning designs have been widely used in the study of medical, education and environmental sciences.

CASE-BASED LEARNING

In case-based learning, a case serves to provide the context and anchor for all learning and teaching activities. Cases have been very widely used in the study and teaching of Law, Business, Accounting and Economics. In these instances, students are required to use the case to explore issues, concepts and problems that they are likely to encounter.

Cases that stand to optimize learning and teaching opportunities are those that have the richness, complexity and variety that is embedded in real life situations and encounters. It is therefore most important that the cases that are selected for study and teaching are carefully selected to match the intended learning outcomes for the subject.

LEARNING BY DESIGNING

In learning by designing, the design task affords the essential anchor and scaffold for all learning and teaching activities. In this learning design students are required to engage in a learning activity which comprises conceptualizing and building something. This is a common learning and teaching activity in the study of architecture, and engineering sciences. As in goal-based learning, in the case of learning by designing, the goal is made very clear to the students. How the students chose to pursue that goal and achieve the targeted learning outcomes is left to their imagination and creativity.

ROLE-PLAY-BASED LEARNING

In role-play-based learning, the role-play provides the anchor and scaffold for all learning and teaching activities. Role-play is widely used as a valuable learning and teaching strategy in social sciences and humanities subjects where very complex processes are prevalent. This learning design comprises the playing out of identified roles by learners which is followed with reflection upon the activity and its analysis in order to focus attention on the expected learning outcomes for the study.

ASSESSMENT, FEEDBACK, AND E-MODERATION

ASSESSING LEARNING OUTCOMES

Assessing learning outcomes is concerned with determining whether or not learners have acquired the desired type or level of capability, and whether they have benefited from the educational experience. A measure of learning outcomes requires learners to complete tasks, which demonstrate that they have achieved the standards specified in the learning outcomes. In order to ascertain the most realistic and valid assessment of performance, these task(s) have to be as similar to on-the-job conditions, that is, as authentic as possible.

A major purpose of assessment in education is the improvement of learning. When focusing on the improvement of learning, it is essential to bear in mind the congruency between the learning outcomes of a course and the measures of learning achievement. It is not uncommon to find measures of learning achievement that do not address the learning outcomes of the course. When this is the case, learner motivation in the course and their performance is adversely affected. Learning outcomes of a course must be given careful thought as quite often, insufficient attention is paid to the learning outcomes of a course. Without a clear set of outcomes, it is difficult to determine criteria for ascertaining whether we have arrived at the place for which we set out. While some skills and competencies are easier to assess, there are many others that are more difficult to assess and grade. Therefore a range of measures of achievement is necessary to assess the wide variety of skills and competencies that need to be acquired. In all cases however, the only fair form of assessment is one that is very transparent, with explicitly stated criteria for students. Therefore, it is important to clearly specify and communicate the basis for all assessment measures. When this is the case, assessment can serve as a powerful teaching tool.

METHODS OF ASSESSMENT

Measures of learning achievement can be classified as either criterion or norm-referenced. A criterion-referenced measure is targeted at the criteria specified in the learning outcome. Criterion-referenced measures require learners to demonstrate presence of learned capabilities in relation to specified criteria. A norm-referenced measure compares a learner's performance against that of other learners in the cohort.

This form of assessment rates student performance against the normal distribution of abilities in the population. In any learning context, a range of assessment methods may be used to determine learning achievement.

These may include:

- Actual performance on an authentic site or a simulated condition such as a model.
- Oral responses which comprise verbal and/or visual presentations to questions.
- Written responses which comprise typed or hand-written responses to questions.

However, as learning becomes more collaborative, situated and distributed in its context, conventional methods of assessment of learning outcomes become inadequate. These have to be replaced with tasks and assessment procedures that can be focused on the processes of learning, perception, and problem solving. Methods that can capture some of these processes are learning logs, critical reflections and portfolios. In situated learning contexts, assessment can no longer be viewed as an add-on to the learning and teaching process, or seen as a separate stage in a linear process of instruction and post-test.

Assessment must become a continuous part of the learning process where it serves to promote and support learning. Assessment that is designed to promote and support learning during the course of the learning and teaching process, may be seen as serving a formative purpose in that it allows skills development to be identified, reflected upon and corrected in a continuous manner. Assessment that seeks to ascertain a final measure of learning capability often at the end of a course, serves as a summative measure. A one-off sampling of students' work is not adequate to make a reliable judgment of the overall quality of their work. We need to examine student's work regularly and continuously without drowning either the students or staff in meaningless tasks.

BEST ASSESSMENT PRACTICES

Principles of best practices in the assessment of learning outcomes are not hard to find. The American Association of Higher Education has sponsored the development of a set of these that are available from the Web. The following are a selection of sound assessment practices drawn from these sources.

- Assessment of learning achievement must be grounded in sound educational principles. Assessment should not be considered as an end in itself. It should be seen as an effective instrument for learning improvement, and especially because students give it so much attention. Its effective use embodies the kind of learning we value for our students. These educational principles should drive not only what we assess but also how we assess. When issues about educational principles, goals and values are overlooked, assessment becomes an exercise in measuring what is easy, rather than a process of improving learning.
- Assessment is most effective when it reflects an understanding of learning as multidimensional, integrated, and revealed through performance over time. Learning is clearly a very complex process. It entails not only the development of knowledge and understanding in a given domain, but what learners can do with that knowledge and understanding. It also involves the development of desirable values, attitudes, and behaviours which affect academic success and performance outside the formal educational setting. Assessment should reflect these

understandings by employing a diverse array of methods, including those that call for actual performance, over time so as to reveal change, growth, and increasing degrees of integration of what has been learned and taught.

- Assessment works well when, what it seeks to improve learning and when its intentions are transparent. Assessment of learning achievement is a goal-oriented process. It entails comparing actual performance and behaviour with intended learning outcomes and expectations. Clear, shared and realistic goals are the pre-requisites for focused and useful assessment practices.
- Assessment requires attention to the achievement of learning outcomes as well as the experiences that led to those outcomes. Teachers and students tend to place a great deal more emphasis on measures of the achievement of learning outcomes. However, to improve learning outcomes, we need to know something about students' experiences along the way. Certain assessment practices such as the use of learning logs and portfolios, for instance, can help us understand which students learn best under what conditions.
- Assessment works best when it is continuous. Learning improvement is best supported when assessment comprises a series of activities performed over the duration of study. This may mean tracking the progress of individual students or of cohorts of students and providing them with the necessary feedback and guidance.

ONLINE ASSESSMENT TOOLS

Moreover, most prominent learning management systems, such as Blackboard and WebCT come with built-in assessment tools which allow the development of questions and surveys with objective type as well as open-ended responses. These are useful in online education as they enable frequent testing and provision of feedback. However, they remain somewhat unsuited for assessing more complex learning activities such as group work and project work.

THREATS TO ONLINE ASSESSMENT PRACTICES

With online education comes increasing problems with security and the authenticity of work that is submitted by students as part of their assessment requirements. As a result there has been growing concerns about the improper use of material from the Internet. In order to combat misuse of material from the Internet, software programmes such as "Turnitin" have been developed. This software can be integrated and used with major learning management systems such as Blackboard and WebCT.

PROVIDING FEEDBACK

Assessment activities are most effective when they are accompanied with feedback. From a review of research on the effects of feedback, Kulhavy concluded that while feedback can be used to correct errors in performance, feedback is more effective when it follows a student response. However, Kulik and Kulik observed that feedback delivered following learners' response is beneficial only under controlled and somewhat artificial conditions. They recommended immediate feedback for conventional educational settings. Schimmel found that the amount of information in feedback was unrelated to its effects and Bangert-Drowns, Kulik, Kulik and Morgan showed that feedback does not always increase achievement. From these general assessments of the effects of feedback, several conclusions can be drawn about feedback and the conditions of feedback in learning.

- At the simplest level, feedback is aimed at correcting errors in understanding and performance. However, like the assessment of learning outcomes, the provision of feedback is a lot more complex process.
  - Feedback is usually designed to inform learners about the quality and/or the accuracy of their responses. This kind of feedback is specific and

directly related to the performance of the prescribed task. It may be delivered directly to the learners, or mediated by information and communications technology.

- Feedback can be directed at different aspects of learning. Some feedback is primarily designed to influence affective learning outcomes such as motivation. Others might be directed at understanding of subject matter content.

• Feedback may differ in terms of its content which is identifiable by:
  - The amount of information proffered in the feedback;
  - The similarity between information in the feedback and that in the learning and teaching transaction; and
  - Whether the feedback restated information from the original task, referred to information given elsewhere, or provided new information.

MODERATING ONLINE LEARNING

Moderation of the learning process comprises supporting learning with the help of a variety of instructional interventions. It is an integral part of any educational context and is often carried out by teachers and tutors as well as students themselves. Moderation of learning can serve several purposes. One of its most important functions is the provision of feedback on learning.

In online learning, where the teacher is not in situ during much of the learning and teaching process, moderation takes on an added degree of importance. E-moderation refers to the acts of managing, facilitating and engendering group based computer-mediated communication. Such communication can be synchronous or asynchronous. In the synchronous mode, even though the participants may be physically separated from one another, the communication takes place in real time. Synchronous computer-mediated communication is quite like a telephone conversation except that the communication channel in the former is normally text-based while in the latter it is voice-based. Synchronous voice-based communication that is mediated by computers is becoming possible with Voice over Internet software. In the asynchronous communication mode, participants involved in the discussion are active at different times, and may be separated from one another by physical distances.

In the asynchronous mode, those who wish to communicate with others can do so in their own time and place without the need for face-to-face contact or being online at the same time. Users can post messages to new or current issues in their own time where these messages are stored for others to view, comment on, and review later.

COMPUTER MEDIATED COMMUNICATION TECHNOLOGIES

Computer mediated communications technologies that enable manage and support such group-based discussion are reviewed. For a review of computer mediated conferencing technologies and a discussion of their uses see Harasim, Harasim, Hiltz, Teles and Turoff, Mason and Kaye, Naidu, Naidu, Olsen and Barrett, and Rapaport.

E-mail: One-to-one Communication

E-mail refers to electronic communication between two individuals with the help of a suitable software application such as Yahoo mailTM, EudoraTM or Microsfot OutlookTM. Wherever the appropriate technology is available, e-mail is being very widely adopted for private and personal communication, as well as for the conduct of business activities.

E-mail List: One-to-many Communication

An e-mail list is an electronic mail facility that allows one-to-many communication via text-based e-mail communication. Mailing lists are often used to support discussions or information exchanges on a certain subject among a group of people who are subscribed to that mailing list. Upon subscribing to the list, each subscriber gets every message that is submitted to the list. A common form of a mailing list is as a newsgroup. There are newsgroups on just about every subject you can think of. Some groups discuss only one subject, while others cover a number of different subjects.

Inter-relay Chat: One-to-one and One-to-many Communication

Inter-Relay Chat or "talk" is a way of communicating electronically with people in "real time", that is, synchronously. In this mode, participants in the chat session are able to send and receive messages almost immediately. Of course, they need to be logged on at the same time.

Electronic Bulletin Boards: One-to-many Communication

Electronic bulletin boards are like good old fashion notice boards, except that the former are electronic spaces and the latter are physical spaces where you can stick a note with thumb tacks. Electronic bulletin boards are electronic spaces where you are able to post information for others to read at their own time and pace.

Computer Conferencing: One-to-many Communication

Computer conferencing combines the functionality of electronic mail and electronic bulletin or message boards. Messages sent to a computer conference are stored in a central location rather than being distributed to individual e-mail boxes such as in a mailing list. Just as in face-to-face conference settings where participants have to move to particular rooms to hear particular speakers, participants in a computer conference are required to actively access the e-mails in computer conferences which will be waiting for action in that conference.

Once they are logged into the conference, participants can read a response and act on it. This is asynchronous communication because a participant can respond to a message or contribute to a discussion at anytime and from any place. The messages sent to the conference are stored on the host computer from where a participant can read it, reply to it, or start a new thread.

ATTRIBUTES OF GOOD CONFERENCING SYSTEMS

David Woolley suggested that no one computer mediated conferencing system has the potential to meet all the needs of someone. Having said that, he has put forth a number of attributes of good computer mediated conferencing systems.

Separate Conferences for Broad Topics

Most conferencing systems will afford this feature. Whether the discussion areas are called conferences, forums, or newsgroups, they provide a basic level of organization. Different conferences enable a focus on different subjects or topics, and allow you to establish small discrete groups or communities who are enthusiastic about particular topics. These communities can grow to cement their interests and relationships beyond the formal educational settings.

Threaded Discussions within Conferences

Most conferencing software also enable posting of messages in response to other messages such that a line of responses can be traced back to the original comment. This is called "threading" and it takes the form of a hierarchical structure, in which the topic is the starting point for a series of responses that follow. Most conferencing systems offer this capability for up to two to three responses to an original thought. Threads can get lost after that which is why it is very important to impress upon participants to keep their comments focused on the topic and to start a new thread when necessary.

Informative Topic List

A conference participant should be able to easily see the list of the topics in a conference and the questions or issues that need a response. At the minimum, the list of topics in a conference should show each topic's title and some indication of the amount of activity in the topic: the number of responses, date of the last response, or both. The topics should be able to be sorted in some form. Participants should always be able to go back to the beginning of a topic and follow it through to the most recent response.

Support for Both Frequent Readers and Casual Browsers

A computer conference should support both, frequent reading and casual browsing. Those who wish to browse should be able to choose a conference manually and scroll through the list of topics, moving backward or forward sequentially through topics, and returning to the topic list. A frequent reader, on the other hand, should be able to move through a list of conferences, skipping topic lists entirely and getting immediately to the new, unread messages. Moreover, readers should be able to search messages by date, author, or keyword.

Access Control

Publicly accessible conferences will require different types of access and control than those within the context of a formal online course. In a publicly accessible conference, a conference host or moderator will need control over who can access the conference and what level of access is allowed to participants. For example, it might be necessary to give some participants read and write permission, and others read only access.

The situation in a conference within a formal course would be different as every participant there will be required to have read and write access. Moreover, the host of a conference should have good tools for managing a conference discussion, such as tools for weeding out obsolete topics, archiving those that are worth saving but no longer active, and moving a divergent thread of a topic to a new topic of its own.

E-MODERATION SKILLS

While creating opportunities for learning, online learning environments also create demands on learners for new skills in managing their own learning. Being successful in such learning environments requires learners to have the ability to organize, evaluate, and monitor the progress of their learning. Not all learners possess these skills, and so they have to be taught how to take advantage of the opportunities that online learning affords. A useful way of conceptualizing key skills for managing and facilitating computer mediation conferencing has been developed by Salmon.

Forming

The first task in the moderation of an online learning environment comprises the orientation of participants for computer conferencing. At this early stage, several skills are necessary for the formation of the group. In a formal educational setting, it is very likely that most of the participants will not know each other. So it will be important to provide them with an opportunity to introduce themselves to others in the group.

This will comprise explaining their academic and other interests but more importantly their specific interest in the subject. Some students will be familiar with the conventions of computer mediated conferencing, while others will not. Some may be threatened by the technology and irritated by many of the conventions of this mode of communications. As such it may be useful to agree on some common ground rules for communicating online. At this early stage the development of respect, tolerance and trust among the group is very important.

The moderator can set the tone of the communication, and try to model those sorts of behaviours for the group to emulate. These would include things like, how much to write in each message, how frequently, and the tone of the language that might be appropriate. Some agreement at this stage on the etiquettes of communicating on the net would be appropriate.

Functioning

This comprises ensuring that the group is on track for completing the assigned tasks. Foremost, it will include making clear the goals and outcomes of the conference. In addition to this, providing some structure and direction for the ensuing discussions will lead to a coherent conversation on the assigned topic. Participants should be encouraged to participate responsibly, and equitably to ensure that everyone is contributing their fair share to the discussions. Participants should also be encouraged to share their ideas and opinions with group members in good faith. They ought to feel free to ask questions, and seek the opinions and support of others in the group.

Formulating Skills

By this stage in the discussion, conference participants are able to build a deeper level understanding of the subject matter. Strategies to support this will include summarizing the ideas and thread of the discussion at regular intervals, asking participants to assist and check each other's understanding of complex ideas, linking theory with practice and elaborating current material with previously learned material.

Fermenting

This is starting to happen when participants are engaging more readily in debate and discussion about the central issues, challenging each other's ideas, meanings, reasoning and concepts. Any controversies in this regard need to be handled very carefully by the moderator, and students should be taught the skills to manage debates. Criticizing ideas without criticizing people is an important but difficult skill to develop. It is important to challenge the ideas of others but it is essential that students learn not to alienate other group members in this process.

For example, ideas can be challenged in subtle ways by asking questions, suggesting alternatives, asking for their reasoning and justification of arguments. Students could be encouraged to find out how the thinking and reasoning of group members' differ and how the different ideas could be integrated into a smaller set of propositions on the subject. At the end of this process, the moderator must bring the discussion to some sort of a close.

ONLINE LEARNING MANAGEMENT SYSTEMS

Online learning management systems are a suite of software tools that enable the management and facilitation of a range of learning and teaching activities and services. In large-scale operations, online learning management systems can save costs and time. In conventional educational settings, online-learning management systems can help to improve the speed and effectiveness of the educational processes, communication among learners, and also staff and students. Use of LMSs in nontraditional educational settings allows organizations to maximize their value by enabling flexible access to its resources and services.

Most online learning management systems also incorporate a learning content management system, which is a set of software tools that enables the, storage, use and reuse of the subject matter content. Contemporary organizations recognize that the use of onlinelearning management systems have the potential to significantly improve their image and value, as well as access to their services. Recent studies conducted by industry analyst Brandon Hall suggest that there has been a steady rise in the use of LMS for education and training over last few years. Most LMSs will have the following features: course content delivery capabilities; management of online class transactions; tracking and reporting of learner progress; assessment of learning outcomes; reporting of achievement and completion of learning tasks; and student records management.

It is likely that the next generation of LMSs will have additional features such as better collaborative learning tools and better integration with other complementary systems, and with portable and wireless devices. It is also suggested that the next generation of LMSs is going to be increasingly browser-based and less reliant on umpteen downloads or plug-ins on the user's desktop. They will have to be easier-to-use, more robust, scalable and more easily customizable. With the growing interest in the sharing of study materials, they are also likely to comply more with industry standards and with complementary systems.

ADHERENCE TO EMERGING STANDARDS

Proprietary learning resources generally do not operate across different platforms, making them difficult and expensive to use easily. To enable learning objects to be reused and managed across various learning management systems, the online-learning industry has embarked on initiatives for the development of industry-wide standards and specifications.

A widely known initiative in setting such industry-wide standards for the sharing of digital learning resources is SCORM. As these standards continue to push for wider recognition and adoption, developers of LMS and LCMS, and learning resources who comply with their specifications are going to strengthen user confidence.

LIMITATIONS OF CONTEMPORARY LMSS

to emulate, as best as possible, conventional classroom-based learning and teaching practices. In beginning with conventional classroom-based practices as the standard the developers of LMSs have continued to perpetuate the many pitfalls of these educational settings. This equates to a false start for LMSs, because developers have failed to capitalize on the critical attributes of LMS tools.

These include features such the flexibility it can afford, the variety of interaction it can support, and the type of study materials it can incorporate. Many contemporary LMSs tend to put learners in a rather passive role, where they can read large amounts of textual material, and engage in on-line discussions.

This does not offer much more than what is possible in a conventional classroom setting. Many of these LMSs lack the tools and capability to engage learners and teachers in the development of complex cognitive and social skills, such as those that involve collaboration, professional judgment and decision-making and where there are many potential solutions, and no single straightforward answers. There is no doubt that many of the contemporary LMSs provide excellent tools for managing learning throughout an organization, however, if not carefully used, they can actually lead to a degradation in the quality and effectiveness of learning. Many LMSs comprise templates for the creation of online course content. These tools help teachers design and create courses easily and quickly in a familiar environment without the need for much training. These built-in authoring tools are fine if one needs to quickly build an online-learning environment where discussion most contemporary LMSs tend to operate as "pageturning" online which consists of a typically linear sequence of screens containing chunks of information.

The level of user interactivity in this activity consists of simply clicking a button or hyperlink to proceed to the next screen. Although sometimes animations, audio, or video elements are added to these sequence of screens, the underlying model of the course that is built using these tools is very uninteresting and a rather poor substitute for conventional classroom-based practices. Another feature of LMSs, which is claimed as a key benefit, is their ability to track learning activities.

Most contemporary LMSs have the capability to collect, organize and report data on learners' activities. These may include data on time spent on a learning activity, when it was started and completed, and number of attempts at an assessment item. The main problem with this kind of tracking of the details of a learner's activities in an onlinelearning course eliminates a key benefit that this environment affords, which is the creation of a safe environment that frees students from the fear of failure and the pressure of time that is endemic of a conventional classroom.

It is possible that learners who know that every time they click something is being tracked and recorded, they are probably likely to feel less comfortable experimenting, taking chances, and pushing the limits of their knowledge. It is possible that instead of learning from their own mistakes, they will work to avoid making any mistakes at all.

THE PERFECT LMS IS STILL EVOLVING

As users become more knowledgeable and comfortable with the use of LMS, they are beginning to demand advanced features and functionality, including support for wireless devices, better collaborative learning tools, and better content management capabilities. The next-generation of LMSs will have to have improved functionalities, customizability, flexibility, interoperability, and scalability. Moreover, as users move beyond the thrills and frills of the technology, they are also focusing attention on the educational functions of the tools. This augurs well for both the developers and novice users, as it signals the development of robust learning management systems that are guided by pedagogical considerations and not by what the developers or the tools can do.

SELECTING A LEARNING MANAGEMENT SYSTEM

Selecting the right online-learning management system and achieving a successful implementation is a large undertaking. This is particularly so for organizations which have historically relied on conventional classroom-based approaches to learning and teaching.

Evaluating the many associated issues that contribute to the acquisition of a comprehensive LMS and ensuring that the organizational infrastructure is able to support it is a major challenge. Foremost, the selection of an online learning management system needs to be an integral part of an overall strategic e-learning plan for the organization. A first step in the LMS decision-making process is to define the learning and teaching goals of an organization and how it seeks to pursue those goals. Being clear about the values and the goals that an organization seeks to promote in relation to learning and teaching will allow one to ascertain how closely an off-the-shelf LMS aligns with those values and goals.

The next step in the process is to investigate all reasonable options by seeking information from potential vendors, as each will certainly offer different features, functionality, support strategies, and costs. Once you have this information, you are in a position to ascertain the suitability of selected systems for your organizational needs. There are several options when deciding to purchase an LMS.

These include:

- Purchasing an off-the-shelf LMS and using it as is;
- Purchasing an off-the-shelf LMS and modifying it;
- Having a LMS custom-developed for your needs; and Developing your own LMS based on the architecture of The Open Knowledge Initiative.

Of course, the best option for anyone will depend upon their readiness, budget, how closely an off-the shelf LMS programme supports their unique needs, and their overall e-learning plan. It is very likely that no single off-the-shelf LMS programme will have all the features or performs all the functions required to comply a 100% with all of anyone's needs. Selecting the right LMS is very user specific and involves a series of tradeoffs between user needs, capabilities and the suppliers of the technology.

DIGITAL LEARNING OBJECTS

Interest in digital learning objects is directly related to the growth of e-learning. Digital learning objects are like books, journal articles and other types of learning and teaching resources that may be found on the shelves of libraries and bookshops. However, unlike most books and journal articles that are found in libraries and bookshops, digital learning objects are stored only in electronic form, hence its association with e-learning. Digital learning objects may include anything from a set of learning outcomes, learning designs or whole courses to multimedia and other forms of resources, as long as they are kept in electronic from. Like books and journal articles, digital learning objects are catalogued and stored in learning object repositories so that they can be easily identified, searched and reused. While standards and conventions for cataloguing books and journals are widely known and adopted, the standards for cataloguing digital learning objects are still in the early stages of their development.

WHAT IS A LEARNING OBJECT

A "learning object" is any item that has the potential to promote learning. As such, a printed book, a journal article, or a newspaper report is a learning object. The term "learning object" is derived from object oriented programming where items of potential educational use are seen as "objects". An object in this context is generally understood as an amalgamation of related variables and methods. Therefore, an object that can promote learning and teaching is seen as a "learning object". A key attribute of learning objects is their discrete nature. Their discreteness enables learning objects to be categorized and stored independently, and reused in a range of educational settings.

Developers of learning objects have used a range of descriptors to capture their discrete character. Some of these descriptors include molecular, organic or granular structure, LEGO or Lincoln Logs. Like any other real-world object such as a car, house or a boat, a learning object will have a commonly recognizable state and behaviour. A car, for instance, will have a name, make or model, and a definition of its engine power and performance in particular settings. In the same way, a learning object can have descriptors of its state and behaviour. Describing and labeling learning objects accordingly will enable them to be easily and accurately identified for reuse by multiple users and in a range of educational settings. This is exactly what cataloguing systems such as the Library of Congress Classification System, and referencing conventions such as the American Psychological Association Publications Style aim to accomplish.

WHAT IS A DIGITAL LEARNING OBJECT

A "digital learning object" is any electronic resource that has the potential to promote learning. Typically these include scripts, images, and multimedia modules etc in digital format. They are often developed as discrete entities so that they can be reused by multiple users and in a range of educational settings. Since the development of digital learning materials is an extremely time-consuming and expensive undertaking, the assumption is that once developed, they ought to be able to be used, reused and shared by a large number of people and in a wide range of settings.

CHARACTERISTICS OF LEARNING OBJECTS

Apart from being discrete entities, learning objects are identifiable by several other notable features. For instance, learning objects must necessarily be able to be easily transported, and reused in a variety of educational settings, otherwise there isn't much point in developing these as discrete entities. They must also be interoperable in a range of educational environments otherwise their potential for reuse is compromised, which will clearly impact their value and use. Moreover, as interest in learning objects grows, there is likely to be a wide variety of learning objects that are developed, just as there are a wide variety of other types of learning resources that can be found in bookshops and libraries.

Some of these learning objects will comprise just the content item. However, others will comprise much more than the content including expected learning outcomes, assessment items to ascertain if these learning outcomes have been achieved as well as metadata on the object. There will also be a wide variety of learning objects that will be developed. These would include learning objects that are factual, procedural, principle-based, and conceptual.

With increasingly more detail being added to learning objects, they are likely to become more context-bound rather remain more context-independent. Moreover, as the focus on the instructional role of learning objects intensifies, there is serious danger that learning objects will begin to drive pedagogical practices rather than pedagogy driving the use of the learning resources. There is already talk of pedagogy in advance of learning objects. Developers of learning objects will need to be aware of the advantages and disadvantages of this trade-off between context-dependence and context-independence of learning objects and the implications for their use and interoperability.

PURPOSE AND MISCONCEPTIONS

It is widely acknowledged that digital learning objects are developed to promote learning and teaching. It has also been suggested that "the future of learning is inextricably linked to the development of quality learning objects". While there is no doubt that learning can benefit from good quality learning resource materials, high quality learning is the result of many more factors than learning objects or resources. The factors that influence learning include learner readiness, their interest and motivation in the study of the subject matter, the nature and quality of the learning experience including the nature of the assessment activities, and the nature and quality of feedback and support that is available to students. Hence it seems unwise to suggest that learning objects are going to determine the future of learning. Just as best selling books have not necessarily improved the quality of learning, there is no reason to assume that learning objects are going to significantly impact the quality of learning.

IDENTIFYING AND DEFINING DIGITAL LEARNING OBJECTS WITH METADATA

In order for digital learning objects to be easily identified and located by users, they have to be uniformly and systematically defined with metadata. Metadata is data about data. They are similar in type and serve the same purpose that is served by data that is found on library catalogue cards about the state and behaviour of various resource items in a consistent format. Work on the development of learning object metadata standards has been led by the Institute of Electrical and Electronics Engineers Learning Object Metadata standards committees.

The metadata standards that have been developed by IEEE LOM standards committees have been refined and simplified by various groups including CanCore. Other similar best practice guidelines include the Dublin Core Usage Guide, the CIMI Guide to best practice, and the online Archive of California Best Practices Guidelines. While work on the development of standards for learning object metadata continues, some concerns have been expressed about the nature and direction of this work.

Some of these concerns include:

- The relationship of best practice guidelines to the

development of tools for the creation of metadata. It is suggested that these tools must be developed so that they are able to be adapted to meet the requirements of particular user groups and specific implementations.

- Partial automation of the creation of metadata. As tools for the creation of metadata are being developed, it is suggested that many of these processes can be automated via content creation tools.
- End-users need not be directly exposed to many of the structures of Learning Object Metadata. The suggestion is that it is not advisable to present less skilled end-users with all the elements for the creation of metadata.
- Learning object metadata does not offer any provisions for version control or digital rights management. Learning object metadata has elements that address some of these concerns, but these are insufficient for a proper management of issues related to intellectual property.

PROCESSES OF PACKAGING, STORING AND DISTRIBUTING DIGITAL LEARNING OBJECTS

Digital learning objects, once they have been appropriately classified and labeled with metadata, are best stored in learning object repositories which can enable them to be easily located, shared and reused in a variety of educational settings. Digital learning object repositories are "the libraries of the e-learning era". When made available in such repositories, digital learning objects are also open to peerreview and scrutiny which in-turn is useful for the improvement of their quality.

It is unlikely, however, that a single repository will be able to house in one place all digital learning resources, just as no one library stores all the books in one location, or no one publisher publishes and distributes all the books. Digital learning objects can be stored and made available to users in a range of ways and from a variety of locations. Therefore, it makes sense to have a "distributed" model of learning object repositories which uses network communications technologies to distribute and share digital learning objects among repositories. These authors also suggest that a successful digital learning object repository is one that promotes the sharing of records along with being able to facilitate access to the learning objects. Like specialist libraries, there might be learning object repositories which will specialize in housing particular types or genre of resources.

Useful specialist repositories might be those that might house only "experiencebased learning designs" or assessment strategies that are congruent with constructivist or collaborative learning designs. Moreover, like different libraries, these repositories may also offer different, and a wide range of services to its users. A number of initiatives in the development of digital learning object repositories that demonstrate a distributed repository architecture have been described by Richards, Hatala and McGreal. These include POOL, POND and SPLASH. Other efforts in building learning object repositories include MERLOT, CAREO, and a growing list of Learning Content Management Systems - LCMSs.

IMPLICATIONS OF AN "EDUCATIONAL OBJECT ECONOMY"

With the growth in e-learning and online learning, there is sure to be increasing interest in the development, storage, and distribution of digital learning objects. Proponents of e-learning and online learning are certain and very clear about the central role that digital learning objects and repositories will play in such educational settings. Some claim that "the future of learning is inextricably linked to the development of quality learning objects", others see digital learning objects as the "building blocks of elearning", and learning object repositories as the "libraries of the e-learning era" with the potential to "fuel e-learning as the stock exchanges fuelled the industrial era". There are some others who are not as enthusiastic or convinced about an educational economy that is founded on the promise of digital learning objects–at least not just yet. However, these are still early days in the development, cataloguing, storing and sharing of digital learning objects. While digital learning repositories anxiously await for a critical mass of learning objects to be developed, there is no doubt that the currently limited pool of resources will grow. The standards for cataloguing digital learning objects with metadata are still evolving.

There are many problems in current practices with the lack of clarity and consistency in the definition of various attributes of learning objects such as in their level of interactivity and their context. There are also unresolved issues with the location and opportunities for viewing suitable items from a digital learning repository as is possible in libraries. A critical issue in the development, storage and sharing of digital learning objects is related to how academics and developers of such material view academic work and intellectual property issues related to it.

Traditionally academic output in the form of publications has been handled by commercial publishers just as to longstanding publication and distribution practices. However, conventions in relation to the production, distribution and sale of digital learning objects are still unclear and emerging. For instance, there are concerns about the rewards to academics and developers for developing learning objects and sharing these across repositories. Making them freely available in repositories is not necessarily in the best interest of academics. A key promise of digital learning objects and its availability across repositories is the opportunity for benefiting from sharing and reusing resources that are expensive and time-consuming to produce.

While this sounds like a laudable concept, it has been suggested that not all content developers are likely to be as enthusiastic about making available their learning and teaching content on repositories without appropriate rewards and safeguards against its use and adaptation. Moreover, not all learning objects may be able to be used as is in different educational settings. This means that there will be a tendency for users to modify and adapt the original version for their use. Naturally this would require the consent of the original owner and developer of the learning resource. Furthermore, once a digital learning resource is modified, there will be issues relating to the ownership of the revised version and how the original work should be acknowledged. Clearly without appropriate digital learning objects rights management conventions, such issues and concerns will hinder progress on the sharing of digital learning objects across learning object repositories.

ONLINE LEARNING COURSE DEVELOPMENT MODELS

CONTEMPORARY ONLINE LEARNING PRACTICES

Contemporary online learning environments are characterized by a growing use of commercially produced learning management systems, which enable online access to subject matter content, asynchronous online discussions, collaborative learning activities, and online assessment. Organizations which seek to adopt online education are quickly realizing that it is not a cheap or easy option. Online education requires a great deal of resources and careful planning.

Some of the strategies used as part of this level of planning include breaking large numbers of students into smaller groups, assigning them specific tasks, and providing them with direction and specific guidance, and setting timelines for discussion. Educators are becoming aware that open, unguided asynchronous online discussion forums can be very ineffective. Students will not give open-ended discussions their time and attention if they are not directed at specific learning or assessment activities.

Most online learning management systems support collaborative learning and small group work, which are widely recognized as desirable educational practices. They enable students to be easily grouped to work on a range of learning activities either online or offline. More importantly, LMSs enable small group work deliberations and activities to be accessible to teachers and tutors to see, critique and comment on. In conventional educational settings, these important aspects of learning would have been accessible only to the group members. Having access to these deliberations gives teachers added insights into group processes and the contributions of individual members to group work. This insight is critical in promoting fairer assessment practices of group work.

Naturally, this kind of educational practice makes student work more visible and open to scrutiny just as the online learning and teaching environment breaks down the barriers to the lecture room walls and makes the teacher and the teaching more visible and open to critique. Some of the operational and administrative issues that are central to developing and implementing a successful online-learning programme include:

- Adopting cost-effective on-line learning management systems that are scalable, and hopefully customizable in order to cope with large numbers of students, and serve the needs of particular contexts and a wide variety of approaches to teaching and learning.
- Adopting learning and teaching designs that maximize the input of the teachers and tutors, and do not leave students floundering in an open and flexible learning space.
- Closely aligning learning and assessment activities in order to ensure that students are more actively engaged in their learning and taking responsibility for their own learning.
- Breaking down the distinctions between "teacher" and "taught" as computer-based conferencing enables students to take on a tutorial role as they learn how to learn from each other.

MODELS OF COURSE DEVELOPMENT

Online-learning environments with their dependence on technology are very different, in several important ways from conventional educational settings. In conventional educational settings much of the responsibility for teaching and learning is in the hands of the teacher who is also the subject matter expert. In online-learning environments, the teacher who may also be the subject matter expert is no longer in complete control of all the activities. The technology for instance is usually managed and serviced by someone else. Someone else may also manage the content that is delivered by the technology, even though the teacher in charge may have developed it. Many of the online-learning environments are the result of a team effort, which brings together a wide range of expertise including subject matter experts, learning management system and web developers, graphic artists, and systems engineers to produce a course.

This team approach to course development has been widely used especially by distance education institutions. Nevertheless, there are less collaborative approaches as well, in which a single subject matter expert might be able to do everything, or do it with minimal and occasional help. The choice of a particular approach to the development of an online-learning course is based on several factors including the academic tradition and resources available to the organization. Institutions that are dedicated to online and distance education have tended to adopt a more collaborative course team approach.

Conventional campus-based educational providers, on the other hand have tended to adopt a lesser collaborative approach. In any event, the development of an online-learning course comprises a new experience for many. It calls for new skills such as in emoderation and some de-skilling as well. Old habits die hard, and when faced with circumstances that render some of one's previous experience "irrelevant" there is quite a lot of uneasiness, loss of confidence, disillusionment, hostility, and at times withdrawal from the activity altogether.

TYPES OF ONLINE-LEARNING COURSES

Robin Mason of the United Kingdom Open University has suggested that most online-learning courses sit on a continuum of a "partially online" or a "fully online-learning course". A "partially online" course is one that integrates existing resource materials that are available either in print or non-print form such as textbooks etc. with some elements of online learning. This might include the use of a learning management system or simply a mailing list for some asynchronous discussion. Such courses promote the concept of what is commonly referred to as "blended learning", where more than one mode is used to teach a course.

Most distance educators have known such courses as "wrap around courses" because much of the teaching and learning activities in such courses are wrapped around existing resource materials such as textbooks. A "fully online" course, on the other hand, is one that will have most of its learning and teaching activities carried out online. I say "most of its learning and teaching activities" because invariably everything about a course could not possibly be carried out online. Moreover, it might not be advisable to do so. For instance, students would always be studying away from the computer from printed materials, textbooks and other resources from libraries. There would be no real need to put these online, and it might not be possible to do so for reasons that have to do with costs and copyright laws. Mason calls this "integrated courses".

WRAP AROUND MODEL

This model of online-learning relies on study materials, which may comprise online study guides, activities and discussion "wrapped" around existing previously published resources such as textbooks or CD-ROMs etc. This model represents a resource-based approach to learning, as it seeks to use existing material that is relatively unchanging and is already available online of offline. Such courses, once they are developed, can be taught or tutored by persons other than the course developers.

Collaborative learning activities in the form of group work, discussion among peers, and online assessments may be supported by computer conferencing, or mailing lists. Unfortunately, quite often, these online learning elements tend to be added to the course and do not form an integral part of the assessment requirements of the course.

THE INTEGRATED MODEL

This model is closest to a full online-learning course. Such courses are often offered via a comprehensive learning management system. They comprise availability of much of the subject matter in electronic format, opportunities for computer conferencing, small group-based collaborative online learning activities, and online assessment of learning outcomes.

For the moment though, some of the subject matter content will be best-accessed offline in already published textbooks and other sources. The learning and teaching in these courses takes place in the computer conferences, in which the prescribed readings and the assigned tasks are discussed. Much of this learning and teaching activity is fairly fluid and dynamic as it is largely determined by individual and group activities in the course.

To some extent, this integrated model dissolves the distinctions between "teaching" and "learning" in favour of the facilitation of learning.

MANAGEMENT AND IMPLEMENTATION OF E-LEARNING

PRECONDITIONS OF E-LEARNING

E-learning, like any organized educational activity is a very complex undertaking. Many organizations seeking to engage in elearning activities quite often overlook the fact that its successful deployment requires the same level of diligence and rigor in its planning, management and implementation that is necessary in setting up conventional education systems.

In fact, e-learning has added elements such as the technology infrastructure that require attention far beyond that is necessary in conventional educational settings. Furthermore, e-learning is neither a cheap nor an easy educational option. It does not offer a quick fix for problems associated with dwindling enrollments, distance education, or poor teaching and learning. Lack of careful planning and implementation of elearning can actually lead to decreasing standards and morale, poor performance in learning and teaching, and wasted resources and loss of revenue.

Any efforts to embark on e-learning must be preceded by very careful planning. This would necessarily comprise, strategic and operational planning that are consistent with the values, mission and goals of an organization. Educational organizations that have a history of employing alternative approaches to learning and teaching such as distance education will have many of the prerequisites and dispositions for e-learning already in place which they can easily capitalize and build upon.

However, conventional campus-based educational organizations that have traditionally relied on residential face-to-face classroom-based learning and teaching activity would need to reconsider their values, mission and goals of educational provision in order to adequately accommodate the adoption of e-learning activities. A critical component of this orienting or reorienting for the successful adoption of e-learning is institutional sponsorship.

For e-learning to succeed in any setting, there has to be complete support for the initiative from the highest levels. This is important not only because it will have implications for funding allocation for any such new initiative, but also because of its implications for the mindset of the rest of the organization. Staff needs to buy into the initiative and be committed to its success.

Without this kind of a ground swell of support and commitment from its foot solders, any such new initiative is doomed for failure in any organization. These are the preconditions for the successful deployment of e-learning, and they have to be in place as part of the preparation for its deployment in any organization. Without adequate attention to these preconditions, e-learning is unlikely to achieve its full potential in any organization, no matter how robust and reliable is its technology and the infrastructure to support it.

ADMINISTRATIVE REQUIREMENTS OF E-LEARNING

Like any organized educational activity, e-learning needs to be very systemically managed. Foremost this will include attention to the technology and the infrastructure that is necessary to support it. It will include different approaches to course design and development and strategies for generating and managing subject matter content from that which is suitable in conventional educational settings.

The Technology

While this is crucial to the success of any elearning activity, technology is not the driver of the initiative. It is there to serve an educational function and such, it is a tool for learning and teaching. However, it has to be robust, reliable and affordable. It is critical to ensure that this is so, just as it is important to ensure that in a classroom-based educational setting, the classroom is available and it is comfortable, and it has the necessary equipment such as tables and chairs and other tools for teaching and learning to take place.

Most teachers and students in such educational settings would take these facilities for granted and they will be unaware of what goes on behind the scenes to ensure that the classroom setting works in the way in which it is expected to work. Staff and students alike would be very agitated if the computer, the projector, or the lights in the classroom did not work, as that would be very disruptive to their learning and teaching activities.

In the same way e-learning technology needs to work just as transparently and fluidly to allow teachers and students to concentrate on learning and teaching and not be distracted by the technology. If teachers and students have to be taught to operate this technology, then there should be processes and programmes in place for this training to occur, routinely.

Course Design and Development

Like any other organized educational activity, e-learning, is a team effort, as a number of people and a range of expertise need to be brought together to make e-learning work. In conventional educational systems, course design and development is the sole responsibility of the subject matter expert who is also the teacher. E-learning will require the delivery of that subject matter content in alternative forms such as online or on a CD-ROM. Some teachers are able to produce their content themselves.

However, this might not be the best use of their time and expertise in most educational settings. A more efficient and effective model of course development is the team approach, which brings together people with subject matter knowledge and expertise in the development of technology enhanced learning materials. However, the establishment and nurturing of such a team process is not to be taken lightly as it has implications on where the boundaries lie for various types of expertise and on the costs of supporting it across a large organization.

Subject Matter Content Management

In conventional educational settings, the generation and presentation of the subject matter content is the sole responsibility of the teacher. In e-learning, while the teacher may still be generating this content, for it to be made accessible to the learners, it needs to be modified, enhanced and presented in a form that is amenable to the technology that is in use. Content once generated will need to be updated in order to retain its currency and relevance.

For this to happen, academic staff and other content developers will need expert assistance with learning and instructional design activities. They will need to be supported in the design and development of such self-study materials in alternative media forms. Permissions will be required in the form of copyright clearance to publish some of this material in such form. In large educational settings, this will create a substantial amount of work, which will require enough trained staff and appropriate procedures and processes.

IMPLEMENTATION REQUIREMENTS OF E-LEARNING

In conventional classroom-based educational settings,

teachers spend a great deal of their teaching time in subject matter content presentation. This activity usually takes the form of lectures where teachers go through a body of subject matter content. Students on the other hand, spend a great deal of their study time in sitting in lectures taking down lecture notes. Irrespective of whether this is a good or bad educational practice; it is certainly an inefficient and ineffective use of teachers' and students' time.

If subject matter content needs to be presented, then there are surely several more efficient and effective ways of presenting it. Sitting students down in a lecture room and having them take down notes, often not so accurately, is certainly not one of those ways. E-learning, with its use of information and communications technology, enables the presentation of subject matter content in alternative forms, as such freeing up lecture time which can now be more usefully devoted to the facilitation and support of learning activity. However, e-learning in itself does not guarantee efficient or effective learning and teaching.

For it to be efficient and effective, a great deal of care and attention needs to go into its implementation. This comprises attention to the recruitment and registration of students, facilitating and supporting learning, assessing learning outcomes, providing feedback to learners, evaluating the impacts of e-learning on the organization, and a host of other issues related to these functions.

Student Registration

Most educational and training organizations have rigorous systems and processes in place to manage student registrations and their graduation. Those who choose to adopt on-line learning would want to also ensure that they are able to recruit, registrar and manage their students online in the fashion of e-commerce and e-business.

Doing so would be consistent with an ethos and philosophy of making one's registration processes accessible online. This would require administrative systems to be in place and that the staff members are appropriately trained.

Learner Support

In the context of e-learning, learner support takes on an added importance, as learners become separated in time and place from the teacher and the educational organization. This does not mean that necessarily more learner support is required. What changes is how learner support is provided, where and when and how often it is provided and who provides it. An online learning course, may not be supported and facilitated by those who developed these courses.

Assessment of Learning and the Provision of Feedback

While in e-learning, the fundamental and guiding principles of assessment of learning outcomes and providing feedback on learning remains the same as that for any other educational setting, what changes is how some of the learning outcomes can and might be assessed and also how feedback may be provided. Most educational settings must also deal equitably and fairly with unfair practices such as plagiarism and authenticity of student work. E-learning because of the flexibility it affords in terms of time and space independence are more prone to unfair learning and assessment practices. Opportunities for these occurrences need to be properly managed.

Evaluation of the Impacts of E-learning

It is crucial to have processes in place for knowing how you are doing with what you have initiated. This will include how your staff and students are engaging in e-learning. Without this kind of evidence, you are in no position to know how you might be traveling and what changes and/or improvements are necessary.

Evaluation of impacts is often neglected or inefficiently carried out in most educational settings. Evaluation of the impacts of your processes should be closely integrated into the planning and implementation of any e-learning activity.

EVALUATING THE IMPACTS OF E-LEARNING

GOALS OF EVALUATION

A major goal of any evaluation activity is to influence

decisionmaking. For any organization to be able to attain its mission, a comprehensive evaluation strategy for ascertaining the impacts of its various teaching, learning and research related activities is crucial. This strategy needs to be systemic and systematic in its approach to gathering different types of data and feedback from a range of sources, and with the help of a variety of instruments.

The gathering of this kind of data and feedback is also crucial to ensuring a high quality of service, and effective utilization of information and communications technology in teaching and learning. The term "evaluation" is being used here to refer to the systematic acquisition of feedback on the use, worth and impact of some activity, programme or process in relation to its intended outcomes. The most basic distinctions between various types of educational evaluation activities are drawn between formative, summative, and monitoring or integrative evaluation.

EVALUATION METHODOLOGY

You should aim to gather data from all stakeholders regularly using a set of evaluation instruments within a consistent evaluation framework which should include front-end analysis, formative, summative and integrative evaluation. You should also aim to collect a variety of data using a range of data gathering instruments. However, you would want to keep the data gathering process as simple and as less intrusive as possible. Front-end analysis comprises a set of ways by which you would plan to ascertain the readiness of students and staff and their preferences in relation to teaching and learning online.

Carrying out such surveys periodically and especially prior to the full roll-out of e-learning will enable your organization to get a better handle on how to align its services to meet the needs of prospective users. The information gathered will help to inform the organization on the nature of its user needs, their perceptions and expectations, and any gaps in the provision of existing support. Formative evaluation would involve gathering feedback from users and other relevant groups during the implementation process. Its purpose would be to identify problems so that improvements and adjustments can be made during the implementation stages of elearning in your organization.

You may wish to plan to carry out formative evaluations routinely and regularly. It would be best that these evaluations use a consistent set of tools comprising surveys, and focus group interviews with users. Summative evaluation will enable you to ascertain the full impacts and outcomes of e-learning on teaching and learning at your organization. You would usually carry this out upon the completion of an e-learning programme, even though there is not likely to be a crisp dividing line between formative and summative evaluation phases.

As part of this process, your aim is to periodically assess the sum impacts of e-learning on teaching and learning activities in your organization. Data gathered should reveal how e-learning is responding to challenges facing teaching and learning in your organization, and the extent to which you are achieving benchmarks and milestones which you have set. Monitoring or integrative evaluation will comprise attempts to ascertain the extent to which the use of e-learning or online learning is integrated into regular teaching and learning activities at your organization. Data gathered as part of this process will reveal the extent to which, and how teaching and learning activities in the organization have been impacted with e-learning.

9

Quality of e-Learning in Europe

INTRODUCTION AND BACKGROUND

The issue of quality in e-learning is both topical and widely discussed. On the one hand, it provides material for political debate at national and European level, and on the other, it leaves those involved in e-learning scratching their heads. How can quality be best developed?

And, even more important, what is in fact the right kind of quality? At first there was an attempt to find the one concept that would be right for all, but we have now become more cautious. Various types of analytical description now head the list. These are intended to ascertain and describe how quality development functions in different sectors of education and in different European countries.

The European Quality Observatory is one such observation platform for quality development in European e-learning. However, there is more to it than 'pure' data collection and description. A key aim is to analyse what actually makes successful approaches successful. In a way, the aim is to find a quality concept for quality concepts. Decision-making and implementation strategies also need to be designed.

One thing is clear today: the main problem is not finding a quality approach *per se,* but rather choosing the right one from among the huge number of quality strategies available. One of the main purposes of this study on 'The use and distribution of quality approaches in European e-learning' is to achieve the following objectives.

- To ascertain the distribution of quality approaches: who uses what?
- To investigate the use of quality approaches: how are they used?
- To identify possible factors for success, on which the development of quality may depend.

As a theoretical yardstick, the concept of quality competence was developed by analogy with that of media competence. This assumes that quality development is a competence that must be possessed by those involved in the learning process–in e-learning, for example, by tutors, media designers, authors and of course learners–if successful quality development is to be made possible.

This competence can be broken down into four dimensions:

- Knowledge of what opportunities are available for quality development;
- Ability to act and experience of using existing quality strategies;
- Ability to adapt and further develop, or to design original quality strategies;
- Critical judgement and analytical ability to enhance quality in one's own field of operation.

This study arose out of the need to establish the usage and state of the art of quality in European e-learning. In this endeavour, quality competence acted as a guiding concept for the analysis of the prevailing situation. In other words, this report aims to analyse the quality competence of those involved in European e-learning and to make recommendations for research and support measures in the medium term up to 2010.

Our work in the European Quality Observatory, the European centre for the observation and analysis of the development of quality in European e-learning, shows clearly that although there are already a wide range of strategies and proposals for quality development, many of those involved in e-learning as decision-makers at an institutional or policy level, as teachers applying e-learning at the operational everyday level, or as media designers developing e-learning, as well as many users, demonstrate too little quality competence to meet the 'quality' challenge. This study therefore investigates primarily what quality strategies there are in European e-learning, which of these are regarded as successful and on what grounds, and what degree of quality competence users, decision-makers and learners demonstrate in dealing with the issue of quality.

RESEARCH DESIGN AND METHODOLOGY

The aim of the study is to arrive at a comprehensive picture of usage and experience of quality in e-learning in the European education and training landscape.

THE SURVEY

In order to achieve a successful survey, the EQO project pursued two objectives:

- to reach as large a number as possible of people involved in e-learning;
- to cover as broad a spectrum as possible of e-learning experts, e-learning decision-makers and e-learning users.

These objectives led to the following survey design: an online questionnaire was placed on the EQO website, accessible to all Internet users. There was no need for prior registration. Versions were available in English, German, French and Greek. The OPST system developed by the 'Globalpark' company was used for the technical administration of the survey. This instrument was particularly helpful as a filter, so that respondents were automatically directed to the questions that were relevant to them. Since not all questions could be answered by all respondents, the online questionnaire automatically jumped these questions.

THE KEY CONSTRUCT OF QUALITY COMPETENCE

In this study, the concept of quality competence was empirically operationalised for the first time, and breaks down into four dimensions. Three general considerations are of particular importance for quality competence in e-learning:

- The term 'quality competence' is comprehensive and refers both to technology-based concepts of education, integrated blended learning concepts and conventional face-toface teaching.
- 'Quality competence' is a matter of learning and experience; it cannot be acquired exclusively from training courses but requires experience and reflection.
- 'Quality competence' is a task of lifelong learning both for learners and providers, such as teachers and tutors. Since educational concepts and objectives are constantly changing, it is necessary to keep relearning afresh how to put new contexts, goals and prior requirements into practice.

Quality competence is thus a key element in the successful implementation of education and training concepts. A description of the four dimensions into which the term can be divided will give a precise clarification of what it covers and includes.

Dimension–Knowledge of Quality

This means the 'pure' knowledge of the potential for present-day quality development, and of current quality approaches. By quality approaches we mean any policies, procedures, rules, tools, checklists or any other verification instruments or measures that have the purpose of enhancing the quality of e-learning products or services. For the purposes of this study, this dimension was evaluated through variables such as respondents' assessments of their level of information or of the present and future importance of quality development in e-learning. Respondents were also asked to provide specific data on the quality strategies with which they were familiar.

Dimension–Experience of Quality

This dimension describes the ability to use quality strategies. It is based on the experience of those involved with quality development activities and the use of quality strategies. This study established whether respondents had experience of quality development in e-learning, and if so, what experience.

Dimension–Design of Quality

This dimension refers to an ability that extends beyond the use of available quality strategies, *i.e.* to the ability to design quality strategies for one's own context. This requires both the innovative ability to change and further develop quality strategies by applying the logic of the media system, and a creative ability to design entirely new forms of quality development. This dimension was operationalised in the questionnaire by asking about respondents' experience of developing their own quality strategies.

Dimension–Analysis of Quality and Criticism of Quality

This dimension refers to the ability to analyse quality development processes critically, comparing and contrasting a range of target systems and perspectives. 'Criticism' originally meant 'distinguishing' and is used to ascertain the ability to reflect on existing knowledge and experience. In the case of learners, this essentially means awareness of their own responsibility for quality in e-learning. In that of providers, it means the ability to undertake quality development through a process of flexible negotiation, allowing a variety of individual and societal target systems to be involved in the issues addressed by education and training. This dimension was not covered by the current questionnaire and can only be analysed indirectly since it is better suited to qualitative procedures.

TARGET GROUPS OF THE QUESTIONNAIRE AND FIELD ACCESS

The questionnaire was addressed to all those involved in any way in e-learning processes. Since the survey was concerned with the issue of 'quality in e-learning', the target groups were defined somewhat differently than in other studies. 'Users' may be schools and institutions of higher education, initial and further vocational training, policy-makers, decision-makers on the client side, and learners. 'Providers' include professionals such as managers of e-learning production, tutors and trainers, media designers and IT administrators.

This restricted set of target groups was selected on the premise that it would give a good impression of its members' views on quality in e-learning. The results of the study largely confirm this assumption, so that this target group model can be recommended for future research on quality. The study covers all European countries. Open access to the Internet also means that people outside Europe took part in the survey. In order to reach as many of those involved in e-learning as possible within the shortest possible time, a wide-ranging information campaign was organised.

This used:

- E-mail shots inviting recipients to take part in the survey,
- E-mails to multipliers, who forwarded or publicised these,
- Banners on the EQO website and other websites,
- Short announcements as links on external websites,
- Telephone calls to multipliers

In this way around 80 institutions were contacted, including:

- Cedefop, Greece,
- Bundesinstitut für Berufsbildung, Germany,
- European Schoolnet, Belgium,
- Le Preau, France,
- Ecole nationale de Ponts et Chausées, France,
- other partners in the EQO network.

There was a very large take-up among these institutions. By passing on the information, many organisations showed that they regarded the issue of 'quality in e-learning' as highly important. Around 75 000 people were contacted direct in this way, 13 000 of them through Cedefop alone. The number of 'chance' contacts via Internet links and banners is certainly even higher, but cannot be quantified exactly. There was thus a very large response to the questionnaire. The number of those who at least glanced at the questionnaire is evidence of respondents' curiosity about the issue. The fact that 1 743 people largely or fully completed the questionnaire demonstrates the huge commitment to the question of 'quality in e-learning'.

DESCRIPTION OF RESPONDENTS

Who Took Part in the Survey

The breakdown of respondents by country shows that all European countries were covered, and even smaller countries are well represented. Some countries are over-represented in proportion to their population, however, including Germany, with almost a fifth of all respondents, and Greece, with 15%. This high take-up may be due to differences in the intensity of the campaign. The availability of Greek and German-language versions of the questionnaire may also have contributed.

The target groups defined are also well represented in the survey sample: around 64% of respondents were professionally engaged in e-learning and almost 40% of the total sample is accounted for by designers, programmers, authors, teachers and tutors working in e-learning. It was to be expected that the group of learners among the 'providers' would be small. This category was only included for the sake of completeness.

It is pleasing, however, that there were a large number of e-learners among the 'users'. As a result, the study also reflects the views of those for whom e-learning is produced. There is also a good balance between the types of institution from which respondents came. Universities account for a large proportion, 28%, followed by companies, with 22% of respondents. It is known from earlier studies that the use made of e-learning by these two groups varies widely. In companies, considerations of cost play a major role. Public administration is also well represented, with 13% of respondents. Among educational institutions, the majority are within vocational training and continuing education and training. School and university education are appreciably less well represented.

This corresponds to current activity in e-learning, in which schools appear to be far less involved. In respect of demographic variables, respondents were almost evenly spread in age and gender.

The number of respondents in each of the four age groups between 21 and 60 years works out between 19 and 30%. However, three respondents were already over 80 years of age. The proportion of men to women in the sample is 57 to 43%.

RESULTS

The data set for this study covers more than 300 variables, which provide material for a variety of in-depth evaluations and reports. The following evaluation of the study centres on key questions of 'quality in e-learning' that are currently being discussed. Each question begins with the statement of a thesis.

Each sub-section:

- Sets out the thesis;
- Describes the findings of the EQO study;
- Places this in the context of overall discussion of 'quality in e-learning';
- Makes recommendations for the further treatment of the issue.

The order of the theses is based on the principle 'from the general to the specific'. They begin by examining in general terms the understanding of quality, and then deal with knowledge about and the importance of quality in e-learning. Next, the actual implementation of quality strategies is considered, and finally the use of particular quality approaches.

MEANING OF QUALITY IN E-LEARNING

Learning outcomes are at the heart of respondents' understanding of quality in the field of e-learning. When we talk about quality in e-learning, we assume an implicit consensus about the term 'quality'. In fact, however, 'quality' means very different things to most e-learning providers. Harvey and Green, have suggested the following set of categories.

- Exceptionality,
- Perfection or consistency,
- Fitness for purpose,
- Adequate return,
- Transformation.

The last perception of quality, transformation, is the most relevant to the pedagogical process. It describes the increase in competence or ability as a result of the learning process as transformation. In order to make these categories manageable for respondents, they were operationalised as follows in the study: Considering everything asked so far, which of the following statements best represents your own personal understanding of quality? Please choose only the one element from the list below which best represents your own opinion.

- Avoiding mistakes,
- A marketing instrument,
- That something meets the standard requirements,
- That something is excellent in performance,
- To receive the best value for money,
- The best learning achievements.

Half of all respondents equate 'quality in e-learning' with the best learning achievements. This means that quality in the educational sense requires not just average performance but the best performance imaginable. This is closely connected with something being excellent in performance. Hence, a fifth of all respondents call for excellence in performance, although this may mean not only successful learning but also, for example, 'carrying out and navigating a learning programme' or 'applying what has been learnt in practice'. Another fifth of respondents expect quality to mean fulfilling a certain minimum standard.

Of all responses, 90% thus relate to the way in which the product or service compares with other products and services. The remaining 10% covers answers associating 'quality' with a specific aspect, namely marketing or value for money. The choice of 'best learning achievements' is particularly high among e-learning providers, medium-sized institutions and universities. These organisations obviously place particular value on the quality of teaching and the standard of learning outcomes. From this it can be concluded that these groups in particular focus in their work on pedagogical quality, while other target groups such as companies, private-sector institutions of continuing education and training, very small institutions and learners pay more attention, for example, to value for money or to meeting a minimum standard. Recommendation: in future work on quality approaches, providers and universities could take the lead in looking at quality standards for teaching. They should be facilitated particularly by the committees of standard-setting organisations.

Furthermore, notions of quality need not automatically correlate with the goals set out when quality measures are introduced in e-learning. Respondents wishing to improve services for their students, for instance, did not exclusively select 'the best learning achievements' as their understanding of quality.

Recommendation: providers should make the effort to present the learning that they offer as transparently as possible. Only if the main content-related, technical and pedagogical criteria are described clearly–perhaps by some kind of 'instruction leaflet'–can users of e-learning decide what particular provision will actually help their learners to achieve the best learning outcomes.

QUALITY COMPETENCE IN EUROPE

There is awareness of e-learning quality throughout Europe, but respondents' quality competence in e-learning nonetheless varies. Although there is a great debate about European reform and harmonisation of education among policy-makers, at the level of practical implementation the question arises as to what is commonly 'European' in education and training.

In the case of quality in e-learning this means enquiring into the peculiarities of a specifically European approach to quality in e-learning. A key question to be clarified by the study in this area was the picture of quality competence in the individual countries or regions. The study shows that the individual dimensions of quality are distributed very unevenly across the regions when it comes to dealing with quality strategies.

The investigation focused on two constructs in particular:

- Knowledge of quality, which ascertains the awareness and familiarity with the topic of those who develop, use or learn from e-learning;
- Experience of quality, which looks at length of experience of putting quality development measures into practice.

The survey also asked how respondents estimated the degree of penetration of quality assurance and quality development in their own country. They were asked the extent to which e-learning products, services, programmes and products focused on quality in their own country, and were invited to pick one of the following answers:

- In my country quality assurance/management and/or evaluation is a requirement in most national funded research programmes about e-learning;
- In my country quality assurance/management and/or evaluation is a requirement for national funded educational programmes;
- In my country quality assurance/management and/or evaluation in educational programmes offered by private providers is required by law;
- In my country quality assurance/management and/or evaluation in e-learning is a major factor in marketing.

People from all 25 European countries took part in the survey. For the purposes of the research, and for reasons of clarity, so that even low sample figures from some countries could be counted in the analysis, country groups were formed for the analysis.

It is very important to point out once again here that countries were grouped into larger units solely for the practical purposes of the research. These do not represent culturally homogeneous areas, and contain wide variations in many respects. This analysis looks exclusively at certain aspects of implementation and affinity in relation to quality development.

What Priority is given to Quality in European e-learning, and how Well Informed are those Involved in e-learning?

There are four dimensions to quality competence. One important dimension consists of knowledge about concepts and possibilities of quality development on the one hand, and awareness of the meaning of quality in respondents' own contexts on the other. These fundamentally determine the capacity of those involved to enhance quality. All those involved in European e-learning regard quality development as very important. Although different conditions obtain in the individual countries and regions, the evaluation is equally high in all regions.

The question read, 'How important do you rate the use of quality strategies in e-learning in general?' Respondents expressed their opinion on a four-point scale. The quality development in e-learning is universally seen as highly significant when the two scale points 'very important' and 'rather important' are combined. Views on the future importance of quality in e-learning are somewhat lower overall, but across all country groups, almost all respondents also regard this as significant. This applies both to respondents' own organisations and to their own countries. In the German-speaking, Scandinavian and Mediterranean countries, around 8 out of 10 respondents, and as many as 9 out of 10 in the Anglo-Saxon countries, regard the issue of quality in e-learning as rather or very important for their own organisation.

The importance of quality for their own country is without exception higher than for their own organisation, which is already at a high level. The group of respondents from other countries shows the same response behaviour. In the quest for what 'binds together' the European debate about quality, the finding that quality in e-learning is of great significance throughout Europe may be identified as a common basis for discussion. This awareness forms the basis for an e-learning

Europe that possesses quality competence. Other responses show that quality is seen by respondents as mainly supra-national. Respondents perceive quality overall to have a strongly international and European significance. Considerably more respondents across all countries would like to see support at international, European and national levels than at regional and local level. The European level stands out in particular.

While there is a high level of awareness of the need for quality and quality development in e-learning, the picture is different with regard to knowledge in this area. Fewer than half of respondents across all European countries consistently feel sufficiently well informed about quality development. Respondents in the new Member States in particular point to a lack of information.

Almost 7 out of 10 respondents state that they are not adequately informed. The lack of information about quality development contrasts with widespread awareness of quality competence, which points to a high level of potential. Information and support measures at a European level, such as the development of country-specific quality strategy portfolios, could be beneficial.

Quality Indicators in Europe

Respondents were invited to go a step further and to assess the extent to which quality in their countries was already enshrined in existing regulations and legislation. Four possible replies to the following question were chosen as indicators: 'To what degree do e-learning services, programmes and products in your country focus on quality?

In my country:

- Quality assurance/management and/or evaluation is a requirement in most national research programmes about e-learning;
- Quality assurance/management and/or evaluation is a requirement for national educational programmes;
- Quality assurance/management and/or evaluation in educational programmes offered by private providers is required by law;

- Quality assurance/management and/or evaluation in e-learning is a major factor in marketing.'

The question deliberately asked for respondents' subjective opinions rather than seeking to analyse the legal situation in each country, since a subjective assessment of the situation would better reflect the quality awareness of decision-makers and learners than the official legal position. The result is a heterogeneous picture. In the field of research programmes, respondents in the Scandinavian countries in particular stated that quality assurance, quality evaluation and/or quality management were compulsory for approval. In the Benelux and Anglo-Saxon, Mediterranean and German-speaking countries, one third of respondents reported regulations of this nature.

However, e-learning is largely–and in some countries overwhelmingly–funded and supported by public research and development programmes. Regulations governing quality assurance have in these cases not yet become sufficiently well established. In the area of education and training programmes, there is a clear difference between provision that is publicly supported and provision offered in the open market. Publicly supported education and training provision is, in the opinion of a third of respondents in Mediterranean and German-speaking countries and up to one half of respondents in Anglo-Saxon, Scandinavian and new accession countries, subject to regulations on quality assurance in the respective country. The open market in education and training is consistently subject to considerably less regulation.

No respondents in the Scandinavian countries state that e-learning is subject to binding regulations on quality assurance, and only 4.5% of respondents in the Anglo-Saxon countries believe this to be the case. This area seems to be most heavily regulated in the new accession countries. More than one in five respondents state that there are binding quality assurance measures for education and training provision in the open education market. All other regions fall between these two. The reflect known quality strategies. Publicly supported provision reveals the strategy of state guidance through legislation and regulations governing quality. In the open education and training market, on the other hand, the market-oriented model of quality tends to apply, poor quality being weeded out. Quality is an essential aspect of marketing.

This applies in particular to the German-speaking and Mediterranean countries and less so in the Scandinavian countries. Support strategies in the field of quality need to take fundamental account of the differing opinions on the market impact of quality in e-learning. There are differing views in Europe of the degree to which programmes, products and services focus on quality. It should be understood, however, that there is not one single correct way of focusing on quality in all sectors. The study shows rather that country-specific circumstances and traditions need to be taken into account.

Implementation of Quality in Practice

In addition to the importance accorded to quality development, and knowledge about possibilities and concepts of quality development in e-learning, one other dimension plays an important role in quality development competence: experience of quality. Respondents were asked whether they had experience of using quality strategies, and what quality strategies they used to develop quality in e-learning. There is a connection between the variables shown.

Anyone using quality strategies generally within an organisation very probably has previous involvement in quality assurance activities specifically for e-learning. The Anglo- Saxon and Benelux countries stand out particularly here. More than 8 out of 10 respondents stated that they used general quality strategies.

Almost as many already had experience of quality development in e-learning. Respondents in the new accession countries, on the other hand, have less experience. This applies in all three areas. Around 6 out of 10 respondents have experience with general quality strategies, and approximately 4 out of 10 respondents have already been involved in quality assurance activities in e-learning. The remaining regions fall in between. If experience of quality development is compared with the importance accorded to the issue, a discrepancy is seen between what is claimed and reality. This is particularly necessary if strategies are to be developed to compare the relationship between general strategies and experience of quality development specifically for e-learning.

The analysis goes one stage further. Respondents were asked to provide specific data on quality development in e-learning. The emphasis was on strategies specifically related to e-learning. It was assumed that organisations always use some form of quality strategy–even if it is not called by that name or described as such and consists rather of internal rules and procedures.

Respondents were asked to choose which of the following four options best described the strategy that applied to their organisation. A distinction was made between socalled explicit quality strategies–official instruments and concepts of quality development, designed either externally or internally–and implicit procedures, in which quality development is left to those involved and is not part of an official strategy.

- Quality strategies or instruments coming from externally adopted approaches;
- Quality strategies that are developed within your organisation;
- Quality development is not part of an official strategy but is rather left to individuals' professional activities;
- We do not use any quality strategies.

That internally and externally developed quality approaches are used in particular. A quarter of respondents work in institutions in which quality development is left to the staff. Around one in six uses no quality strategies for e-learning. Overall therefore, around four out of ten respondents do not use any official quality strategy. Recommendation: it should be noted here, however, that the heterogeneity in e-learning that without doubt exists in Europe has an impact on findings on quality, but overall–even in the new accession countries–there are already numerous approaches and experiences. It is suggested that a permanent European quality reporting system be set up for education and training, and specifically for e-learning, to investigate the longitudinal effect of support measures. The results of the study thus confirm the expected division into explicit and implicit approaches. 'Explicit quality development' predominates, while 'implicit quality strategies' shift responsibility for quality in e-learning to individuals, such as teachers and developers, and are appreciably less common.

It requires a very high degree of competence to develop one's own quality strategies. This calls for knowledge, experience, design skills and critical judgement. Instead of adopting a strategy devised externally, it means examining one's own needs, developing, implementing and evaluating one's own special instruments and guidelines, and constantly updating them. From the aggregated country comparison it is apparent that the order identified is reproduced in all regions: external strategies come first, and internally developed strategies come second, followed by implicit strategies.

The Anglo-Saxon and Benelux countries, the Scandinavian countries and other countries have a preference for internally developed strategies. Around one quarter of all respondents in the German-speaking, the Anglo-Saxon and Benelux and the Mediterranean countries stated that they used external strategies. This is around one in five in the new accession countries, the Scandinavian countries and other countries. Overall, it became clear in relation to the 'experience of implementation' dimension that although there are already many different experiences of quality development for e-learning, these have not yet had an impact everywhere in terms of external and internal quality strategies. The Anglo-Saxon countries are playing a major role, while the new accession countries still demonstrate a need for further support.

Summary and Recommendation

The aggregated country comparison shows that quality is perceived as something overarching and specifically European. In respect of the competence dimensions referred to as knowledge, awareness and experience of practice in quality development, it can be concluded that quality development is on the verge of becoming the norm in Europe. Experience is still very varied, and the use of instruments, concepts and strategies specifically for e-learning is still not universal, but there is a very high level of awareness of the importance of quality in European education and training. Suitable support strategies are therefore needed to equip countries with appropriate, country-specific portfolios of quality strategies.

Country-specific and European forums for the exchange of experience will play an important role in this. The average values of aggregated regions. From a methodological point of view, this can only be treated as a preliminary indication, however. It does not so much show that individual regions can be classified as 'better' or 'worse', as that both of the dimensions examined can in fact be used to show up differences in quality competence. The dimensions of the analysis thus make clear distinctions–although the aggregated presentation does not permit differentiation at country level. France, for example, should be rated higher on the experience dimension than the aggregate of the Mediterranean group. Both dimensions should be supported separately.

A permanent system of reporting quality in e-learning in European countries would give an insight into the effects of support measures. In terms of a strategy for implementation, this could mean either greater activity among target groups as a result of information campaigns on the subject, or encouragement for individuals to become involved in quality in e-learning in a variety of ways, thereby increasing the importance of the issue. For those who do not yet feel very familiar with the issue, however, support strategies must be found.

QUALITY IN TERMS OF STRATEGY AND EXPERIENCE

Attitudes towards, experience and assessment of quality development in e-learning vary just as to the target group. The concept of quality competence includes both the area of knowledge and that of experience of implementation. While there is considerable agreement overall as to the importance of quality development, by no means all respondents have yet been able to gather experience of activities in this field. There is a clear 'quality gap' between respondents at decision-making level, at operational level and at learner level on the one hand, and between providers and users of e-learning products and services on the other.

In response to the question 'Have you already been actively involved in activities aimed at improving the quality of e-learning, over half of all respondents stated that they already had experience of quality development in e-learning. There is, however, a clear gap between providers and users of e-learning provision. Among e-learning providers, over 70% had already been involved personally in quality management measures, while the proportion is almost reversed among users of e-learning. A similar picture emerges in respect of the differences in view between respondents who are decision-makers, at the operational level, or learners.

Among decision-makers, 77% already had practical experience of activities serving to ensure improved quality, while two thirds of respondents in the operational sphere had not yet been involved personally in such activities. Very few learners have experience in the area of quality management. If the groups of e-learning providers and users are divided by decision-making authority. In both groups, decision-makers have the most experience: 81.9% among providers and 63.4% among users.

The operational-level groups have less experience in each case. This group includes media designers and course authors, for example, among providers, and teachers and facilitators among users. The learners in both groups lag well behind. Overall, this makes clear first of all that users, especially learners, are seldom involved in quality development, which is thus a process guided by providers that normally excludes learners. There is no evidence of a participatory understanding of quality, in which quality is worked out in collaboration between providers and users and automatically involves learners in the process. Another area of research interest was whether respondents felt sufficiently well informed about the issue of quality and quality assurance/development/ management. Overall, more than half of all respondents felt that they were not sufficiently informed about possible measures of quality management.

When the group is divided by decision-making authority, this shows that the information situation is very unequal. Of decision-makers, 56% said that they felt sufficiently well informed, while a roughly similar proportion of respondents at the operational level feel insufficiently informed. Among learners, as many as two thirds felt insufficiently informed. Among e-learning providers, almost as many respondents felt sufficiently well informed as insufficiently informed. On the user side, however, two thirds of respondents did not feel sufficiently informed. If we examine the connection between personal involvement in quality management measures and the subjective impression of level of information, the data show that only a quarter of respondents who had as yet gained no experience of quality measures felt sufficiently informed about possible measures.

This suggests that comprehensive knowledge and hence potential competence are considerably strengthened by practical experience. That said, 38.1% of respondents who had been involved in such measures themselves still stated that they felt insufficiently informed. There is thus a clear shortfall in information on the user side, which is a barrier to quality development in e-learning. Given the differing perspectives and positions in respect of quality and quality development, there is a need to develop concepts of quality for specific target groups.

The primary concern is not to design new quality concepts, but to devise channels of communication and ways of providing information which transparently and understandably convey existing options. There are already plenty of quality strategies, but there is too little knowledge of which strategy is appropriate in any particular case. Although at a higher level overall, this also applies to the provider side. Over 40% of decision-makers and more than half of those at the operational level also felt insufficiently informed. An information and advice strategy must be matched not just to the needs of the relevant target groups but also to the particularities of the institutional context in which those concerned operate.

There is most satisfaction with the level of information about quality development in the universities and among public institutions of education and training. Schools and private education and training providers feel least secure. The picture is thus similar to that in relation to previous experience. Another question ascertained whether methods or instruments of quality management were used generally in respondents' organisations. It became apparent that respondents as a whole were relatively conscious of measures of quality management. Almost three quarters of respondents overall stated that quality approaches were used in their organisations. Among e-learning providers, quality approaches were used in almost 77% of organisations, while the proportion was less favourable among e-learning users, although still relatively high.

If respondents are divided by level of decision-making authority, it becomes clear that quality awareness among decision-makers is appreciably higher. Of decision-makers, 83% stated that quality approaches were generally used in their organisations, while this applied in only 70% of cases among respondents at the operational level. Among learners, the proportion was yet lower; in this case only 60% stated that quality approaches were used in their organisation. Interestingly, a further question revealed that 86% of respondents regarded certification as important in the choice of e-learning courses for their own personal use and in this case there were few differences between the groups of respondents.

This suggests that these measures will find broad acceptance among all groups of respondents, assuming the requisite understanding of the function and benefits of quality approaches. Certificates provide a relatively 'tangible' instrument for determining quality, so that in this case a uniform level of information can be assumed, extending beyond the groups of respondents. This in turn implies that lack of information must be overcome on the operational level and among e-learning users if quality management is to be successful, and that management needs to ensure that all those concerned are involved equally.

The question about which quality strategy had been found to be the right one in practice, and which had in fact been used in the organisation, revealed the following distribution among groups of respondents. Overall, it was stated in half of all cases that an explicit quality strategy was used in the respondent's organisation. The group of decision-makers was heavily over-represented while respondents at the operational level were slightly under-represented. Among learners, however, a majority stated that no quality strategies at all were used in their organisation.

Among providers, over half of respondents picked the explicit strategy option, while the rest chose more or less equally the implicit strategy option or the no strategy option. On the user side, however, almost equal numbers of respondents stated that an explicit strategy was used as that no strategy was used. These data demonstrate that there is a considerable lack of information about quality management measures among those working at the operational level since a large proportion of respondents in this group are evidently not aware of the use of quality measures in their organisations. This lack of information is even more pronounced among learners, among whom a below-average number of respondents stated that an explicit quality strategy was being used, and an above-average number stated that no quality strategy was used in their organisation.

The overwhelming majority of all respondents could not explicitly name a quality approach. Up to five quality approaches could be listed, but only 10% of respondents were able to name even one. E-learning providers were far more likely to be able to name quality approaches than e-learning users. If the distribution is examined by level of decision-making, it can be established that decisionmakers could consistently name more quality approaches than respondents at operational level, who could in turn consistently name more quality approaches than learners. Overall, a third of decision-makers were able to list one or two quality approaches, and only just over half as many respondents at the operational level could name one or two quality approaches.

Among learners, this proportion sank to just over 7%. In summary it can be said that there is generally a great lack of information about possible quality strategies. Respondents could not think of the names of many quality approaches, and the subjective impression among respondents that they felt sufficiently well informed about possible quality measures is obviously deceptive. It is therefore necessary to begin by finding suitable information strategies with which to overcome or at least reduce this general lack of information so that the most appropriate quality measures can be selected. Once the decision has been made to select a particular quality strategy, the process of implementing it within the organisation needs to involve all levels of staff considerably more than at present. The awareness of quality currently demonstrated at the strategy level must permeate all levels of the organisation if there is to be the prospect of truly integrative, comprehensive and successful quality development.

QUALITY AS REFLECTED IN INTENTIONS AND REALITY

Quality is high on the agenda but is not reflected in the actions of individuals and organisations. What priority do e-learning providers and users give to quality? From the findings it is already evident which groups are particularly well informed, *i.e.*, to what extent they are aware of quality and put this into practice.

But how high a priority is given subjectively to this issue, and how will the situation change in the opinion of respondents? The question also arises in this context as to whether there is a gap between the subjectively felt importance of the issue and its actual implementation. The question in the study was, 'How important do you rate the use of quality strategies in e-learning in general? Quality strategies in this context are any policies, procedures, rules, criteria, tools, checklists or any other verification instruments or mechanisms that have the purpose of ensuring or enhancing the quality of e-learning offerings.' Respondents could express their opinion on a four-point scale.

The high level of importance accorded to the issue is not surprising, particularly given the general theme of the survey. Of respondents, 72% stated that quality strategies were very important, and another 26% said 'rather important'. However, a difference in opinion between target groups is also apparent, albeit at a very high level overall. The trend in quality awareness already is confirmed here in respect of the importance of quality. While an above-average figure of 77% of decision-makers rated quality development very important, the proportion is average at the operational level, and the figure of 56.7% of learners saying quality development was very important is below the average.

The trend to choose 'rather important', on the other hand, runs in the opposite direction, with the result that all groups gave either a 'rather important' or a 'very important' rating. It might be thought that the importance of quality in e-learning could rise no further if a clear majority of respondents already state it to be very high. But the importance of the issue as a whole can obviously be increased: most of those who stated it now to be very high also expected that it would be higher in future. All respondents were in agreement that quality in e-learning would be more relevant in future.

Of respondents, 85% were of the opinion that quality in their organisation would in future be more relevant than it is now, and another 15% thought that it would have the same importance as today, while only 1% believed that it would be less relevant. In response to the question about the future relevance of the issue in their country in future, 87% of respondents stated that this would increase, another 1% thought that would have the same relevance as today, and fewer than 1% again thought that it would be less relevant. Surprisingly, there was little difference in the distribution of responses between respondents either by level of decision-making authority or by provider versus user status. However, if we now look at what actually happens in organisations, almost as many respondents stated that quality was a goal of the organisation as that quality in e-learning was left to individuals. In other words, in over half of the organisations in question, quality measures are perceived by respondents only at a very abstract level or as an implicit requirement. Only 13% of respondents stated that methods and instruments were used which were explicitly aimed at ensuring quality in e-learning products and processes. Even fewer respondents were aware of the use of an integrated quality management system in their organisation. However, 16%, stated that a quality strategy which related to e-learning was currently being implemented in their organisation.

If these estimations are looked at in terms of distribution within the various target groups, it is noticeable that specific instruments are rated more or less equally highly by all respondents. This confirms the impression that arose from the importance given to certification as a specific quality instrument in the choice of e-learning course for personal use. The more tangible and concrete the way in which quality strategies are implemented in methods and instruments, the more homogeneous will be the reaction to them from the various groups of respondents. Differences do appear in the subjective assessment of importance, depending on what strategies were used or proposed for the implementation of quality in e-learning.

- Involvement in quality activities: respondents who were already involved in quality in e-learning stated this issue to be considerably more important than those who were not yet actively involved —this may be a result of interaction between the two variables.
- Good level of information about quality in e-learning: the situation was similar among respondents who already felt well informed about the issue. Those who were 'into it' were significantly more likely to choose 'very important' while those who were less well informed chose this assessment in 68% of cases.
- Use of quality approaches/quality strategy: there was

a close connection between the rating of quality as very important and the use of external quality strategies. Those who used no quality strategy or left it to individuals, tended to regard quality instead as 'rather important'.

- Future use of quality approaches: among those who stated quality to be 'very important', the proportion of those intending to implement a quality approach in future was higher.

This also shows clearly that there is an interaction between the estimation of the importance of quality for e-learning on the one hand, and respondents' knowledge about the subject and own activities on the other. The more people have to do with the issue, the more important it is, and vice versa.

SUPPORT FOR QUALITY DEVELOPMENT

Quality development calls for a range of different support strategies since information and advice can only cover existing needs if they are designed for specific target groups. Appropriate support strategies must be found for those who are not yet very familiar with the issue of 'quality in e-learning'. What support strategies have respondents used to date, and what do they want to use in future? The EQO study asked about different types of information and made a distinction between respondents who already felt well informed about the subject and those who had as yet had little to do witl. it. The former were asked about the sources of information already used, and the latter about sources which they would prefer to use to find out more about the issue.

Many respondents used three different sources to become familiar with quality issues in e-learning. Essentially, there is little difference in percentage terms between current and anticipated future sources of information. The most important sources of information are Internet websites and examples of good or best practice, from which it is possible to learn in different ways. It was to be expected that provision which has to be paid for would be less popular. It is curious that there was appreciably less enthusiasm for Internet discussion forums, which are another free service. This may be because it is difficult to join in a group discussion without a firm foundation of knowledge. It may also be that forums for beginners are either not good enough or not sufficiently informative. Recommendation: provision that is free of charge, especially via the Internet, could certainly be one future information strategy for increasing awareness of quality in e-learning, provided that this provision is easy to find and suitable for all target groups. If a target group is more used to relying on consultants or other paid provision such as courses or fairs, consideration should be given to the provision of such services. Significant differences in current information behaviour between the various target groups are only found in relation to a few sources of information.

- Discussion forums are used largely by providers at operational and decision-making levels with experience of the Internet, who tend to prefer this medium. Otherwise, decisionmaking providers tend to seek information from specialist fairs;
- Providers at operational level also rely more frequently than others on examples of best practice. The same applies to staff in companies generally and universities.

Recommendation: in any information campaign on quality in e-learning it is important to take into account target groups' preferences for sources of information.

USE OF SPECIFIC QUALITY APPROACHES

The use of specific quality approaches tends to be more widespread among those in positions of responsibility than those at the operational level.

A detailed description of the use of a variety of quality strategies:

- quality strategies or instruments coming from externally adopted approaches;
- quality strategies that are developed within your organisation;
- quality development is not part of an official strategy but is rather left to individuals' professional activities.

The following analysis looks at the 25% of respondents belonging to the first group, *i.e.* those using an external quality approach. Which respondents, and which institutions, make greater use than other groups of external resources?

The following groups can be identified as 'frequent users' of external quality approaches:

- Companies, commercial continuing education and training institutions, establishments of public administration;
- Providers of vocational training;
- Decision-makers among providers and users, and e-learners;
- Senior management and researchers.

It is apparent that these groups are generally those who have already been seen in the preceding parts to have a high level of awareness and active involvement. The fact that learners are over-represented among users of a specific quality approach–which is also the step with the greatest level of investment–may be due to the fact that they are eager to turn to what is already available because they do not know enough to develop their own quality approach. The analysis also shows which groups have as yet made little or no use of external quality approaches: these include schools, and all universities. It may be that this reflects the ability of the latter to devise their own yardsticks for quality in e-learning even though they do not make these assessments binding. The target groups which make the least use of external quality approaches are those working at the operational level. Recommendation: the information campaign about quality approaches should be strengthened in future for these groups in particular, if the aim is to achieve the widest possible support for generally accepted standards of quality. This is a specific challenge for the EQO project and for the other EU projects working on this topic.

MAKING EUROPEAN QUALITY APPROACHES USABLE

The respondents were asked to provide the names of quality approaches which they knew. A total of 650 quality strategies were named, covering a vast range of different strategies known to and used by respondents. The strategies listed come from all fields of quality development. They include official quality management approaches such as EFQM and ISO 9000, evaluation approaches such as Kirkpatrick's four-level approach, benchmarking approaches such as 'Quality on the line' and catalogues of criteria such as 'MEDA' and 'AKAB'.

The data collection produced a comprehensive list of quality strategies with descriptions and recommendations on how to use them. Among the answers there were also a large number of other, informal descriptions such as 'Quality development through evaluation' or 'Transparency towards learners'. Respondents thus listed not only official quality strategies but also their implicit 'home-made' strategies. A second report on the EQO study to appear probably in autumn 2005 will provide an analytical summary and comparison of the individual strategies.

For those not concerned on a daily basis with 'quality in e-learning', such a list of different quality strategies may appear unwieldy since it is difficult to put the individual approaches into any particular order. Together with a summary of the results of the study, the next subsection, which looks in greater detail at 'standards' and sets out the requirements for future standards, is therefore included as a digression to round off this analytical part of the report.

QUALITY STANDARDS

Quality standards have the aim of underpinning the process of quality management and assurance, using a variety of methods–and these methods are explicitly intended to provide support rather than standardisation. In the context of this study, it is relevant to ask what requirements can be deduced for the current and future design of standards.

In the discussion of quality, the term 'standard' is often taken to mean merely a technological standard or standardised methodology. We use the term 'open standards' deliberately to counter this perception. What we mean is an open methodology which can be used in a variety of contexts and provides a set of instruments for a variety of purposes, to support quality development in each individual case.

Are Standards of Quality Management and Quality Assurance Generally Sensible

Given the variety of potential standards, it is not possible to give a straightforward general answer. Standards are taken to mean harmonisation or formalisation of products, services and processes in the form of rules, guidelines or specifications that are based on a consensus. Standards are intended to make things simpler. The term standard is also used even where there is as yet no formally recognised document from a standards institution. There are also quasi-standards, which usually arise out of practice and are recognised among a particular group of users. The term norm is used for formally recognised documents.

Standards are as numerous as quality approaches themselves, and can be classified just as to the following features:

- *Context*: In what context is the standard developed and used?
- *Purpose*: What is the aim of the standard?
- *Quality dimension*: What items are investigated?
- *Perspective*: What actors are involved?
- *Methodology*: What methodology is followed by the standard?
- *Measurement*: How is compliance or success measured and checked?

No standards have yet achieved general recognition in the field of quality management and quality assurance. Norms such as ISO 9000:2000 are not suited to all quality aims or types of organisation, and other approaches have not yet come to dominate the market. Nonetheless, the study shows that the adoption of a standard would meet a pressing need for support: the development of generally accepted certificates and procedures is seen as a sensible element that would take the process forward. The reason for this statement is that certificates provide some outside evidence and are helpful in marketing, as well as acting as internal guidelines so that internal development occurs automatically and skills can be built up to meet the requirements of certification. It follows that a standard must be developed which is transparent and achieves wide acceptance, thereby combating the lack of information that has been found above to exist among users. The requirements of such a standard can be deduced from the study.

What Requirements can be Deduced for Standards?

The study has revealed several requirements which must definitely be taken into account in the future development of standards if a successful solution is to be delivered:

- *Participation*: The greatest weakness in current approaches is the lack of equality between those involved. This must be addressed on two levels. First, all groups need to be involved in the standardisation process. Unless all groups are involved, the outcome cannot be a balanced consensus, and there is no guarantee of acceptance. The learner group should be involved more strongly, *e.g.* by involving consumer protection or student organisations. Secondly, the quality standard itself must incorporate a guarantee of participation by all those concerned. Here too, learners must be included in order to close the quality gap identified between them and other users;
- *Transparency*: The study has shown that there is a demand for and some awareness of quality standards, but that there is a lack of transparency. This needs to be remedied in three ways. The standardisation process has to be transparent, so that all those concerned are involved and can influence development, and a genuinely consensual process of standardisation can result. The standard to be developed must itself ensure transparency of processes, products and services. This is the only way of achieving benefits for all and taking differing interests into account. Examples are making

information available through strategies, processes and products, and the publication of quality guidelines. Should a standard lead to a certificate, the certification process must also be transparent. Procedures must be clearly specified, comprehensible and consistent to avoid disadvantaging anyone and creating a negative impression. This is the only way of achieving the requisite level of acceptance and confidence;

- *Familiarity and acceptance*: Standards will only be adopted on a large scale if they succeed in the market and are accepted both internally and externally;
- *Openness*: The study has shown that in Europe in particular, the goal cannot be strict standardisation. Differing perceptions, perspectives and circumstances must be taken into account. No one-fits-all solution can therefore be created, but the standard must be open and hence expandable;
- *Suitability and scalability*: It must be possible to adapt a standard to the needs of individual users and to accommodate cultural, organisational and individual requirements and peculiarities. This affects methodological procedures, for example. In many organisations, for instance, all that is required is measures to support individual components, while in other situations complete quality management concepts need to be introduced;
- *Harmonisation and integration*: It has become apparent that a variety of approaches and methods have already been successfully implemented. These existing approaches must feed into a new quality standard so that existing approaches and methods can still be adopted. This applies equally to the implicit quality approaches used in organisations;
- *Integrated methodology*: It has become apparent that a standard cannot be restricted to individual components, *i.e.* that account must be taken of different aspects. These include strategies, processes,

competences, products and services;

- *Quality awareness*: The study has demonstrated that quality is not yet perceived as equally necessary and important by all groups, and that where its importance is appreciated, it is not put into practice. A quality standard must therefore lead to an increase in awareness of quality-oriented action;
- *Measurability*: One important requirement is successful measurement of processes, products and services. Instruments must therefore be provided to facilitate measurement and to be used as guidance tools. Examples would be statistical references or benchmarks.

These requirements may serve as a framework for the future standardisation process. The study has thus provided an empirical profile of requirements for the success of the process.

What Standards Meet these Requirements, and what Form Should the Future Development of Quality Standards take?

The standards EFQM and ISO 9000 are used in initial and continuing training in particular, together with a large number of isolated approaches and certificates. These approaches have at least led to a widespread awareness of quality in organisations. However, it is apparent that these standards do not fully meet requirements such as transparency, adaptability and scalability, and especially participation. Current developments in standardisation already provide a framework for individual quality development.

A brief description will therefore be given here of what these standards offer, and how they should be further developed in accordance with this investigation. On the basis of national approaches, a common approach has been defined by the ISO/IEC JTC1 SC36 working group which is the standardisation committee for learning technologies. A crucial contribution was the German reference model, DIN PAS 1032-1. The ISO/IEC standard contains the following components. The Reference framework for the description of quality approaches contains a descriptive framework and a process model, so that process-oriented quality approaches can be described in identical terms and made transparent. The components of the descriptive framework. A standardised process model was also developed to act as a reference model for comparing and describing process-oriented quality concepts. As a result, quality development is being conducted for the first time on a common basis.

The processes and sub-processes. Another element is the specification of reference quality criteria. These contain a collection of some 800 criteria which may be used for evaluation purposes. From these, it is possible to deduce requirements for further standardisation on the basis of the ISO/IEC 19796-1 standard:

- *Quality standards should use frameworks and reference models*: The RFDQ model meets many of the requirements. However, it is primarily only a framework and does not provide for specific instruments or procedures. It serves rather as an outline, a structural aid and a basis for the development of computer-supported tools;
- *Reference models need to be completed and updated*: The use of individually adaptable reference models may be seen as promising. However, only reference processes and criteria are currently specified. For other categories, similar collections should be compiled. This particularly concerns reference methods, potential participants and reference metrics;
- *Guidelines and good practice need to support implementation*: Reference models can only be adapted successfully if adaptation aids are made available. Guidelines should be developed as an aid to individual adaptation, embracing scenarios for application, criteria for success and solutions. Such approaches are currently being discussed at European level in the CEN/ISSS Workshop Learning Technologies;
- *Participation must be introduced at all levels*: Standardisation committees may be open, but they

do not always involve all individuals and groups concerned. New ways must be found of conducting a broad consensual discussion;

- *Transparency creates acceptance and support for the decisions taken*: Despite various positive approaches, learning resources and courses are still not described in standard terms, so that users and learners are not given the information to make well-founded choices of products and services;
- *Every quality standard needs an implementation strategy*: There are currently few aids to the implementation of a quality standard for processes and products. Support measures must be made available to simplify the complex process of implementation;
- *Education and training organisations need a culture of quality*: A standard must offer organisations ways in which they can make quality the guiding image for organisational and individual action. These can obviously not take the form of rules or regulations but must offer opportunities and potential for the implementation of quality in an organisation at all levels;
- Tools support quality development: the successful use of standards depends on ease of application and use. In particular, ICT tools need to be further developed to provide both for integration into the entire operation of an organisation and for individual support functions. Without effective tools, even well-designed approaches with good methodology will not succeed.

The discussion of standards should take up and build on these proposals so that quality becomes an integral part of action in the medium and long term.

QUALITY COMPETENCE

The study shows that there are numerous quality strategies and concepts in the European environment, and that the competence to use these varies widely among those involved in e-learning who took part in the survey. However, it is this competence which determines the degree to which strategies and concepts of quality development are implemented. The core results of the study are summarised once more and related to the individual dimensions of quality competence.

Knowledge about Quality and the Challenges Ahead

This dimension covers knowledge of the possible ways of developing quality in e-learning. In this study, data were collected on five areas:

- Global importance of quality strategies for e-learning;
- Expectations of the future importance of quality strategies for e-learning in respondents' own organisations;
- How well informed respondents felt about quality development in e-learning;
- Expectations of the future importance of quality strategies for e-learning in respondents' own countries;
- Whether respondents knew of a quality strategy.

The results show that there is broad agreement among respondents that quality is now and will in future be of great importance for e-learning. On the other hand, it is evident that there is generally a great lack of information about possible quality strategies. Respondents could not think of the names of many quality approaches, and the subjective impression among half of the respondents that they were sufficiently well informed about possible quality measures is obviously deceptive.

In terms of knowledge about quality, there is thus a gap between the perceived importance of and demand for quality, and the knowledge available to meet that demand. It is therefore necessary to begin by finding suitable information strategies with which to overcome or at least reduce this general lack of information so that the most appropriate quality measures can be selected. Once the decision has been made to select a particular quality strategy, the process of implementing it within the organisation needs to involve all levels of staff considerably more than at present. The awareness of quality currently demonstrated at the strategy level must permeate all levels of the organisation if there is to be the prospect of truly integrative, comprehensive and successful quality development.

Experience of Quality and the Challenges Ahead

This dimension refers to an ability that extends beyond the use of available quality strategies. This means creating a quality strategy for each individual context, calling for both the innovative ability to change and further develop quality strategies by applying the logic of the media system, and a creative ability to design entirely new forms of quality development.

This dimension was operationalised in the questionnaire through questions about respondents' experience of developing their own quality strategies.

- Did respondents already have active experience of quality development?
- What quality strategies were used by respondents?
- How were quality assurance, evaluation and development reflected in policies guidelines and research and support programmes?

Overall it is apparent that users, especially learners, are seldom involved in quality development, which is thus a process guided by providers that normally excludes learners. There is no evidence of a participatory understanding of quality, in which quality is worked out in collaboration between providers and users and automatically involves learners in the process.

However, almost three quarters of respondents stated that quality approaches were used in their organisations. Among e-learning providers, quality approaches were used in almost 77% of organisations, while the proportion was less favourable among e-learning users, although still relatively high. A detailed analysis showed that in over half of the organisations in question, quality measures were perceived by respondents only at a very abstract level or as an implicit requirement. Only 13% of respondents stated that methods and instruments were used which were explicitly aimed at ensuring quality in e-learning products and processes. Even fewer respondents were aware of the use of an integrated quality management system in their organisation.

However, 16% stated that a quality strategy which related to e-learning was currently being implemented in their organisation. The gap between what is claimed and the real situation can only be reduced if those involved are given better targeted, more transparent information about possibilities of quality development. Instruments and methods must be collected in a quality strategy portfolio and made available together with decision-making aids.

Design of Quality and the Challenges Ahead

This dimension relates to respondents' ability to design quality strategies for their own contexts. This calls for both an innovative and a creative dimension. In the questionnaire, this dimension was operationalised largely through questions on respondents' experience of developing their own quality strategies and on suitable ways of supporting quality development.

Respondents were also asked to make recommendations for successful quality development. The institutions in which respondents work handle the use of quality approaches very differently. Some do not use them at all, while others develop a checklist for their own use or a kind of 'rulebook' for 'good e-learning'.

In yet other cases, a standardised but internally developed system is used in a company or institution. Some institutions also use a quality approach developed elsewhere. Where organisations develop their own quality strategies–34.8% of respondents stated that they developed their own quality strategies internally–those involved need a high degree of e-learning competence, operationalisation ability and creativity. Respondents were actively seeking information about possible designs for quality development, and the most important sources of information were Internet websites and examples of good or best practice. It is also evident that discussion forums are used largely by the target groups which have experience of the Internet, providers at operational and decision-making levels, who use this medium.

Decision-making providers also tend to seek information from specialist fairs. Providers at operational level also rely more frequently than others on examples of best practice. The same applies to staff in companies and universities organisations generally. In relation to design competence, further investigation will be required to show exactly which processes and abilities are the key to successfully adapting externally developed quality strategies that are already available.

It can be assumed that a low level of design competence will mean that quality approaches are simply imported directly and not adapted independently, so that users are obliged to use what is offered. This will result in low levels of acceptance.

Analysis and Criticism of Quality, and the Challenges Ahead

This dimension refers to the ability to analyse quality development processes critically, and to compare and contrast different sets of objectives and perspectives. This study has not examined this dimension since it is qualitative analyses and case studies in particular which can provide information about the individual critical and analytical ability of those involved in the e-learning quality development process. The results do show that there is a high degree of critical awareness in individual areas.

Respondents are aware of the importance of quality, in their own contexts as well as in general terms, and they see quality as an overarching, international or European concern. An analysis of individual assessments of actions and decisions cannot be provided, however, in a study such as this.

Our work in the European Quality Observatory and in other contexts shows nonetheless that the understanding of quality has shifted from standardisation to individualisation.

Quality systems must therefore be able to reconcile the objectives of the individuals involved–both learners and teachers–or to take these into account through a process of negotiation.

Quality is thus no longer something static and immutable but a dynamic process of adaptation to the needs of the stakeholders, and primarily those of the learners. This process calls for a high degree of analytical competence and discrimination. The analysis and criticism dimension of quality competence is therefore of great importance.

Bibliography

Allan, B.: *Blended Learning: Tools for Teaching and Training*, New Jersey: Facet Publishing, 2007.

Allan, M.: *e-Learning and Teaching in Library and Information Services*, New Jersey: Facet Publishing, 2002.

Anderson, T.: *Theory and Practice of Online Learning*, India: Cambridge University Press, 2008.

Depuis, E.A.: *Developing Web-Based Instruction*, India: Neal Schuman Publishers, 2003.

Hodges, C. B.: *Designing to Motivate: Motivational Techniques to Incorporate in E-Learning Experiences*, Scotland: University of Glasgow 2004.

Johnston, P.: *After the Big Bang: Forces of Change and e-Learning*, UK: Clarkson University, 2001.

Jolliffe, A: *The Online Learning Handbook: Developing and Using Web-based Learning*, UK: Taylor and Francis, 2005.

Kapoor, Bupesh.: *e-Learning Content Advisory Paper*, India: Cambridge University Press, 2003.

Khan, B.H.: *Web-Based Training*, India: Educational Technology Publications, 2001.

Lee, S.: *Supporting e-Learners throughout Wales and Beyond*, Minnesota: Univesity of Minnesota, 2003.

Lewis, D.: *Facilitating Virtual Learning Communities*, India: Open University Press, 2006.

Moshinskie, J.: *How to keep e-Learners from e-scaping*, UK: Univesity of Minnesota, 2000.

Newton, R.: *Staff Attitudes to the Development and Delivery of e-Learning*, India: Cambridge University Press, 2005.

Rowlands, J.: *A Field Guide to e-Learning*, California: Sandia National Laboratories, 2002.

Salmon, G.: *e-moderating: The Key to Teaching and Learning Online*, UK: Taylor and Francis, 2002.

Salmon, A.: *E-tivities: The Key to Active Online Learning*, UK: Taylor and Francis, 2006.

Schank, R.: *Designing World Class e-Learning*, Scotland: University of Glasgow, 2000.

Scholten, E.J.: *Learning Online-putting 'e' into Education*, Switzerland: Elmepress International, 2004.

Index

M

O

P

Q

S

U